THE RISE AND FALL OF DÉTENTE

THE RISE AND FALL OF DÉTENTE

Relaxations of Tension in US–Soviet Relations, 1953–84

Richard W. Stevenson

Foreword by Hedley Bull

University of Illinois Press
Urbana and Chicago

First published in the United States of America by
University of Illinois Press, Urbana and Chicago

Printed in Hong Kong

Library of Congress Cataloging in Publication Data
Stevenson, Richard W. (Richard William), 1955–
The rise and fall of détente.
Bibliography: p.
Includes index.
1. United States—Foreign relations—Soviet Union.
2. Soviet Union—Foreign relations—United States.
3. Detente. 4. United States—Foreign relations—
1945–   . 5. Soviet Union—Foreign relations—
1945–   . I. Title.
E183.8.S65S74   1985   327.73047   84–23965
ISBN 0–252–01215–1
ISBN 0–333–36283–7 (UK edition, Macmillan)

Contents

Foreword

The rise and fall of détente between the United States and the Soviet Union is one of the grand themes of international politics since World War II. Already during the classic period of cold war confrontation, from the Truman Doctrine of 1947 to the death of Stalin in 1953, voices were raised that called for an understanding between the super powers, as Winston Churchill did in his advocacy of a parley at the summit. In the mid-1950s, most notably at the Geneva summit conference of July 1955, a relaxation of tension was proclaimed to have taken place, although this did not issue any specific agreements about matters of substance. In the 1960s, in the wake of the Cuban missile crisis of October 1962, specific agreements about arms control and the control of international crises did establish the foundations of a framework for the conduct of relations between the super powers, which promised to hold the danger of nuclear war at bay. In the early 1970s, centring upon the Nixon–Brezhnev meeting in Moscow in 1972, there began a more ambitious attempt to bring about a comprehensive relaxation of tension, to create a structure of peace binding the United States and the Soviet Union not only to coexistence but also to a programme of co-operation. But in the late 1970s there followed breakdown and disillusion, and in the 1980s we find that there is a new cold war, and that the era of détente and the hopes that went along with it have receded into the past.

Richard Stevenson's book is the most thorough and penetrating study of the phenomenon of super power détente that, to my knowledge, has so far been produced. He has been prepared to wrestle with the difficult conceptual question of the meaning or meanings of détente, where others would have shied away, while also steering clear of the foolish notion that détente is something tangible or measurable or the proper subject of purely abstract analysis. He has been assiduous in assembling the historical record of the successive détentes that are said to have taken place between the United States and the Soviet Union, in showing to what extent they have involved substantive relaxations of tension and to what extent mere changes of rhetoric or political atmosphere, and in setting out the causes of their coming and going. Most importantly, he has raised the question whether the successive alleged détentes of 1955, 1959, 1963–4 and 1972–5 have conformed to a cyclical pattern, leading in each case to a return to the *status quo ante*, or whether there is evidence that a cumulative advance has taken place.

Dr Stevenson's study deals only with détente between the two super powers. He does not encompass the United States–China détente, nor the détente between West Germany and its eastern neighbours, nor the wider détente between the Western and Eastern halves of Europe, except in so far as these bear on détente between the United States and the Soviet Union. Nor does he attempt an analysis of the wider subject of détente or relaxation of tension as a recurrent phenomenon in relations among states in all times and places (wisely, perhaps). His study has the inevitable limitation that the evidence we would need for a full understanding of Soviet decisions relating to the subject is not available, and may never be. His book, however, fills a gap of which students of recent international politics have long been conscious, and represents a significant advance in our understanding of the subject.

Balliol College   HEDLEY BULL
Oxford

Acknowledgements

Several months ago my father observed that if one were to take all of the people with whom I have spoken about 'the nature of détente' and lay them end to end . . . they probably would be much more comfortable. For the patience and support I have received in this effort, I am thankful: first, to my supervisor, Professor Hedley Bull, who not only gave generously of his time but also supported this rather ambitious approach to the study of détente; second, to the Royal Institute of International Affairs, the International Institute for Strategic Studies and, especially, the United States Library of Congress for research guidance and services rendered; third, to the late Senator Henry M. Jackson, Peter Jennings, the Laings, the Spowers, the Hardmans, the Leans, the Lundquists, the Frys, the Rolfes, the Malans, the Chapmans, Michael Hoffman, Steve Cope, Mark Bentley, Andy Paterson, Denny Miller, Ann Holladay, Jane Stromseth, Jennifer Eklund and my brothers Mark, Frank, Dan and Doug for their encouragement, assistance and/or spiritual wisdom; finally, and most importantly, to my family whose overall support was unparalleled and unfailing.

University of Oxford   RICHARD W. STEVENSON

Introduction

Détente is an ambiguous term and an amorphous topic. It has become such a political shibboleth that the polemics surrounding it tend to obscure the meaning of the word and the basic issues involved. For most of us, détente carries images from the 1970s of summit meetings, ping-pong diplomacy and secret negotiations – images that are now fading. At its prime, détente was credited with having ushered in a new era in which the cold war would be brought to an end. When this did not occur and the great expectations surrounding détente were disappointed, détente became the focus of a debate which has raged in political and academic circles in the Western world. While much has been written on the topic, many works have been distorted by political bias. In fact, the majority of authors have been more interested in whether détente is good or bad than in trying to discover what it is. Even those who have managed to eschew the temptation of taking sides still cannot agree on the basic meaning of the word; thus détente has been defined by some as a condition, by others as a process, a policy or a historical period. Given the inability to agree on a common definition of détente, it has been difficult to ascertain the nature of it. With such confusion in the theoretical study of détente, it is no surprise that there is so much chaos in its practical application.

Central to this study is the proposition that détente is an essential concept in the study of international relations and that an attempt should be made to understand it conceptually. While the concept has been generally taken, over the past decades, to describe an easing of tension between various states – especially the superpowers – the misunderstandings, misinterpretations and disillusionment surrounding détente have actually contributed to a marked rise in tension. Perhaps a clearer understanding of the nature of détente would augment its utility in the practical conduct of international relations.

While the terminology might in some respects be peculiar to

our own times, some form of détente has occurred regularly and between numerous states throughout the history of world politics. From the ancient city-states of Athens and Sparta to the religious alliances in medieval Europe and the contest of France and the Habsburg Empire in early modern times, détentes may be said to have occurred. In this study, however, we are concerned with détente in the relationship between the United States and the Soviet Union.

We will attempt to ascertain the nature of détente by discussing three fundamental questions. First, what is the meaning of the term détente? Second, what factors work for and against détente? Finally, is détente cyclical or progressive in character? That is to say, looking back on the various détentes that have occurred between the superpowers, does the evidence suggest that each détente led simply to the resumption of the *status quo ante*, or can we discern an overall trend towards improved relations? By applying the experience of détente in US–Soviet relations in the post-war years, a consistent and interesting examination of these questions is possible. Chapter 1 explores the meaning of the term détente to a degree that may seem excessive, but, nonetheless, is necessary for clarification of the term. Chapter 2 examines the setting for détente – specifically the extent to which relations broke down during the cold war years. Chapters 3, 4, 5 and 6 analyse respectively what are commonly said to have been the four periods of easing tension in contemporary US–Soviet relations. They include the 'spirit of Geneva' (1955), the 'spirit of Camp David' (1959), the Post-Missile Crisis détente (1963–4) and the Moscow détente (1972–5). In each chapter, the setting, occurrence and aftermath of détente will be discussed as a means of revealing those factors working for and against détente. In addition, the legacy of each period will be reviewed. Finally, Chapter 7 will conclude with an examination of the nature of détente by way of its meaning, those common elements working for and against it and the logic of détente. The epilogue will bring us up to date on the course détente has taken under the Carter and Reagan administrations. While this study will cover much of the history of the contemporary US–Soviet relationship, it does not aim to present a full history of superpower relations, but rather to analyse the Soviet–American experience only so far as it helps to reveal the nature of détente.

This study has a number of limitations. First, it focuses on détente between the superpowers; it does not deal directly with détente between the European alliances, or between Germany and its eastern neighbours, or with Sino–American détente, or with other historical examples of détente. This problem is inherent in the selection of the US–Soviet relationship as the case of détente to be assessed. While European détente cannot be divorced from any study of superpower détente, it has a special character that is not adequately covered in this study. For reasons of manageability, European détente will be discussed only as it relates to the progress of superpower détente; this study is already an ambitious one. Equally, anything narrower in terms of time or subject matter would fail to produce the necessary overview by which to assess détente.

Second, the study of détente does not admit measurement. As 'an easing of tension', détente is too fluid a concept and is too uncertain in its boundaries and limiting conditions to admit quantitative analysis. Previous attempts at measuring tension have only served to oversimplify the complexity of the subject. While this study demands some assessment of the relative levels of tension between one period and another, it proceeds with full awareness of the limitations and ambiguity of such observations. Furthermore, the problem of assessing levels of tension is exacerbated by the fact that in each country different groups within the élite and within the nation at large perceive the adversary country in different ways. Moreover, very little is firmly known about decision-making within the Kremlin and the Soviet Communist Party, and, indeed, it is difficult enough to determine precisely what is the level of tension being experienced within the 'open' system of foreign policy-making prevalent in the United States. Once again, we will have to proceed with full awareness of the limitations of the present inquiry.

Thirdly, this study is complicated by the disagreement that has prevailed between the United States and the Soviet Union over the meaning of the term détente. Each side has pursued détente in its own preferred sense, while rejecting détente in the sense preferred by the other; perceptions of the 'success' or 'failure' of détente are largely determined by these differences of meaning.

Finally, in a study of this kind there is no way of avoiding bias; the most that can be hoped is that in seeking to illuminate this concept, we remain aware of the numerous forces that shape our views of the world and attempt to place them in perspective.

1 The Meaning of Détente

Détente is an amorphous, not to say cloudy, subject and, like all clouds, susceptible to a variety of interpretations. Hearing experts argue about détente, one is reminded of the famous colloquy between Hamlet and Polonius. As you will remember, Hamlet seizing Polonius by the arm, says, 'Do you see yonder cloud that's almost in shape of a camel?' 'By the mass, and 'tis like a camel indeed', agreed Polonius. 'Me thinks', says Hamlet, 'it is like a weasel'. 'It is backed like a weasel', agrees Polonius. 'Or like a whale?' 'Very like a whale'.[1]

Arthur M. Schlesinger, Jr

While the term détente has been popularised over the past several years by the media, few people actually understand what it means.

THE AMBIGUITIES OF DÉTENTE

Détente is ambiguous for several reasons. First, it has been used to describe a very wide range of relationships. As former Secretary of Defense James Schlesinger pointed out, détente 'has included everything from mutual reconciliation to a nuclear alert during the 1973 War'.[2] Theodore Draper adds, 'the concept of détente is like an accordion: it can be stretched out or pulled in. It can be as broad as it seemed after the summit meeting of May 1972 or it can be as narrow as it became after October 1973'.[3]

Second, the term has been used to describe actual or possible relationships between different powers – between the USSR and the United States, between the United States and the Peoples' Republic of China, between the USSR and the Peoples' Republic of China[4] and between the Eastern and the Western alliance systems taken as wholes. Détente in these relationships not only demands varying degrees and types of impetus; what works for détente in one may work against it in another. For example, efforts

1

at improving the superpower relationship sometimes lead to an increase of tension in the relationship of one or both superpowers to China, and vice versa. Just as the Chinese leaders have denounced superpower détente as a Soviet tactic in the quest for world hegemony, the Soviet Union has nervously denounced Sino–American attempts at improving relations as a 'dangerous game' aimed at upsetting superpower détente.[5]

Similarly, while superpower détente and European détente have been basically complementary, each relationship has worked to define the limits of the other. For instance, the extent of trade and cooperation between Eastern and Western states has sometimes been determined by the requirements and vicissitudes of the Soviet–American relationship. However, while West European leaders have learned that the success of their détente depends somewhat upon the success of superpower détente, they have also sometimes feared 'the emergence of a US–Soviet condominium that would sacrifice their vital interests on the altar of détente'.[6] The current debate over the 'divisibility of détente', over whether Western Europe's détente with the Soviet Union and the Soviet bloc can be separated from the détente between the United States and the Soviet Union, has illuminated this ambiguous relationship. The 'test of wills' between the Reagan Administration and West European governments over the Soviet natural gas pipeline represents but one example. As one can see, these various dimensions of détente are intricately intertwined and cannot be totally divorced from one another.

Third, while both superpowers agree that restraint is the primary element of détente, they have failed to agree on a common set of rules or guidelines defining the nature or limits of restraint to be observed. For instance, the United States has claimed that détente requires a diminution of the ideological struggle, while the Soviet Union has claimed that détente is consistent with an intensification of that struggle. These conflicting views are a direct result of the differing perceptions and expectations of détente. The Soviet government views it as a dynamic process within which the socialist revolution will flourish.[7] While détente involves superpower cooperation in the maintenance of peace and security, it in no way imposes obstacles to competition in other spheres. As Brezhnev stated in his speech to the Twenty-Fifth Party Congress in February 1976:

Détente does not in the slightest abolish, nor can it alter, the laws of the class struggle . . . we make no secret of the fact that we see détente as the way to create more favourable conditions for peaceful socialist and Communist construction.[8]

For this reason, the main Soviet interpretation of détente is summarised in the concept of 'peaceful coexistence', where states of differing social systems can compete without resort to war.[9] This doctrine was formalised at the Twentieth Party Congress in February 1956 when Khrushchev departed from the strict Stalinist interpretation of the doctrine on 'the fatal inevitability of war between the social systems'. Soviet views on this matter, however, have continued to shift with time. The fall of Khrushchev in October 1964 symbolised the renewed influence of political hardliners and the Soviet military. In contrast to Khrushchev's position that nuclear war would have no victors, the military and hardliners claimed that, while war was not an expedient instrument of policy, the Soviet Union needed to maintain the ability 'to wage and seek to win a war if it could not be averted'.[10] This position was seen as essential in terms of supporting Soviet military programmes and maintaining vigilance. However, with the emergence of SALT and the Moscow détente in the 1970s, Brezhnev sought to find a domestic policy that would strike a balance between the demands for détente and the demands for a high state of military preparedness. Détente was pursued in concert with continuing increases in arms procurement and an intensification of ideological warfare; '. . . peaceful coexistence means neither the preservation of the social and political status quo nor the weakening of the ideological struggle and activity of the Communist Parties . . .'.[11] As Soviet military power grew, deterrence increasingly moved from 'defensive themes of war prevention and protection of prior political gains to more emphasis on themes that included the protection of dynamic processes favoring Soviet international interests'.[12] Given these influences, Soviet concepts of détente have continued to involve strong elements of competition as well as co-operation.

Conversely, the American government has tended to view détente not as a dynamic process, but rather as one guaranteeing peace and security through the maintenance of stability. Both Nixon and Kissinger 'sold' détente to the American people on the premise that it would not only limit the arms race but also control

Soviet behaviour and expansionism. For this reason (and others which will be explored in Chapter 6), most Americans tended to view détente optimistically – as a way by which the Soviet Union and the United States would become partners in the maintenance of world peace.

In the early 1970s, the American inclination to transpose Anglo-Saxon concepts of domestic law into the international field[13] led many to view détente as a contract which suggested Soviet acceptance of an adherence to a specific international order in which peace and stability were the overriding priorities. There was a belief that peaceful coexistence reflected a 'mellowing' of Soviet objectives rather than a strategy of means. Furthermore, the concept of a 'legal' code of détente removed the competitive elements inherent in equilibrium, power politics and spheres of influence – considerations alien and distasteful to the traditional Wilsonian concept of world order.[14] As Kissinger states in *White House Years*:

> There is in America an idealistic tradition that sees foreign policy as a contest between evil and good. There is a pragmatic tradition that seeks to solve 'problems' as they arise. There is a legalistic tradition that treats international issues as juridical cases. There is no geopolitical tradition.[15]

While it is important to point out that Americans hold many different views about the cold war conflict – views which range from perceiving the Soviet Union as a revolutionary power bent on world domination to accepting it as a great power acting under the guise of ideology[16] – the debate over détente has taken place primarily within the scope of this specific world outlook. For this reason, the American concept of détente has identified it with co-operation and has seen competition as antithetical to the very idea of détente.[17]

In the light of the barriers to finding a common definition of détente, it is not surprising that the superpowers have been unable to arrive at a common language placing limits on such activities as ideological warfare, the arms race, and support for 'national liberation' movements. The superpowers' formal agreements regarding détente are vague statements of general principle, whose content can be ascertained only by the interpretations provided by each side. Robert McGeehan observed, 'détente's ambiguity, which (was) so useful in its initiation, (is) becoming counterproductive as each superpower accuse(s) the other of violating its nebulous code'.[18] James Schlesinger noted that détente had been 'reduced to an ever changing set of verbal formulas'.[19] Hence, given the proper semantic and legalistic manipulation, détente has been and continues to be applied as a blanket concept covering a number of divergent actions and goals.

Finally, the meaning of détente is ambiguous because the word has suffered the fate of 'semantic hijacking', a modern political art in which, Paul Seabury claims, 'powerful words may be seized and used as slogans for purposes their creators did not have in mind . . .'.[20] In 1976, Theodore Draper wrote that détente had become an 'obstacle to thought' because it had been 'defined and redefined virtually out of existence'.[21] Two years earlier, John Herz observed that détente was already undergoing 'a transformation in meaning similar to that which appeasement underwent in the earlier period, namely, from a genuine effort to arrive at mutual understanding to a policy of unilateral concessions'.[22] Today, détente has suffered the same fate as words like appeasement, imperialism, and neo-colonialism. As early as 1974, Senator Edward Kennedy noted that 'the word détente itself has fallen into disfavour among some Americans thus requiring new thinking and a new and more precise vocabulary'.[23] During the 1976 United States Presidential elections, President Gerald Ford found it necessary to drop the term détente from his political vocabulary because, while it was interpreted positively in some circles, it was viewed negatively as a 'sell-out' or a 'one way street' in others. Hence, not only do states differ on the meaning of détente; the pejorative images associated with the word cloud its meaning and obstruct the achievement of a consensus within those states. Because of the ambiguities arising from these differing views, détente lacks utility as a concept upon which policy can be based. As former Secretary of Defense James Schlesinger stated on 13 April 1976, 'If détente means everything, it means virtually nothing . . .'.[24]

It is unclear why, or at what point, the term 'détente' came into contemporary political parlance and what has happened to its meaning, since Harold Nicolson defined it simply as 'an easing of tension'.[25] In the four short periods covered by this study, during which an easing of tension took place in superpower relations, it is important to point out that the term was only popularly applied to the most recent period – the Moscow détente. Perhaps its very ambiguity in describing a transition from the cold war contributed to its widespread acceptance. Nonetheless, the term 'détente' has found its place in the contemporary parlance of international politics and, since it will be legitimately applied to earlier instances of relaxations in tension, it seems essential to find a clearer definition of its meaning. Given the ambiguities explored above, it is possible to define détente while, at the same time, respecting its complexities?

DEFINITIONS OF DÉTENTE

In diplomatic terminology détente describes 'an easing of tension'. Its etymological roots lie in the French word 'détendre', meaning the archer's action in releasing the tension on his bow string as the arrow goes on its way. Hence, détente expresses *the action of reducing tension* between two determinate units, in this case, states. As currently applied to international relations, this usage of the word has been confused.

For instance, the political application of détente has led to its use as a shorthand term to describe a *policy* such as the one pursued by Nixon and Kissinger in the early 1970s. Some students of the subject have endorsed this view. Keith Eubank, for example, has defined détente as a policy leading to the relaxation of international tension.[26] In *The Diplomacy of Détente*, Coral Bell describes détente as the management of adversary power – a policy or strategy by which to achieve the objective of peace.[27] Josef Korbel defines détente 'as a policy . . . which tries to solve the problems which, as a consequence of World War II and the Cold War, have divided the East and West'.[28]

Détente has also been used as a shorthand term to describe a *specific historical period*. Thus it has been claimed that détente describes the period between 1963 and 1976 by contrast with the period of the 'cold war' from 1947 to 1963; or (to quote Arthur Schlesinger, Jr.) that it is 'a new phase in the evolution of the cold war'.[29]

While the definitions of détente as a policy or as a historical period at first sight appear to have some force, these common applications distort the term by confusing causes or results of détente with détente itself. The Nixon–Kissinger policies of

1969–73, for example, can be credited with bringing about an easing of tension, but they are not themselves that easing of tension. An easing of tension can occur in the absence of such policies, for example because two states become preoccupied with the rise of more dangerous adversaries or because the passage of time defuses old conflicts and issues, and replaces them with new ones.

Similarly, the present period of Soviet–American relations is certainly more relaxed than the cold war period of 1947–63, but this is the product of an easing of tension – not the actual easing of tension itself. Various historical periods may be brought about by processes of détente, but they are not synonymous with détente itself. Given these misinterpretations, an important first step is to determine whether détente is a condition or a process.

Détente as a condition

If détente is a *condition*, then it logically represents a 'state of eased tension'. Thus, one writer has described it as a 'logical spectrum of relations (along) which conflict either increases or decreases'.[30] This suggests that a détente relationship exists when two states reach and maintain a specific level of tension in their relations. If we construct a 'logical spectrum of relations' (see Figure) depicting a given state of relations between two states, and arbitrarily assign labels representing specific levels of tension (i.e. cold war, détente, entente), then détente can be categorically defined as a 'condition'. Within the classification of détente, states might merely maintain peaceful coexistence, or their level of intimacy might be extended to an adversary partnership as tension decreases.

HIGH TENSION	war	cold war	détente	entente	alliance	LOW TENSION
		peaceful coexistence		adversary partnership		

Levels of tension between states A and B

If tension increases sufficiently between two states, they may
move out of the condition of détente and into the condition of cold
war, or even into a state of war. Conversely, if tension decreases
sufficiently those states might move from the condition of détente
into a relationship of entente or alliance.

There are, however, a number of problems in viewing détente
in this way. First, because détente, in its generic sense, is an easing
of tension, a preceding state of tension is inherently presupposed.
In other words, détente is achieved only through the relaxation of
a previously existing tension. But if détente is defined as a
condition on the 'logical spectrum of relations', then it can be
achieved not only through a decrease of tension but also through
an increase of tension – the antithesis of what the word détente
connotes.

Thus, if two states move from an alliance relationship to a cold
war relationship as the United States and the Soviet Union did
between 1945 and 1950 then, under the 'condition' definition,
they passed down the spectrum and through the state of détente as
tension increased. This application not only violates the essence of
détente; it also contradicts the widespread assumption that
détente follows, rather than precedes, a cold war.

Secondly, viewing détente as a condition complicates the
problem of measurement. If détente is one classification on the
'logical spectrum of relations', at what point does détente begin
and end, and what are the alternative classifications? In other
words, can one draw only an arbitrary or subjective line marking
the point where détente becomes entente on one side or cold war
on the other? Furthermore, is there a set of criteria that might be
employed to demarcate these categories? Assuming that there
were some set of criteria which must be fulfilled in order for a
bilateral relationship to move from one category to the next
(agreement to practise restraint in the use of military power may
represent a step in moving from cold war to détente), would not
the classifications become ambiguously relative as the criteria
change with the passage of time and events? For instance, the
threshold of tension during the 1950s differed greatly from the
threshold of tension during the 1970s. This fact was revealed in
the changing United States response to 'Soviet influence' in the
1950s and early 1960s in Korea and Vietnam, and to 'Soviet
adventurism' in the 1970s in Africa. As Senator Edward Kennedy
pointed out in the late 1970s, 'the contrast with the late 1950s is

striking. Neither we nor the Russians (apparently) now automatically view every action by the other as intrinsically hostile.'[31] While each case is individually complex, it is clear that the impetus which elicited a military response in the 1950s no longer elicited such a response in the 1970s. The threshold of tension had changed, thereby shifting the criteria in relation to which the shifts in the bilateral relationship had been judged to take place.

A second example of the fallibility of criteria involves the emergence of a common intention to avoid nuclear war. Many have claimed that this common intention is a signpost or criterion of détente.[32] However, as will be seen, this intention to avoid nuclear war existed during the period of the cold war. It was simply more implicit than explicit. Furthermore, some claim it was based more on the fear of nuclear war than on the desire to establish peaceful relations through a relaxation of tension. As Hans Morgenthau pointed out, 'peace between the superpowers has been preserved not through détente but through the nuclear balance of terror'.[33] The relationship between détente and the avoidance of nuclear war is still somewhat unclear.

Finally, can any existing level of tension between two states be empirically measured? Are there identifiable and measurable variables in a bilateral relationship that determine where that relationship is located in the 'logical spectrum of relations'? For instance, is it possible, as some claim, to measure the level of tension in the Soviet–American relationship by such yardsticks as the extent of vilification in the press, or by the responses of one state to a provocation or insult by the other? In short, there are many problems with viewing détente as a condition or state of relations.

Détente as a process

Alternatively, détente can be defined as a *process*. During the 1974 Hearings on Détente before the Senate Committee on Foreign Relations, Former Secretary of State Dean Rusk claimed that détente was a 'process' not a 'condition'.[34] Secretary of State Kissinger concurred that détente was a 'continuing process, not a final condition'.[35] Former UN Ambassador Daniel Patrick Moynihan strengthened this consensus by stating: 'Détente . . . is not a condition, such as peace or war, but a process that can lead away from or toward either accordingly as we successfully manage the process – or fail to do so.'[36] On the Soviet side, Foreign Minister Gromyko defined détente as 'a process of relaxation of tension, not an accomplished phenomenon or an entity which has already taken shape'.[37] All agreed that détente was the process of reducing tension between two states, and was not the end product of such a reduction.

At first, this view of détente seems more convincing. However, taken to its logical extreme, the process definition is not without its faults. First, if it occurs every time tension is eased in a bilateral relationship, détente cannot be regarded as a phenomenon that necessarily follows a cold war relationship and precedes a relationship of entente; it loses its unique relative position. Furthermore, détente, seen simply as a process of easing tension, can occur between any two states, at any time, regardless of the degree of affection or disaffection between them. For instance, a significant degree of tension exists among the Western allies, especially between France and the United States. Events like the 1973 Arab Oil Embargo serve as a catalyst accentuating differences in national interest and priorities, thereby increasing the underlying tension inherent in those differences. However, when crises pass, or new challenges demand unified action and co-operation, a relaxation of tension usually occurs. When this happens, is there détente? Under the process definition, détente does indeed occur. This violates the widely held assumption that détente occurs only between bitter adversaries who are divided much more deeply than allies.

Second, relations between states are characterised by a continuous saga of tension-raising and tension-reducing events and policies that alter the nature of the 'complex whole'. If détente is defined as a process of easing tension, then the frequent aberrations to the contrary make détente an ambiguous phenomenon. This is complicated by the fact that some events which initially raise tension (thereby working against détente) may ultimately contribute to an easing of tension (thereby aiding détente) and vice versa.

The purpose of taking these two definitions of détente to their logical extremes is to illustrate the immense complexities and ambiguities surrounding the term. Simplistic definitions, phrases or graphs all too often do violence to these complexities. It is necessary to find a workable definition that does not ignore the complexities or ambiguities of the term but attempts to make them manageable.

Given the core meaning of détente as an easing of tension, the 'condition' definition is less appropriate because it inherently suggests that détente can be achieved through an increase as well as a decrease in tension. It is more appropriate to describe détente as a continuing process rather than a static condition or state of relations. How then do we deal with the aforementioned problems surrounding the 'process' definition of détente?

DÉTENTE DEFINED

First, *detente cannot be defined as simply the process of easing tension*; as stated earlier, tension constantly rises and falls even in the closest bilateral relationship. We rather define détente as the *process of easing of tension between states whose interests are so radically divergent that reconciliation is inherently limited.* In other words, détente presupposes a bilateral relationship between powers whose perceived interests are basically in conflict. These conflicting interests and perceptions continually inject tension into the relationship, thereby causing conflict. Détente is the process of easing tension within this context.

Détente, by this definition, does not apply to an easing of tension between those states which are allies or which together form an entente; it applies only to states emerging from a condition of intense conflict. It is the process of reducing tension between states whose differences are not likely to be completely reconciled. After the Second World War, the United States and the Soviet Union found their political–ideological, strategic–military, and socio-economic interests to be in such direct conflict.

SOURCES OF CONFLICT IN SUPERPOWER RELATIONS

The US–Soviet relationship in the post-1945 era has been conditioned by three basic realities, providing the foundation for a general conflict of perceived interests. First, the strategic power, and, to a lesser extent today, the political and economic power of the United States and the Soviet Union has created a bipolar international system. After World War II served to weaken or destroy the old centres of power, the United States and the Soviet Union emerged to a large extent unrivalled and unchecked in power and influence except by each other. Each power represented the greatest potential threat to the other; furthermore, there was no third power capable of coming to the rescue in case of attack. For this reason, security for each has depended upon vigilance and military preparedness; neither side can afford to gamble its ultimate security and existence on the peaceful promises of the other.

Secondly, despite their geographical separation, the United States and the Soviet Union have become chief military adversaries through their new-found capability of destroying one another's social and economic life virtually at a moment's notice. In the 1950s, the development of nuclear bombs and the means to deliver them brought the United States and the Soviet Union within the same geo-political sphere. Neighbouring states, because they are vulnerable to attack by one another, have often been hostile, while geographically distant states, being invulnerable to one another, have been friendly or at least indifferent. Just as the development of sea power challenged this invulnerability conferred by distance in previous centuries, the advent and advancement of nuclear weaponry has 'dwarfed' the world and brought the two military superpowers face to face. This constant threat has resulted in the maintenance of a high level of military preparedness and vigilance in the interests of security.

Finally, the United States and the Soviet Union espouse ideologies that are inimical and threatening to one another. No doubt it is easy to overestimate the importance of ideological differences as a source of the conflict of interests. As we shall note in the next chapter, the emergence of a 'communist' Russia after the Bolshevik revolution in 1917, led only to a temporary interruption of US–Russian relations. Conflicting ideologies did not long prevent the development of economic ties and the eventual achievement of a normal, and later of an allied relationship. But their commitment to ideologies that are apparently mutually exclusive has, in fact, added a third source of tension to that provided by the bipolar distribution of power and the new factor of strategic or geo-political propinquity.

The combination of these three realities has provided the basis for competition and conflict in the US–Soviet relationship over the past thirty-five years, and while it is impossible to predict the future, it is likely that they will continue to do so throughout the remainder of the twentieth century. First, while the world has witnessed and continues to witness many changes, conflicting ideologies will continue to divide the superpowers with or without détente. For instance, the leaders of the Soviet Union have defended détente internally on the claim that peaceful coexistence provides the most suitable environment within which to infiltrate and destroy Western capitalist states. Regardless of the extent to which ideological considerations influence Soviet decision-making, any stated claim to move beyond peaceful coexistence into entente or fraternity with the West is tantamount to denying the relevance and truth of basic Marxist doctrine. The class struggle and the inevitable fall of the West form the underlying foundation of Soviet ideology as well as providing the legitimacy of the present ruling circles. Conversely, no American President can afford politically to embrace the Soviet Union as a friend while it remains openly committed to the undermining of Western economic and political institutions. Beyond this, American public concerns regarding the Soviet treatment of dissidents and Jews as well as Soviet control over satellite states such as Poland, and Soviet support of guerrilla movements in Central America and Africa, have served to limit the popularity of proposals to extend economic, cultural and scientific ties. The outcry against President Ford's refusal to greet Soviet dissident Alexander Solzhenitsyn at the White House, in addition to various Congressional actions like the Jackson Amendment to the US–Soviet trade bill, have demonstrated the power of these concerns. The declining popularity of the Nixon–Kissinger policies with the approach of the 1976 Presidential election illustrated the problems of pursuing a policy insensitive to American ideological and moral convictions.

Secondly, while other powers such as China, Japan, and West Germany rose during the 1950s and 1960s in political and/or economic terms, the international system continued to be polarised in strategic terms. The arsenals of the superpowers are unrivalled in military power and sophistication and seem set to remain so, at least throughout the twentieth century. A constant sense of threat fuels the arms race which, in turn, augments the strategic superiority of the superpowers and reinforces bipolarity.

While détente has enabled the initiation of the Strategic Arms Limitation Talks (SALT), little success has actually been achieved in slowing down the arms race or reducing the amount the superpowers spend in their military budgets.

Third, technology seems likely to continue to 'shrink the globe' bringing us closer both to our friends and to our enemies. This factor will continue to increase the vulnerability of states to one another.

The continuing influence of these three realities has been demonstrated repeatedly over the course of US–Soviet relations in the last three decades. While notable advances have been made in the contemporary US–Soviet relationship, it has not been characterised by a steady progression of easing tension. It is rather the case that tension has risen and fallen in reaction to a series of events, policies and trends. Because there are both tension-reducing and tension-producing forces at work in the relationship, there are two competing processes which represent the manifestations of those forces. Détente is the process of easing tension, and occurs when the tension-raising forces outweigh the tension-producing forces; conversely, the opposite process of the raising of tension (which has no name due to the absence of a proper antonym for détente) occurs when the tension-producing forces outweigh the tension-reducing forces. With the advantage of hindsight, it is possible to identify specific periods during which one process dominated the other. For instance, from 1945 until 1953 it may be argued that the process of increasing tension characterised Soviet–American relations, while in the early 1970s the détente process characterised those relations.

This study will consider the contemporary US–Soviet relationship in the context of the four periods during which détente is said to have occurred. These were the 'spirit of Geneva' (1955), the 'spirit of Camp David' (1959), the 'Post Missile Crisis Détente' (1963–4) and the 'Moscow Détente' (1972–5).

Each of these four détentes will be reviewed in relation to the three phases through which it passed, so as to facilitate a consistent examination of détente in US–Soviet relations between 1953 and 1976. There is a need in the present study not to focus exclusively on the moments of maximum détente, the phases of what we shall call 'high' détente. In most cases, the phases leading up to and away from détente are equally relevant in identifying those factors contributing to and detracting from it. Therefore, each of the four periods of détente will be discussed in terms of three phases: the setting, the 'high' détente, and the aftermath. This will be followed by an analysis of those factors contributing to the emergence of détente and the decline of it. Finally, we shall consider what legacy each specific period of détente left to the following period. Do the numerous advances and setbacks in the US–Soviet relationship support a 'cyclical' view of the history of Soviet–American détente or does the notable progress that has been achieved in the last three decades support an evolutionary view? An identification of the legacy of each period of détente will help to answer this question.

TENSION: PROBLEMS OF MEASUREMENT

Before we proceed, however, it is first necessary to examine the most fundamental element of détente – that is, tension. Perhaps the greatest obstacle to gaining a general understanding of détente lies in the immeasurability of tension. Numerous attempts to measure and chart the flow of tension in US–Soviet relations have, thus far, met with little success.

Tension is partly a product of the human mind. For this reason, when we say that there is tension between two states, this is a product of the collective perceptions held by the leaders and/or citizens of State A in regard to State B and vice versa. As Plato claimed, 'States are as the men are, they grow out of human characters.' States 'grow out of human characters' because they are conceived by and composed of human beings. Hence, when tension is said to exist between two states, we legitimately refer to the state as a personified abstraction.

The human emotions that collectively cause tension between states range from fear, hatred and anger to covetousness, competitiveness, moral righteousness and jealousy. Tension is caused then, by a wide spectrum of emotions, including fear of war on one hand, and the frustration resulting from an adversary's policies on the other. As Hedley Bull argues, tension 'is the product not merely of the likelihood of an immediate eruption of a conflict into war, but of the assessments made by each side of the other's basic and long-term capacity to frustrate its objectives. . .'.[38] Hence, the level of tension in a bilateral relationship corresponds with the extent to which various forces and factors elicit these human emotions.

SOURCES OF TENSION

As previously stated, three basic realities have characterised the contemporary US–Soviet relationship. These underlying realities are the basic tension-producing factors, in relation to which the forthcoming discussion of détente will be presented. First, the ideological factor produces a combination of fear and moral indignation. As previously stated, Marxist–Leninist doctrine has come to represent the ultimate anathema to a majority of Americans. It is perceived as being totally contrary to the American experience, posing a serious threat to the cause of individual economic and political freedom.

On the Soviet side, there is fear and indignation over American 'imperialism' and capitalism. Communist doctrine requires a constant struggle against these forces and legitimises an authoritarian policy to combat ideological pollution from the West.

Since ideology serves to legitimise the activities of both superpowers, unite the people and convince them to make sacrifices, as well as providing a peaceful means to compete, ideological conflict acts as a cause and effect of tension. Fear and moral indignation breeds hate, which, in turn, breeds more tension.

Second, the bipolar factor creates fear, competitiveness and covetousness as both sides strive for political, strategic and economic advantages. Bipolarity acknowledges the frightening fact that if vigilance and security are not maintained, there will be no other power capable of coming to the rescue. Hence, the fear that the bipolar factor produces weighs heavily in the security considerations and propaganda of both superpowers. While peace is strengthened by parity, both sides are constantly tempted to upset the balance by seizing unilateral advantages. The nature of competition in a polarised system is a zero sum game. Each unilateral gain by the opposing side causes fear and jealousy and injects new tension into the relationship. As one side attempts to equalise or neutralise the gain of the other, competition becomes its own engine. The relationship develops the dynamics of a race, and the pace varies according to the gains and losses achieved. For this reason, bipolarity fosters a high and continuous level of tension.

Third, the geo-political factor contributes to the continued maintenance of fear. As previously stated, the advent of nuclear weapons and the ability to deliver them brought the United States and the Soviet Union face to face with the potential of imposing total destruction on each other within hours. In strategic terms, modern technology made them neighbouring states, each holding the power of life and death over the other.

In short, the factors of ideology, bipolarity and geo-politics based on nuclear weapons have served to inject a consistent level of tension into the US–Soviet relationship. While various incidental factors cause that level of tension to fluctuate, détente must function within the limits of these constant factors. The influence of these factors on US–Soviet relations during the cold war will be displayed in Chapter 2.

2   The Setting for Détente

There are, at the present time, two great nations in the world which seem to tend towards the same end, although they started from different points: I allude to the Russians and the Americans. Both of them have grown up unnoticed; and whilst the attention of mankind was directed elsewhere, they have suddenly assumed a most prominent place among nations . . .

Their starting point is different, and their courses are not the same; yet each of them seems to be marked by the will of Heaven to sway the destinies of half the globe.[1]

Alexis de Tocqueville

In this prophetic passage from *Democracy in America*, Alexis de Tocqueville predicted the rise of the United States and Russia to the apex of the hierarchy of nation-states. What Tocqueville did not foresee was the emergence of two antithetical ideologies whose basic tenets involved 'swaying the destinies of "the whole of" the globe'. Furthermore, Tocqueville did not foresee the creation of nuclear weapons, which would enable each superpower to hold the destiny of the other in its own hands. In this chapter, we will consider the consequences of US–Soviet rivalry when it first surfaced in the immediate post-war years (1947–53). More particularly, we shall explore the extent to which the US–Soviet 'cold war' was restrained or unrestrained. If we are to assess periods of détente, it is essential to contrast with them the period from which détente emerged.

BEFORE THE COLD WAR

The 'Cold War' was an unexpected development in post-war US–Soviet and international relations. While the US–Soviet relationship had been born in conflict, the preceding years had led to the establishment of diplomatic relations, economic co-operation and, eventually, a wartime alliance. Following the

18

October Revolution in 1917 and the subsequent withdrawal of the Soviet Union from the war, the Allied and Associated Powers had intervened in Russia in an attempt to defeat the Bolsheviks. The Communists had not only deprived the Allies of a badly needed Eastern front but had justified their withdrawal with a barrage of propaganda appealing to the workers of all capitalist countries to rise in revolution and bring down their warring bourgeois governments. Following numerous Soviet appeals for peace and promises to 'cease propaganda' and 'recognise creditors who are nationals of Allied Powers', the Allies withdrew, having been unsuccessful in their joint efforts to defeat the Bolsheviks.[2] While intervention had been deeply resented by the Bolsheviks, the demands of survival drove them to seek diplomatic and economic ties with the West. Soviet participation in the international conference at Genoa in 1922 provided the Moscow régime with a measure of respectability, and recognition was granted in 1924 by Great Britain, France, Italy, Austria, Sweden, Norway, Denmark, Greece, Mexico and China, and in 1925, by Japan.

The Americans, however, withdrew into post-war isolation and refused to recognise the Soviet Union due to 'the irreconcilability of the revolutionary communist theory and practice of government with the theory and practice of American democracy and capitalism'.[3] Non-recognition was a 'moral' luxury the United States government could easily afford during this period of economic prosperity and isolationism; there was no need to seek the goodwill of the Soviet government or even come to terms with it.[4] While limited economic ties were established between the two powers throughout the 1920s, various events in the 1930s negated America's 'moral luxury' and brought about recognition. First, the Depression forced America to look outwards in the hope of reclaiming its lost prosperity. Seemingly unaffected by the Depression, the Soviet Union was increasingly viewed as a power deserving of recognition. As a leading economist stated in the *New York Times*, '. . . the Russians are more dependable financially than Wall Street'.[5]

Second, strategic considerations served to bring the two sides closer together. As Joseph Whelan observed, 'A mutual awareness of immediate and potential dangers stemming from the excesses of Japanese imperialism and the recrudescence of Germany under Hitler provided the necessary catalyst.'[6]

Finally, the domestic political environment became more

favourable to reconciliation upon the election of Franklin Roosevelt in 1932. While the Soviet Union had been anxious for the establishment of diplomatic relations from the start, the American public came around to supporting the granting of recognition on 17 November 1933 – a step which European governments had taken and benefitted from for almost a decade. Therefore, by the early 1930s, economic, strategic and political factors served to subordinate American ideological concerns and bring the two sides closer together.

Throughout the decade, the Soviet government strengthened its ties with the West by playing a more active role in diplomacy. Protocol was established and non-aggression treaties were signed with numerous states. In 1934, the Soviet Union joined the League of Nations, and in 1935 the Third International repudiated its revolutionary past by proclaiming the need for a 'Popular Front' with the Western powers to check fascist aggression and support rearmament. When Germany and Japan concluded the Anti-Comintern Pact in 1936, with Italy and Spain adding their signatures in 1937 and 1939, the Soviet Union moved even closer to the West.

While the signing of the ill-fated Nazi–Soviet Pact in 1939 led to an immediate resurgence of anti-Soviet feelings in the United States and the League countries, Hitler's invasion of the Soviet Union in June 1941 and declaration of war on the United States in December 1941 brought the United States and Great Britain into alliance with the Soviet Union against the Axis powers. Throughout World War II, the Soviet Union and the Western Powers were drawn and held together by the common threat posed by Germany and Japan. The United States provided large sums of lend-lease aid, and the Western Allies eventually launched a second front thereby relieving pressure on the Soviet Union. While traditional prejudices and suspicions troubled US–Soviet relations, allied co-operation succeeded in defeating the Axis powers. Therefore, by the end of World War II, US–Soviet relations had moved from a state of conflict and nonrecognition to one of recognition, economic exchange and allied co-operation. Furthermore, the war had left a legacy of great power co-operation upon which the hopes for the reconstruction of the post-war world were placed.

THE COMING OF THE COLD WAR

These hopes were not realised, however, as the Great Powers were faced with the question of how to fill the power void in the heartland of Europe. While great power consultations at Tehran in 1943 and Yalta and Potsdam in 1945 produced various agreements, the post-war political map of Europe was in fact to be determined primarily by the location of each country's occupation forces. After liberating Eastern Europe (March 1944–February 1945) at great cost, Stalin felt justified in demanding the installation of governments friendly to Moscow. At the Yalta Conference, Roosevelt and Churchill had little leverage by which to oppose these designs. The 'Declaration on Liberated Europe' represented a Western attempt to guarantee democracy in Eastern Europe but was open to 'wide' interpretation.[7] Poland was of special concern to all three powers and the resolution of its 'two governments' problem was finally achieved when the parties settled for a 'reorganisation of the present government . . . pledged to the holding of free and unfettered elections'.[8] It was the failure to reach a precise understanding on the Polish issue, however, that produced the first major conflict leading to the cold war.[9] While it is difficult to know what Stalin's intentions were, it seems almost certain that achieving Soviet control of Poland and gaining influence over other Eastern European states was a fundamental goal of Soviet foreign policy – one founded on the needs of security as well as the just rewards of victory for a great power. It was, in part, the American refusal to accept these claims that laid the foundations of the cold war. In fact, the lack of clarity as to the nature and extent of each power's 'spheres of influence' was to be a major contributing factor to its perpetuation. Having had little previous experience in this area, the United States and the Soviet Union were unprepared for such uncertainty. Without agreement on specifically defined boundaries, a genuine and inevitable feeling of insecurity emerged as each side suspected the other of constantly seeking to undermine its authority.[10]

The question of 'spheres of influence' directly affected the fundamental interests of all of the major powers when it came to the future of Germany. In March 1946, Churchill made his famous Fulton speech asserting the need for Anglo-American power so as to counterbalance the Soviet Union. While the American government was not yet convinced of the wisdom or the necessity of such a move,[11] it was watching the Soviet actions with increasing concern. Concurrently, at the Twenty-Ninth Anniversary of the Bolshevik revolution in November 1946, Stalin observed that the world was being split into socialist and imperialist camps and asserted the need for militancy within the Soviet bloc. Few observers had expected, or wanted to see, the rise of a new conflict so soon after the Allied victory. Nonetheless, the lines of conflict were being drawn.

It was not until 1947 that the United States determined its future course of action. Caught between the traditional forces of isolationism and the growing burdens of international responsibility, the Truman Administration had been hesitant to commit more American resources to Europe. However, in February 1947, due to economic difficulties, Britain could no longer provide troops to support the right-wing governments in Greece and Turkey. With communist guerillas waiting in the wings, Truman was compelled to reach a decision regarding the future of United States involvement in Europe. On 12 March, Truman recommended that $400 million be allocated in military and economic aid to Greece and Turkey – a move that touched on a highly sensitive area in Soviet security interests. With this, the Truman Doctrine was issued, the policy of containment launched, and the 'Cold War' begun.[12]

THE COLD WAR

The 'Cold War' assumed the character of a conflict unforeseen by the powers involved. At no point was there direct armed conflict between the United States, Great Britain and the Soviet Union. However, the battle was fought on every other front – political, economic, ideological – and by almost every other means. While both sides continued to co-operate in the control of Germany and diplomatic relations were maintained, East–West relations broke down in many other areas and the structure of international relations changed radically as Britain's role diminished.

While American support for Greece and Turkey through the Truman Doctrine had been prompted by Britain's economic difficulties, it represented an extension of American influence in Europe closer to Soviet borders. Roosevelt's plans for a post-war America that would slowly pull back militarily within its borders were now history. To the Soviet leaders, the United States appeared to be embarking on a policy to expand its influence throughout the whole of Europe. Their suspicions deepened when in June 1947, American economic aid was announced in the form of the Marshall Plan. Following the lead of British Foreign Secretary Ernest Bevin, most European states accepted the offer, including such Eastern European states as Poland, Hungary and Czechoslovakia. However, when the Soviet leadership rejected Marshall aid on the grounds that it represented an American attempt to infiltrate and control Eastern Europe, these 'satellite states' were forced to withdraw their acceptance.

In turn, the Soviet government opted for even tighter control in Eastern Europe. By August 1947, the freely elected Smallholders' Party in Hungary had disintegrated as a result of communist pressure. In September 1947, the Cominform was finally organised, uniting all of the principal communist parties in Europe – including those in France and Italy – under strict Soviet leadership. Less than nine months later, Yugoslavia was expelled for allegedly placing itself 'outside the united Communist front'.[13]

When the Council of Foreign Ministers' Conference of December 1947 broke up in disagreement over German reparations, patience with negotiations ran out on both sides. In January 1948, a plan for the consolidation of Western Europe was proposed by Bevin. The following month, a communist seizure of power took place in Czechoslovakia. This event was a major alarm signal for the West[14] and no doubt increased the incentive to organise. In March, the Brussels Treaty was signed representing the first major step in the consolidation of Western Europe and the integration of western German occupation zones into it. The Treaty also established the principle of collective defence.

The first major confrontation of the cold war occurred over Berlin. In response to currency reforms which sought further to integrate Western occupation zones with the West, the Soviet government raised a blockade. In response, Truman declared that the West would remain committed to Berlin and a massive airlift of supplies was begun. Tension flared as both sides appeared committed to winning this test of wills. It was in this atmosphere that NATO was created. As the first peacetime treaty committing American forces to Europe, the agreement signed in April 1949 represented American acceptance of the responsibility of Western leadership as well as the 'collective' Western commitment to the containment of communism in Europe. The creation of this Western security block hardened further the division between East and West. Meanwhile, in Berlin, restraint prevailed and negotiations at the ambassadorial level led to the Soviet withdrawal of the blockade. Both sides agreed to convene a Foreign Ministers' Conference in May 1949 to discuss the German question. The meeting produced no agreement, however, because both sides had already taken steps to create separate states in East and West Germany. Thus, by the summer of 1949, a divided Germany existed in Europe which statesmen increasingly came to accept as being divided.

Following this episode, three events took place which were to set the tone for the 1950s. First, sometime in late August–early September 1949, the Soviet Union tested its first atomic bomb. Sooner than had been expected, the Soviet Union was beginning to close the gap between Western and Eastern strategic strength.[15]

Second, in October 1949, the Chinese Communists triumphed in the civil war in China, thereby causing a shift in the East-West balance of power; over 500 million people were added to the Soviet bloc, now boasting one-quarter of the world's land mass and one-third of the world's population. This event shook American confidence and confirmed Western fears that the Soviet Union was seeking world domination.

Finally, this 'frightening spectre' of the 'Red tide' sweeping over the earth was augmented in June 1950 by the outbreak of the Korean War. When the Western forces rose to meet this challenge in the Far East, it became clear that the East–West conflict had taken on global dimensions.

These three events had the effect of raising tension to new heights and alerting the new superpowers to the long struggle ahead. Fear in America was registered in the form of McCarthyism, and United States foreign policy was characterised by immobility. Likewise, Soviet foreign policy under Stalin was cautious and the fear of 'capitalist encirclement' paralysed any efforts aimed at mitigating tension. While ideological warfare served to exacerbate tension even further, there was no rational military recourse to take as the ultimate means in settling the conflict. In fact, Soviet conventional superiority in Europe and American strategic superiority served, to some degree, to cancel each other out. Both sides became entrenched in their relative positions.

THE CONSEQUENCE OF US–SOVIET RIVALRY

Despite high levels of tension, the cold war was in some ways remarkably restrained. First, and most significantly, the United States and the Soviet Union managed to avoid direct military conflict. While various crises brought the superpowers to the brink of conventional and nuclear war, neither side stepped over it. This restraint was based primarily upon the imagined consequences of superpower conflict.

While the United States clashed with Soviet-backed forces in Korea, the war demonstrated the limits that were placed on the conflict. After great expense in terms of human and financial resources, both sides were willing to settle for a 'stalemate'. In Berlin and Eastern Europe, restraint was practised as each side ultimately respected the vital interests of the other.

Second, while areas of common interest and co-operation were limited, both sides continued to co-operate in the control of Germany. If the future of Germany was at the centre of the cold war debate it was because neither side could agree on the best means by which to achieve that control; there was never any question as to the common commitment to prevent a strong, reunited Germany from rising again.

Finally, despite a series of provocations, neither side broke diplomatic relations with the other nor was there a serious move to close the channel of access and communication through the United Nations. Furthermore, both sides continued to participate in international conferences aimed at solving various post-war problems.

In other areas, however, relations did break down and the rivalry arising out of feelings of insecurity on both sides was less restrained. First, the United Nations Security Council system broke down thereby taking the teeth out of the only international organisation entrusted with conflict resolution and peace-keeping. Superpower and East–West competition was reflected in the 'bloc' votes of the General Assembly.

Second, the rising level of subversive activities conducted by both sides led to the breakdown of consular relations. As mutual suspicion grew, restrictions were tightened and general harrassment was practised as a means of expressing dissatisfaction with the relationship.

Third, the Soviet rejection of the Baruch plan, which was designed to establish the United Nations inspection of atomic production, reduced initial hopes for international management of atomic power. This represented a major setback for the cause of disarmament as well as the opportunity to place limits on the arms race.

Fourth, after maintaining an active economic relationship throughout the war, the superpowers sharply curtailed their economic relations. The United States placed barriers on trade and revoked most-favoured-nation trading status. At the same time, the Soviet Union announced its intention not to repay American lend-lease aid, thereby undermining confidence in East–West trade.

Fifth, US–Soviet dialogue, which had flowed so freely during the war, was eclipsed by the cold war. While diplomatic relations were maintained, high level consultations disappeared almost entirely. Almost no agreements were signed between the United States and the Soviet Union for ten years. While the United Nations provided an open channel for communication, it was used primarily as a forum for propaganda. Instead of being used as a means to communicate, modern communication techniques were being applied as a means of fighting the cold war. Ideological warfare was waged from the United Nations assembly rooms in New York to the air waves of Europe. Vilification was applied with increasing intensity as the conflict grew. Through this means, the participants defined the enemy and justified their actions in such a way that reinforced the cycle of tension.

Ideological warfare not only involved portraying the enemy as a group of warmongers; it involved portraying the other side as having a monopoly on immorality and evil. Given the nature of this vilification, little communication was possible as both sides branded diplomacy as a compromise with the devil. Herbert Butterfield summed up the problem: 'The process of détente, which can be hastened or delayed by the conduct of statesmen on both sides, is completely held up so long as each rival party regards the other as a monolithic slab of unredeemed evil.'[16] In short, this was the state of US–Soviet relations in 1953. Such was the setting for détente.

3 The 'Spirit of Geneva'

> We may be likened to two scorpions in a bottle, each capable of
> killing the other, but only at the risk of his own life.[1]
>
> J. Robert Oppenheimer

At the time Robert Oppenheimer compared the contemporary
US–Soviet relationship with that of two scorpions trapped in a
bottle, the fate of the world appeared to be hanging precariously
in the balance. The Berlin Crises, the stalemate over Germany,
the 'fall' of China, and the coming of the Korean war provided
startling evidence that the United States and the Soviet Union
were headed on a collision course. As both sides moved to
consolidate their allies politically and militarily, the spectre of a
third world war became all the more real. With the growing
destructive potential of nuclear weapons and technology, however, war as an instrument to settle differences was no longer a
rational alternative. Because there was no guarantee that ration-
ality would prevail in the high-pitched environment of the cold
war, both sides felt a need to reach some sort of accommodation
which would keep the contest within bounds.

The 'spirit of Geneva' was the term which came to be applied to
such efforts in the mid-1950s when they culminated in the first
great power summit since the beginning of the cold war. Like
many labels, it was somewhat misleading and by implication
oversold the product. Nonetheless, the Geneva Conference in July
1955 brought a significant easing of tension, as well as the
re-establishment of a dialogue between the two sides. The most
notable and lasting aspect of this dialogue was the joint enuncia-
tion of the necessity of avoiding nuclear war. In this way, the
adversaries acknowledged an element of restraint in their competitive relationship.

27

THE SETTING: MARCH 1953–MAY 1955

The foundations for the Geneva détente were laid in the two years preceding the Geneva summit meeting in July 1955. The first and most important development involved the changes of leadership in both the Soviet Union and the United States. The death of Stalin in March 1953 represented no less than the end of an era. Stalin had singlehandedly shaped and ruled the Soviet Union for almost three decades; moreover he had been the primary architect of Soviet foreign policy. With the death of Stalin came a generation of leaders who were more willing to try new initiatives with the West. Malenkov, Stalin's immediate successor, declared in Stalin's funeral oration that the Soviet Union would increasingly follow a 'policy which stems from the Lenin–Stalin formulation on the possibility of prolonged coexistence and peaceful competition of the two systems, capitalist and socialist'.[2] Soviet Security Chief Beria made a similar plea for the peaceful resolution of international problems.[3] The most eminent Western statesman, Winston Churchill, seized the opportunity and renewed his call for a summit meeting between the principal powers. The French government, anxious to find a way out of the stalemate, was sympathetic to Churchill's suggestion. The Eisenhower Administration, however, branded it as premature and the Adenauer Government expressed suspicion over any move which would place the future status of the Federal Republic of Germany on the auction block.

For several reasons, this initial opportunity for progress was lost. First, the primary proponents of an East/West initiative were frustrated in their efforts by a variety of unexpected factors. In the West, Churchill and Eden were struck by illness and the French government suffered a major defeat in the assembly, taking several weeks to reorganise. In the East, Beria was arrested and purged for 'criminal anti-party and anti-state actions . . . intended to undermine the Soviet State'.[4] In fact, the initial energies of the new Soviet leaders were consumed primarily by the task of sorting out the new 'collective' leadership. Throughout 1953 and 1954, Malenkov, who held the governmental–bureaucratic powers, and Khrushchev, who controlled the party apparatus, competed for leadership and power. By taking the tougher line and supporting investment in the military and heavy industrial sector over the consumer sector, Khrushchev won the backing of the military and was eventually triumphant.[5] This power struggle, however, was waged partly at the expense of pursuing new opportunities in US–Soviet relations.

Likewise, the newly elected Eisenhower Administration was ill-prepared to handle any new peace initiatives. Having just been elected on the premise that America needed to 'get tough' with the Soviet Union, and with the forces of McCarthyism in full swing, Eisenhower was reluctant to explore the opportunities at hand. Eisenhower's reservations, however, appeared mild next to Secretary of State Dulles' hardline stance – a position that was to prove to be a source of conflict within the administration in the years to come. Dulles had condemned the previous administration's 'policy of containment' as weak and defensive – one that could never win against the aggressive designs of the Soviet Union. Instead, he advocated a 'policy of liberation' through such 'processes short of war as political warfare, psychological warfare and propaganda'.[6]

Nonetheless, by 1955, the trend began to change. In America, the public fervour that had, in part, driven the new administration to pursue a more aggressive foreign policy, was beginning to subside. The excesses of McCarthyism demonstrated to many Americans that the threat to freedom was not exclusively a communist one. Various events abroad and the growth of bi-partisan support for President Eisenhower allowed his administration more flexibility in dealing with the Soviet Union.[7]

Similarly, a transition was taking place in the Soviet Union. By February 1955, Khrushchev had consolidated his power and thus was prepared to take new initiatives, both domestically and internationally, for which he had previously criticised his opponents. In short, by mid-1955, both Eisenhower and Khrushchev were ready to pursue new alternatives to the cold war. Having established their credentials as hardliners, both gained the support necessary to explore the benefits of negotiation without falling prey to accusations of appeasement or 'sell-out'. Eisenhower enjoyed popular domestic support, and Khrushchev's position within the Kremlin was strong.

Beyond the change of leadership, many other factors served to reverse the tide of tension during this period. The Soviet Union contributed to this process in three ways. First, Soviet rhetoric and propaganda began to reflect a desire for a relaxation in international tension. The initial 'peace' speeches made by

Malenkov, Beria and Molotov on 9 March 1953 were followed by a series of articles welcoming peace efforts and introducing the language of peaceful coexistence.

Progress in the Korean peace negotiations elicited the optimistic claims from *Pravda* and *Izvestia* on 21 June 1953 that 'events in the past months have persuaded the peoples that it is possible to achieve peaceful settlement of all international differences'. By August, a Korean truce had been signed and the Soviet press was suggesting the expansion of East–West trade.[8] By the end of 1953, the Soviet leaders were pushing for a four-power conference 'for the purpose of reducing international tension'.[9]

Throughout 1954, Soviet rhetoric and propaganda continued to reflect the Soviet desire for détente. The language of peaceful coexistence was spoken with increasing frequency but the Soviet press was far more important for what it did not say than for what it did say. Not since the commencement of the cold war had there been such restraint in the vilification of American life, society and politics. The usual polemics regarding the class struggle and bourgeois imperialism continued but with less specific reference to the United States.

The second way in which the Soviet Union contributed to the process of easing tension was through a series of actions suggesting that the oppression of the Stalin years was coming to an end. On 28 March 1953, Moscow granted amnesty to most prisoners condemned to less than five years. As André Fontaine observed:

> From then on, almost every week brought good news: lower prices for basic commodities, a reduction in forced loans, a purge of the police, the elimination from non-Russian republics of those groups which had persecuted 'bourgeois Nationalists', the renewal of relations with Israel, the abandonment of territorial claims against Turkey, the appointment of an ambassador to Belgrade, the liberation of the American journalist Oatis, condemned in Prague in 1951 to ten years' imprisonment, etc.[10]

Also, beginning about this time, significant reforms eased political terror and restrictions throughout Eastern Europe and Soviet relations with the whole of Eastern Europe were subjected to change. By 1955, liberalisation was seen to have taken a large step forward when the new Soviet leadership attempted to reconcile differences with Yugoslavia. During his visit to Belgrade in May, Khrushchev made the astonishing admission that the split had been the fault of the Soviet Union and that the new Soviet government supported differences in practical forms of socialism. This theme of liberalisation was to be developed further during the Party Congress in February 1956 and through the dissolution of the Cominform soon thereafter.

Finally, the Soviet Union contributed to détente by taking steps to settle some sources of conflict and tension in the East–West relationship. Most significantly, the Russians used their influence to gain a settlement in Korea.[11] On 27 July an armistice was signed. While it represented a formalised stalemate, peace was welcomed on both sides as a major source of tension in US–Soviet relations was removed.

In addition, an East–West dialogue was slowly re-established through a series of conferences during 1954. Despite an unproductive Foreign Ministers' conference in Berlin during January and February, the Geneva Foreign Ministers' conference on Indo-China during April produced significant results. By April 1954, French management of the war had reached a crossroads; either the West would have to escalate the war in the hope of achieving a military solution or the conflict would have to be settled by negotiation. The French government was primarily interested in ending the war and therefore was opposed to its expansion. The British government realised that total victory was unattainable without the risk of general war, and so wished to negotiate the partition of the disputed area. To the American government, such an arrangement represented a communist victory – one which would undermine the defence of Southeast Asia on the whole. Despite British attempts to obtain American support for a compromise, Dulles left the conference so as to dissociate the Eisenhower Administration from an agreement that, he believed, would be interpreted as a 'sell-out'. In reality, the American government could not decide what steps to take. It was not prepared to accept further communist advances in Indo-China nor would American public opinion allow the placing of troops in another Korean-type situation.

In contrast to American intransigence, the Soviet government appeared willing to negotiate a settlement. The most likely explanation for this Soviet interest has been suggested by Devillers and Lacouture in *End of a War*: 'Moscow was eager to conciliate France, not for the sake of Indo-China (which the USSR was willing to leave to its own fate), but because of the situation in Europe and the German question in particular.'[12] The Soviet desire to achieve a *quid pro quo* in Europe in exchange for a settlement in Southeast Asia was prompted by the debate over the establishment of the European Defence Community (EDC) in the French Assembly. Despite pressure from the United States, Britain and West Germany, the EDC faced serious opposition within France. Nonetheless, the new Soviet government was probably anxious to reach a settlement for another reason; any conflict that threatened to involve the Chinese Communists held the potential for escalation.[13]

Accordingly, on 21 July, the parties issued a Final Declaration (unsigned) which set a date for Vietnamese elections and signed three important agreements 'on the cessation of hostilities' for disengagement in Laos, the pacification of Cambodia and the military partitioning of Vietnam. Neither the Americans nor the South Vietnamese signed the agreement – a fact that would contribute to the renewal of hostilities in the years to come. Nonetheless, while the American government refused to support the Geneva Foreign Ministers' conference, the success of the meeting contributed to the growing hope and belief that East/West negotiations could produce mutually advantageous results.

Further proof of the potential advantages to be gained by negotiation came during the meetings of the Subcommittee of Five of the UN Disarmament Commission in 1954 and 1955. After months of unfruitful proposals presented through the forum of the General Assembly,[14] both sides agreed to pursue more serious negotiations through the Subcommittee. When differences over priorities continued to block progress, the British and the French governments developed a means to bring the two sides closer together. Their plan, which was submitted in June 1954, called for phased disarmament and attempted to strike the balance between reducing American nuclear power and Soviet conventional power so as to leave neither side vulnerable.[15]

The United States expressed its support for the plan and on 10 May 1955 the Soviet government suddenly presented its own version which accepted the fundamental points of the Anglo-French plan. What looked like a significant breakthrough proved to be shortlived, however, when the Eisenhower Administration expressed new reservations about it. These reservations were partly a product of the reappraisal of United States disarmament policy based on the emergence of the hydrogen bomb. The major reservation came from Dulles, however, who simply felt that the Soviet government could not be trusted; the new Soviet proposal still lacked an effective means of international inspection and control. Furthermore, stabilising conventional arms, at a time when German rearmament had become a likelihood and new problems were arising in the Middle East, was viewed by Dulles as being contrary to Western interests. In fact, Bulganin's additions to the 10 May plan at Geneva in July were to include a proposed limit on the force levels of all other states – a move aimed at prohibiting the rearmament of West Germany.

While this opportunity of partial disarmament was lost, the Soviet concessions of May 1955 were symbolic and provided further indication – especially to some Europeans – that progress could be made. To others, however, this incident was to expose East–West disarmament talks as a futile game.

For its part, throughout 1953 and 1954, the new American Administration was exceedingly slow and cautious in responding to overtures by the new Soviet leadership. There was great uncertainty about the political consequences of negotiating with the Soviet communists. In response to the growing chorus of calls for a four-power summit conference, Eisenhower gave a stock reply:

> I would not go to a summit merely because of friendly words and plausible promises by the men in the Kremlin: actual deeds giving some indication of a Communist readiness to negotiate constructively will have to be produced before I would agree to such a meeting.[16]

While the eventual termination of the Korean conflict removed one cause of East/West tension, its very occurrence and magnitude had further convinced the United States of the seriousness of the communist threat. Many lives and great resources had been sacrificed, and despite the widespread yearning for peace, the tide of public opinion was not to be turned quickly. American policy had been one of outright anti-communism and any change was rooted in a series of problems. As Walter Lafeber explained:

The American response to these Soviet changes was slow and unsure. The Washington bureaucracy was fearful and confused, partly because of its terror of the ubiquitous McCarthyism, partly because of the usual problems found in changing governments. Underneath this confusion lay a deeper problem. Soviet Communism, Dulles told the Senate Foreign Relations Committee in January, 'believes that human beings are nothing more than somewhat superior animals . . . 'I do not see how, as long as Soviet communism holds those views', Dulles concluded, '. . . there can be any permanent reconciliation. . . . This is an irreconcilable conflict'. By defining the conflict as so intensely ideological, Dulles severely limited the possibility of easing tensions through a flexible diplomacy.[17]

Dulles' comment encapsulated the essential position and problem of American foreign policy. First, while the politics of Soviet détente involved preserving the status quo or seeking recognition for their post-war sphere of influence, the American politics called for 'liberation' and 'roll-back'. Americans viewed the state of the world as unnatural. As Norman Graebner observed, 'American policy continued to regard Communist leadership or power as no more than a distasteful and temporary phenomenon on the world scene.'[18] What naturally followed was the illusion of American omnipotence – the belief that communism in China and Eastern Europe could be rolled back. In short, America was not prepared, and did not know how to deal with the Soviet détente initiatives in 1953 and 1954 and was somewhat blinded by the same illusions in the immediate years to come.

In May 1955, however, a significant step was taken by both sides that was to have the paradoxical effect of formalising and solidifying the opposing cold war power blocs in Europe while, at the same time, giving both sides the security and confidence to pursue peace. In April 1949, the North Atlantic Treaty had been signed between twelve Western states as a military alliance to repel Soviet aggression towards Europe. However, the all-important question involving the future of Germany left an unsettling power void in the heartland of Europe. The Korean War had convinced the American government of the need to rearm West Germany, but previous attempts to form a European Defence Community had been unsuccessful. When West Germany joined NATO in May 1955, the security question that had plagued the West was at last resolved. Eisenhower stated in his memoirs that this step toward Western unity had been significant in his decision to accept the idea of a summit meeting. Dulles began to soften his opposition after West Germany joined NATO and a 'western' European security system had been negotiated. By 1955, the United States had concluded a series of security agreements or treaties of alliance with states throughout the world including Japan, Australia, New Zealand, the Philippines, the Republic of Korea, Thailand, Pakistan, Turkey, Iraq, and Iran. By drawing all of these states into the Western security system, the United States significantly augmented its own security and felt more prepared to negotiate from a 'position of strength'.

Concurrently, by May 1955, the Russians had concluded a series of agreements forming their own security system throughout Central and Eastern Europe. Following World War II, nineteen bilateral treaties were signed that had the same characteristics and effects as multilateral pacts. Such agreements were signed with China, Bulgaria, Finland, Poland, Rumania, Hungary, and Czechoslovakia to name a few. In January 1949, the Soviet leaders formalised their influence over Eastern Europe in the establishment of Comecon. In October 1949, they concluded a treaty of mutual assistance with East Germany. Finally, in May 1955, the Treaty of Friendship, Co-operation and Mutual Assistance (the Warsaw Pact) was concluded giving the Soviet leaders the political, economic and military security blanket they had desired. Khrushchev recorded in his memoirs that the formation of the Warsaw Pact had given the Soviet Union an extra measure of security in pursuing negotiations with the West. The Pact legitimised Soviet troops in Europe and gave them command control over all the armed forces.

After both the United States and the Soviet Union had consolidated their respective European security systems in May, the process of détente gained momentum. While these security arrangements tended to split Europe into two opposing power blocs, they drew boundaries and acknowledged the political and military realities of the cold war. This enabled both sides to negotiate from a self-perceived position of strength.

HIGH DÉTENTE:
MAY 1955–OCTOBER/NOVEMBER 1955

With the conclusion of the respective security systems, there came a mutual willingness to explore the possibilities of co-operation. The Soviet Union encouraged this trend by signing the Austrian State Treaty on 15 May. The treaty represented a landmark in superpower relations because it was the first US–Soviet agreement on a mutual troop withdrawal from central Europe in ten years. This agreement, along with Soviet disarmament 'concessions' and approaches to Tito, helped to convince the West that the Soviet leaders were ready to put their words into deeds and that the West must respond favourably. The security agreements coupled with the Austrian State Treaty in May caused both parties to seek summit talks in anticipation of further progress.

The events leading up to the Geneva summit in late July exemplified the desire of both sides to ease tension. First, an exchange of athletes and chessplayers took place. Next, when in June 1955, a United States Navy patrol plane was shot down over the Bering Strait, the Soviet Union apologised and paid half of the damages. Eisenhower recorded that this was 'something it had never previously done following an incident of this type'.[19] On both sides of the world, vilification and propaganda declined while each government prepared its people for the anticipated changes to come. The *Manchester Guardian* (4 July 1955) noted this change in *Pravda*. On 7 July, in Washington D.C., Richard Rovere commented on the new practical, non-ideological attitude in the city: 'It is rather an odd thing to hear people here discussing detailed systems of disarmament not as theoretical exercises or propaganda gambits but as programs that are well within the realm of the possible.'[20]

The shift in American opinion played an especially important role in the events leading up to the Geneva Conference. On 2 December 1954, after four long years of leading the American 'spiritual' assault on communism, Joseph McCarthy had been censored by his colleagues in the United States Senate. Having single-handedly fanned the flames of the cold war by his ability to elicit and capitalise on the fears of the American people, McCarthy's fall was a triumph for those advocating a new approach to US–Soviet relations. When his true colours became known, the appeal of McCarthy's black/white views of communism faded. While the frenzy of McCarthyism had blinded Americans to the changes that had been occurring since 1953, it was the excesses of McCarthyism that forced Americans to reassess their views in 1955. It was this reassessment that persuaded Eisenhower to explore alternatives to the stalemate in the cold war, and helped him politically to do so. On 7 July 1955, Richard Rovere reported from Washington D.C.:

No significant body of public opinion at present opposes the President's leadership in foreign affairs. The Gallup poll finds only 16 percent of the people expressing dissatisfaction of any sort with the Eisenhower administration and the causes of this trifling amount of discontent are thought to be wholly domestic. . .

. . . it is a decade at least since there has been anything approaching the present degree of national unity. . .

. . . At Geneva he can take any course that appears to him to be sensible . . . he can be confident that anything he does at Geneva will now be accepted by the people and, if it should come to that, ratified by the Senate.[21]

Indeed, the vast majority of Americans were supportive, anxious and optimistic. Millions responded to Eisenhower's request for prayer on the eve of the conference. Several churches held special services and the unity expressed gave Eisenhower even greater confidence. In his radio and television address to the nation before leaving for Geneva, Eisenhower optimistically proclaimed that his approach would be one 'of conciliation and tolerance and understanding'.[22] Alastair Buchan commented in *The Observer* that the President was not going to Geneva to seek evidence of Soviet good faith – he was assuming it. In this way, Buchan added, Eisenhower's mood was reflective of the American mood. A poll taken for official purposes revealed that 89 per cent of Americans expected good results from Geneva. Buchan concluded that this liberal swing represented a reaction to McCarthyism.[23]

On 19 July, the opening day of the conference, the *Manchester Guardian* observed that the stock market rose sharply and credited this boom to the tremendous optimism surrounding Geneva. It was this optimism which greatly constituted what was to become known as the 'spirit of Geneva'.

This 'spirit' reigned supreme at the Geneva Conference and was characterised by the approaches and statements of both sides. The Soviet leaders displayed a new, patient and relaxed form of diplomacy. Eisenhower credited them with an earnest desire for peace and even the sceptical Secretary of State, Foster Dulles, concurred.[24] On 23 July 1955, political observer Joseph Harsch declared in the *Christian Science Monitor*, 'East and West have established a precedent for speaking to each other in the careful, measured, restrained and non-ideological term of diplomacy, rather than in the vigorous and unrestrained idiom of the so-called cold war.'

The 'spirit', however, and the language that was used to proclaim it, were far from reality in terms of making any tangible progress towards solving those problems plaguing the East–West and specifically the US–Soviet relationship. The discussions were characterised by deadlock after deadlock. On the first day, the powers discussed the German question which lay at the centre of the East–West conflict. Since the Federal Republic of Germany had become a full member of NATO in May 1955, Eisenhower demanded free elections in East Germany and defended the right of a reunited Germany to join NATO if it elected to do so. Soviet Premier Bulganin countered Eisenhower's demand by insisting that a general European security pact be signed which would include the withdrawal of all foreign troops from Germany – thereby dismantling NATO. Khrushchev then declared that the Soviet Union would not allow free elections in East Germany until West Germany had been disarmed. No progress was made.

In response to the Soviet disarmament proposals of 10 May, Eisenhower presented his 'open-skies' proposal involving the exchange of plans of each nation's military facilities, and the right of aerial reconnaissance to check against surprise attacks. For the Soviet Union, this proposal represented a poor substitute for disarmament and reflected the desire of the United States to overcome its disadvantages in intelligence while maintaining nuclear superiority. This plan was rejected by Khrushchev on the grounds that it would violate Soviet territorial sovereignty.

Finally, the issue of East/West contacts was discussed. While both sides expressed a willingness to expand contacts, there was general disagreement as to how this should be done. The Soviet leaders claimed that the first means of contact should involve trade. The American government, having just recently legislated a series of barriers against trade with communist countries, claimed that a free flow of information and exchanges between peoples was the most important means of establishing East–West contacts.

Beyond these three issues, mutual discussion was impossible. The West wanted to question Soviet leaders on the 'enslaved' peoples of Eastern Europe and on the aims of international communism. The Soviet leaders wanted to question the West on its involvement in Indonesia as well as the future status of the Peoples' Republic of China in the United Nations. Each side refused to discuss the other's questions.

Despite their inability to agree on any substantive issues, the four Heads of Government issued a final directive committing the leaders to have their foreign ministers meet again in October in Geneva. Additionally, it declared a mutual commitment to the relaxation of international tension. To this end, the powers had achieved a measure of success. While observers attributed the 'spirit of Geneva' to everything from 'atmospherics' to the realisation that one's adversaries were people too, it clearly represented a manifestation of all preceding efforts at easing tension. The 'spirit' was a real and authentic feeling among peoples built upon the joint foundations of fear and hope – fear of war and hope for peace. It brought widespread hope and speculation that the political winds were changing. The four Heads of Government were the first to express this hope.[25]

Walter Lippmann observed the tremendous change in friendliness which had occurred independently of any change in declared policies. He concluded that political differences had been, at least for a time, subordinated. The downgrading of issues that had divided the powers made possible the progress of détente.[26]

Laudatory comments continued to flow from both sides. Eisenhower made the extraordinary claim that 'he had spoken to every member of the Russian delegation and found them all sincere men' – a statement that might have been political suicide six months before.[27] On 25 July, the White House released a statement following a bipartisan meeting on Geneva stating: 'The President expressed the belief that the outstanding feature of the meeting was the apparently sincere desire expressed by the Soviet delegation to discuss world problems in the future in an atmosphere of friendliness and a willingness to sit down together to work out differences. . . .'.[28]

Concurrently, Khrushchev admitted after Geneva that 'neither side wants war'. This was a notable concession for a leader whose power base had partially rested on the continued threat from the West.[29] For years, *Pravda* had been portraying Americans as a people bent on war. After Geneva, *Pravda* credited Eisenhower with a powerful desire for peace.[30] On 5 August, *Pravda* reported Bulganin's speech to the Supreme Soviet:

> The Geneva four-power conference of government heads can be considered an important historical event, since it marks a turning point in relations among the USSR, the USA, Britain and France. . .
> . . . Different countries have different ways of life . . . but all agree on one thing: they are equally interested in preserving and strengthening peace.[31]

Two weeks later *Izvestia* announced Soviet armed forces would be reduced by 640 000 men in the interests of achieving this goal of peace.

Eisenhower's most important challenge upon his return from Geneva was to explain the proceedings to an anxious and hopeful American public. In his national address, Eisenhower defended the lack of substantive progress on the issues by stating: 'We must never be deluded into believing that one week of friendly, even fruitful negotiations can wholly eliminate a problem arising out of the wide gap that separates so far East and West.'[32] Unfortunately, this comment inadvertently raised unfounded hopes for the doomed Geneva conference of foreign ministers in October.

In the interests of not disappointing the hopes that had been raised, however, Eisenhower reiterated time and time again, the discovery that the West could actually talk with the Russians. In a press conference on 27 July, the President declared:

> One thing is indisputable. For one week of argument and debate that sometimes was, to say the least, intense, never once did we have a recurrence of the old method of merely talking to constituencies in terms of invective and personal abuse and nationalistic abuse. This in itself is a great gain and one that I hope we shall never lose. . .[33]

Despite the lack of progress, it seems that the East and the West had rediscovered the means to negotiate. This realisation contributed significantly to the 'spirit' of Geneva.

Writing in the journal *Foreign Affairs*, one observer commented: 'The Geneva meeting of the heads of government ushered in a new period in international relations. Only time will tell whether we are on the threshold of the "era of orderly peaceful change".'[34] Time did tell and sooner than anyone predicted. One of the first to recognise Geneva as 'all spirit and no substance' was political observer Roscoe Drummond. As early as 3 August 1955, he expressed his extreme disappointment that the Soviet leaders had come to Geneva with 'all smiles' with the intent of preventing settlement on anything.[35]

As this feeling became more prevalent, the administration began to 'backpedal'. At the end of August, Walter Lippmann observed that in the face of growing domestic criticism, Eisenhower's speech on 24 August to the American Bar Association represented an attempt by the administration to prove that America had not become soft on communism.[36]

In reality, the Eisenhower Administration was uncertain and unimaginative as to the next step to take. This inability to put the 'spirit of Geneva' to work for United States foreign policy gave credence to domestic concerns about its substance. Any hope of action was deflated by the occurrence of Eisenhower's stroke in September 1955. In some ways, his condition personified the condition of United States foreign policy.

In contrast, the Soviet leaders made good use of the 'spirit of Geneva'. Significantly, the Conference had marked a turning point in the Soviet commitment (whether rhetorical or real) to German unification. In mid-September, they negotiated formal diplomatic relations with the Adenauer government in West Germany. A week later they gave East Germany full powers in foreign affairs, thereby preventing Adenauer from ignoring the Communist regime indefinitely. This helped to ensure the future division of Germany.[37] Furthermore, the Soviet leaders attempted to extend their influence into the Middle East by the procurement of Czechoslovakian arms for Egypt – a move that was to have a tremendous impact on East–West relations in the near future.

As the foreign ministers' conference neared in late October 1955, it became increasingly clear that, in Eisenhower's words, the conference would be the acid test of the conciliatory 'spirit of Geneva'. Within the first couple of days of meetings, it was apparent that the 'spirit' had waned. The mood of the conference was summed up in the headlines of the *New York Times* on 30 October: 'Dulles Charges Moscow Flouts Spirit of Geneva', 'Molotov Assails West', and 'Geneva Mood: Less "Spirit", More Realism'.

The United States claimed that the Soviet Union had breached the summit directives and promptly ended the conference. The Soviet government immediately expressed extreme disappointment and blamed the failure on 'sinister elements opposing an easing of tension'.[38] The failure of the foreign ministers' conference had dealt the 'spirit of Geneva' and the first US–Soviet détente a damaging blow.

THE AFTERMATH: NOVEMBER 1955 UNTIL NOVEMBER 1956

The following months in US–Soviet relations witnessed a series of conflicting trends. On the one hand, the disappointed expectations of many Americans produced both recriminations and warnings. On 30 October 1955, Thomas Hamilton warned in the *New York Times* that the relaxation of tension was causing the democracies to lower their defences. On 11 November, in a speech at the University of Virginia, presidential aspirant Adlai Stevenson warned:

> Let us, I say, not deceive ourselves. . . . since the death of Stalin they (the Soviet leaders) have sharply altered their tactics and stepped boldly forth from the shadows of conspiracy and secrecy. To our dismay, they are competing openly and directly with the West. We must take care lest the illusions of their charm policy further weaken our defenses, moral and physical.[39]

On the other hand, despite the disillusionment with the 'spirit of Geneva', many Americans seemed to feel that, somehow, things had changed. While little or no progress had been made, the legacy of civilised negotiation at Geneva lingered on. The next few months were characterised by this paradoxical marriage between disillusionment and faith.

Nonetheless, the evidence kept mounting in the West that the Soviet Union was pursuing détente for mainly tactical reasons. For instance, the Soviet leaders began experimenting with a series of new foreign policy ventures. During November and December 1955, Khrushchev and Bulganin toured India and Afghanistan promising trade and economic assistance of the kind previously provided by the Western powers. In February 1956, they offered trade and economic assistance to Pakistan if it pulled out of its military commitments to the United States. Similar 'aid' packages were offered to Latin America.[40]

The split in Germany was reconfirmed in January 1956 when East Germany entered the Warsaw Pact. At the NATO foreign ministers' meeting in December 1955, Dulles predicted that, due to the stalemate in Europe, the Soviet leaders would begin to employ 'indirect' threats 'primarily developed in relation to the Near and Middle East and Southeast Asia', with special emphasis on controlling Middle Eastern oil so 'essential to the industrial life of Western Europe'.[41] As predicted, they increasingly sided with the Arabs against Israel in the United Nations. Behind the scenes, aid agreements were in the making, one of which would eventually finance the building of the Aswan Dam in Egypt.[42]

While all of this was taking place, the Soviet leaders were proposing a treaty of friendship and co-operation with the United States. In response, Eisenhower wrote to Premier Bulganin: 'A further deterioration has taken place because to us it has seemed that your Government has, in various areas of the world, embarked upon a course which increases tensions by intensifying hatreds and animosities implicit in historic international disputes.'[43]

These events were occurring, however, at a time when a revision in Soviet domestic policy was about to astonish both the communist and the western worlds – as well as reinforcing the faltering détente. At the Twentieth Party Congress of the Communist Party in February 1956, Khrushchev announced what was to amount to a significant liberalisation of Soviet policies. These speeches covered three main points. First, Khrushchev denounced the personality 'cult' of Stalin as well as several of his policies and methods. Second, in denouncing Stalin's policies, Khrushchev formalised the doctrine of peaceful coexistence, thereby denying the inevitability of war between the two social systems. Finally, he announced his doctrine of 'Independent Roads to Socialism' in what amounted to be a loosening of the Soviet grip on Eastern Europe.

Khrushchev's denunciation of Stalin 'surprised his listeners, shocked the satellites, and astonished the West by detailing Stalin's crimes against the Communist Party and (the same thing) Russian national interest'.[44] Never before had there been any official Soviet admission that Stalin had been subject to human error. Khrushchev was, of course, careful to base his criticism on the classic doctrines of Marxism–Leninism. He claimed that pure communism demanded collective leadership and hence, Stalin's construction of the 'cult of the individual' was not a fault of the communist system, but of Stalin himself. This 'fault' had led to a series of domestic crimes and mistakes in foreign policy.

Khrushchev's special efforts to exonerate the Party and the Army from blame led observers to conclude that he was trying to expand his own power base while, at the same time, loosening Stalinist restrictions on both domestic and foreign policy. This 'loosening of restrictions' included a formalisation of Khrushchev's doctrine of peaceful coexistence. In a departure from Lenin's classical view of peaceful coexistence which included the fatal inevitability of war, Khrushchev declared that war was not inevitable and that peaceful coexistence was the only rational option in the nuclear age.[45] Claiming that 'negotiation must become the sole method of settling international problems', Khrushchev declared, 'We want to be friends with the United States and to co-operate with it for peace and international security, and also in economic and cultural spheres.'[46] The message was clear. Soviet foreign policy would no longer be dictated by rigid Stalinist principles: Khrushchev sought the manoeuvrability and flexibility to establish business-type relations with the West when such relations might prove fruitful.

In terms of East–West relations, Khrushchev's most significant departure in his speeches to the Twentieth Party Congress dealt with his declaration of 'different roads to socialism'. Challenging the Stalinist maxim that every socialist country must follow the Soviet example, Khrushchev again based his interpretation on classical Marxist/Leninist doctrine. Quoting Lenin he claimed, 'All nations will arrive at socialism – this is inevitable, but not all will do so in exactly the same way.'[47] While Khrushchev was careful to maintain Moscow's command position over its client states, his new ideological interpretation did extend a significant degree of autonomy to Eastern Europe. As Joseph Korbel pointed out, this move served to salvage détente:

> This period of liberalization contributed substantially to the development of a climate for détente. Not only did it offer a precious opportunity for developing contacts with the West, but West European governments, comprehending the significance of liberalization and fully grasping its potential for a relaxation of tensions, began to treat the East European countries as individual national entities rather than as Moscow's obedient satellites.[48]

Because these new policies were presented in a secret session of the Congress, it took several months before the full interpretation and impact was realised in the West. However, as the reports began to leak out, the news was received with great interest. Soviet control over Eastern Europe had long been one of the fundamental sources of conflict between East and West. While the new liberalisation was far from the political and economic freedom demanded by the West, the new Soviet policies were viewed as favourable signs.

Over the next few months, de-Stalinisation appeared to give substance to Western optimism. In April, the Cominform was abolished in order to stress the new independence of socialist countries. Khrushchev also announced a variety of internal reforms. One new law abolished the practice of using special criminal procedures for political prisoners. In addition, Khrushchev ordered the release of hundreds of political prisoners from concentration camps. Finally, a new decree repealed the 1940 law which made absenteeism and leaving a job without official permission a criminal offence.

In late April, Khrushchev and Bulganin visited Great Britain. While nothing of significance was accomplished during the visit, it did symbolise the fact that things had changed for the better in East–West relations.

The potential for salvaging détente, however, from these Soviet initiatives was ignored by the United States. Despite the changes occurring in the Soviet Union, 1956 was a presidential election year and the polls showed that most Americans supported a 'get tough' policy with the Russians.[49] Eisenhower's trip to Geneva had met with mixed results and an election year was no time to be experimenting with new ventures in foreign policy. In fact, 1956 was a rather uneventful year in US–Soviet relations until late October, when the entire situation exploded, threatening the foundations of the respective alliances and shattering any remnants of the 'spirit of Geneva'.

Two events – the Anglo-French–Israeli invasion of Egypt and the Soviet invasion of Hungary – caused this explosion in October. These crises were precipitated by a series of smaller events occurring in the preceding months.

The Suez crisis had its roots in President Nasser's new course of Arab nationalism which came into conflict with Britain's remaining imperial interests and Israel's fear for its security. Nasser's growing relationship with the Soviet Union which was symbolised by the arms purchase of 1955 was both a cause and effect of Dulles' decision to withdraw the American offer to finance the Aswan Dam[50] – a project which represented the nucleus of Nasser's modernisation efforts. On 26 July, exactly one week after the withdrawal, Nasser announced the nationalisation of the Suez Canal and justified the move in terms of Egypt's inherent rights to the canal as well as the need to gain the necessary funds to finance the Aswan Dam. This action caused fury among the British and French who held the major historical, strategic, and financial interests in the canal. Over the next three months, both powers applied a variety of pressures to elicit the return of the canal, but with little success. Without United States knowledge or support, Britain and France made a secret agreement with Israel to arrange a pretext for military intervention to re-take the canal. On 29 October 1956, Israel launched a 'preventive' strike against Egypt. Britain and France then issued an ultimatum declaring that if the fighting did not stop, they would be forced to intervene to separate the combatant forces, 'protect' the canal and ensure its continued operation. When peace was not forthcoming, the French and the British moved in to take the canal. Any military success was immediately negated by the widespread political condemnation of these old colonial powers, seeking to impose their will upon a weaker Third World state by the traditional means of 'gunboat diplomacy'. The United States immediately led the fight in the United Nations for a ceasefire, against the opposition of the British and the French. A potentially dangerous conflict was in the making as the Soviet Union attempted to exploit the situation to divert attention from the events in Hungary. On 5 November, claiming that a spread in the fighting could lead to a third world war, Bulganin proposed joint US–Soviet intervention.[51] Eisenhower quickly discouraged such 'folly' by placing the responsibility with the United Nations and stating the United States would not allow such action.[52]

The Suez crisis soon subsided, but not without serious repercussions. In its wake lay an alliance torn by competing interests and perceptions. The British and the French earned the condemnation of world opinion, as well as rejection by the Americans, who were not prepared to identify themselves with the forces of 19th Century imperialism. As a result, the West suffered a damaging blow in the Middle East which had become a scene of East–West competition and rivalry.

The second event – the Soviet invasion of Hungary – had its roots in Khrushchev's policies of liberalisation announced at the Twentieth Party Congress in February 1956.[53]

Following Khrushchev's speech on 25 February 1956, most of the countries of Eastern Europe anxiously began to build their own 'independent roads to socialism'. The governments of Hungary and Czechoslovakia made significant attempts to improve their relations with neutral Austria and with Yugoslavia. In May, the Hungarian Prime Minister declared that the 'iron curtain' fortifications along the Austrian border could be dismantled, and he extended a similar promise to Yugoslavia in August. Such moves were made possible by Moscow's reconciliation with Tito, who visited Khrushchev in Moscow and attempted to convince him of the wisdom of getting rid of such incompetent and unpopular communist puppets as Rakosi in Hungary. While Khrushchev considered his options, an event in Poland marked the first violent by-product of Khrushchev's policies of liberalisation. In June, a group of Polish workers and youths seized the Communist Party and police headquarters in Poznan. The vacillating communist regime took two or three days to restore order.

In Hungary, the spirit of 'national independence' was on the rise. Throughout June and July, an increasing number of calls were heard for the ousting and punishment of the hated Moscow-backed leadership. As the crowds grew larger, the cries grew louder for the return of the popular Hungarian nationalist,

Imre Nagy. Wishing to remain on the right side of events, the Soviet Government sent a representative to Budapest during the third week of July. Eventually, Nagy was reinstated in the Communist Party.

By October, national passions in Poland were reaching uncontrollable heights. About this time, Gomulka, the popular Polish leader who had been released from prison in 1954, became the master of events. Poland's Congress was scheduled to meet on 19 October, and from the Soviet precedent, great changes were anticipated. Suddenly, without warning, Khrushchev and an entourage of Soviet Marshals flew into Warsaw and the Soviet government practised some military posturing. In response, arms were distributed among the Polish workers and Gomulka stated that Poland would not give in to military pressure. When the possibility of national war arose between two fraternal socialist states, Khrushchev relented. Impressed by Gomulka's determination, and wanting to avoid a divisive and costly conflict, Khrushchev promised Gomulka his support. In return, Gomulka responsed with wisdom and restraint. Euphoria reigned throughout the streets of Poland and Gomulka and the Party leadership maintained control, always mindful of the consequences of wandering too far from Moscow's paternal hand.

At the time of the Polish 'revolution', there was a similar event in Hungary that was to have a different and tragic ending. Encouraged by the events in Poland, crowds began swarming through the streets of Budapest chanting nationalistic slogans and protesting against repressive Soviet influence. Revolution broke out on 23 October. By the following day, the army, the police and the workers' organisations were joining the revolution. By the time the remnants of the Communist government announced that Imre Nagy would be appointed as Premier, Soviet troops had already been called in to restore order. As bloodshed increased, so did the demands of the people. Demands for reform of the Communist Party gave way to calls for its abolition. Demands for the withdrawal of Soviet troops from Budapest gave way to calls for the total withdrawal of Soviet troops from Hungary.

The Soviet Union reacted by giving their support to Nagy who, in turn, announced a series of extraordinary reforms. By 28 October, Soviet tanks began to withdraw from Budapest. Despite these conciliatory moves, the tide of public fervour could not be turned. The people refused to rest until the last vestiges of Soviet influence had been eradicated from Hungary.

In a last and final attempt at pacification on 30 October, the Soviet government issued extraordinary statements admitting that mistakes had been made and asking for a reconciliation on new terms:

> . . . there have been many difficulties, unresolved problems and downright mistakes, including mistakes in the mutual relations among the socialist countries.[54]

The Soviet Union then offered to renegotiate its role in Hungary and recalled its advisors. Finally, the Soviet government announced its readiness to negotiate the presence of Soviet troops in Hungary.

Suddenly, on 1 November, significant numbers of Soviet troops and tanks began to cross into Hungary. When the new Hungarian government demanded an explanation, the Soviet ambassador claimed that the additional units were simply replacements. The seizure of Hungarian airfields, however, suggested more devious Soviet designs. In a final attempt to save the revolution, Nagy issued a protest, announced Hungary's withdrawal from the Warsaw Pact and declared neutrality.[55]

Despite having a major impact on world opinion, Nagy's appeal had little practical effect. On 4 November, in a sign that the Soviet decision makers had reached their threshold of tolerance, Soviet forces 'attacked' Budapest 'to help the Hungarian people crush the black forces of reaction and counter-revolution'.[56] The following day, 50 000 Hungarians were reported dead or wounded in Budapest. The Soviet Union installed Janos Kadar as leader and declared the formation of the 'Hungarian Revolutionary Workers and Peasants Government'. With one swift and powerful Soviet blow, the revolution was crushed and the crisis terminated.

The events in Hungary caused a dual reaction among Americans. On one hand, the efforts by the satellites to break free from the Soviet grip were welcomed and encouraged. The desire for the 'liberation' of the 'enslaved masses' of Eastern Europe was, at long last, being fulfilled, or so it seemed. On the other hand, the Administration feared the Soviet Union would be forced to try something dangerous in the interests of maintaining its security.[57] In his memoirs, Eisenhower claimed that the United States considered providing military assistance to Hungary but decided against it for two reasons. First, the United States could have had no access to Hungary without violating Austrian neutrality. Second, intervention probably would have led to a major conflict.[58] Perhaps the main reason, though, was revealed by Joseph Harsch in the *Christian Science Monitor* on 7 November: 'It was recognized that the Soviet Union regards its military alliance with satellites as the essential feature of its military security system.' In other words, the United States had implicitly acknowledged that Hungary was within the Soviet Union's security sphere – an admission that the Administration could not afford to make publicly. In terms of foreign policy, American inaction demonstrated that the 'policy of liberation' was political rhetoric; any real action would have to be taken by the countries concerned.

The effect that the Suez and Hungarian crises had on détente or the 'spirit of Geneva' was devastating. Once again, propaganda and vilification characterised the East–West dialogue as each side attempted to divert the world's attention. On 28 October, *Pravda* claimed that United States agents were instigating the revolution in Hungary and that similar attempts at fomenting unrest were occurring in Czechoslovakia. When Vice President Nixon led an aid mission to Austria to help thousands of Hungarian refugees, *Pravda* condemned the mission as a subversive attempt to aid counter-revolutionaries.[59]

The American response was articulated in no uncertain terms. On 4 November, the *New York Times* declared:

We accuse the Soviet Government of murder. We accuse it of the foulest treachery and the basest deceit known to man. We accuse it of having committed so monstrous a crime against the Hungarian People yesterday that its infamy can *never* be forgiven or forgotten. . . Gone now are the last illusions. Moscow now stands self-exposed . . . Those bullets killed first of all the picture of a reformed, penitent Russia seeking to repudiate Stalinism and practice coexistence.[60]

The American public was outraged. Calls were heard for such actions as the withdrawal of diplomatic relations, expulsion from the United Nations, the application of economic sanctions and so on.

. By the end of November, it was clear that the 'spirit of Geneva' was gone. While the crises of 1956 had not exploded into world war, they demonstrated that little had changed since the cold war. Once again, mutual vilification characterised the superpower dialogue. In reaction to a speech by Eisenhower condemning Soviet crimes in Hungary, *Pravda* stated: 'Such a speech can only be evaluated as a ... step toward the deterioration of the international situation and a resumption of the cold war.'[61] By the end of 1956, tension was again on the rise and the cold war resumed.

FACTORS CONTRIBUTING TO, AND DETRACTING FROM, DÉTENTE

Having observed the fall and rise of tension surrounding the 'spirit of Geneva', it is now possible to assess those factors which contributed to, and detracted from, détente. In retrospect, six factors appear to have contributed to détente, representing steps on the stairway to the 'spirit of Geneva'. The first step came in early 1953 with the change in leadership in the Soviet Union and the United States. The death of Stalin and the election of a new American president opened up new opportunities in US–Soviet relations.

The Western reaction to Stalin's death was one of cautious expectation and hope for Stalin had come to epitomise the very evils of communism. The public, exhausted by war, worried over the growing tension in the post-war world, and frightened by the disastrous consequences if that tension got out of hand, was ready to give the Soviet Union 'a new chance'.[62] While it is difficult to assess accurately the 'mood of public opinion' or its significance in the Soviet Union or the Eastern bloc, the long series of positive steps taken by the new Soviet leaders immediately following Stalin's death most certainly augmented hopes that things would change for the better.

The election of Eisenhower elicited a similar response. To millions of Europeans, Eisenhower was the man who had liberated Western Europe from Hitler. To the Soviet leadership, he appeared to be a practical military man and a great improvement over President Truman. After all, the worst years in US–Soviet relations had occurred under the Truman Administration and practically any other leader was thought to be an improvement.

The American people also viewed Eisenhower's election with hope and confidence. 'Truman's war' in Korea was becoming increasingly unpopular and his Administration had been tainted with allegations, even if unfounded, of communist infiltration. Eisenhower's strong electoral mandate reflected the faith and confidence that Americans had in his ability to meet both the internal and external communist threat. Given the influence of McCarthyism on American thought and politics in 1952–3, the election of Eisenhower worked to restore faith and confidence in American domestic and foreign policy. The early conclusion of the Korean War in July 1953 further augmented hopes that Eisenhower could meet the communist threat by peaceful means.

In short, the change of leadership in the United States and the Soviet Union in 1953 was a major factor in initiating the process of détente. The widespread feelings of hope that accompanied the transitions in power worked in favour of the process of détente by simply increasing the expectations of a new era. As Herbert Butterfield pointed out in describing the relaxation after the fall of Robespierre and the 'reign of terror' during the French Revolution in 1795: 'détente, which was unplanned and unintended, was brought about because it was assumed that this was the natural coorollary.'[63] Or as Richard Rovere wrote from Washington D.C. on 7 July 1955, 'There can be an easing of tensions in the world by the simple assertion of a desire for tensions to be eased.'[64] The transitions in power fired the hopes of millions and provided the psychological environment in which détente could prosper.

The second factor was both a manifestation and cause of the 'spirit of Geneva'. It involved the lessening of ideological warfare between the two superpowers. This change in superpower dialogue and propaganda was initiated by the new Soviet leadership and was not reciprocated by the United States until 1955. As previously recorded, the new Soviet leaders made a series of unprecedented appeals for peace and co-operation with the West. New disarmament packages were proposed and high level conferences were requested to settle differences. While it would be incorrect to claim that the Soviet communists dropped their ideological campaign against the United States, it is clear that between 1953–1956, there was a notable decline of anti-Western propaganda and vilification in the Soviet press.[65]

The Western response was varied. Churchill called for seizing the moment of opportunity and establishing a meaningful peace with the Soviet Union. Conversely, Dulles viewed the new Soviet 'image' with cynicism, and remained cynical throughout the 'spirit of Geneva' primarily because he believed that 'no totalitarian society (could) afford to acquiesce in the easing of tension'.[66] The 'centre' view was taken by Eisenhower, however, who looked on with caution but curiosity as well. While American politics in 1953–4 did not allow for great flexibility in pursuing peace with the communists, the Soviet leaders continued to speak the language of peace, and as McCarthyism began to wane, Americans became increasingly receptive to Soviet appeals. Eventually the Eisenhower Administration began to temper anti-Soviet language and propaganda. By May 1955, as the spectre of a conference loomed on the political horizon, it became wise domestic politics to speak more kindly about the Russians.

The lessening of ideological warfare raised hopes on both sides that progress was being made. The oldest and seemingly most basic conflict between the United States and the Soviet Union was ideological, and the willingness to subordinate this basic difference in the interests of peace was perceived as a positive step toward détente.

The third event that provided the groundwork for the 'spirit of Geneva' was the testing of the hydrogen bomb – by the United States in late 1952, and by the Soviet Union in August 1953. This development, seemingly so inimical to the cause of peace, had a dual effect on the level of tension between the superpowers. First, despite the limited ability of both powers, especially the Soviet Union, to deliver the weapons effectively, the creation of a bomb many times more powerful than those dropped on Japan had a great psychological impact on the populations of many countries. Nowhere was this impact greater than in the United States. Having been isolated and virtually invulnerable from attack for much of its history, the United States suddenly became susceptible to unprecedented degrees of destruction. This produced a wave of fear, thereby escalating tension. At the same time, however, this fear of nuclear annihilation became a unifying element in the struggle to prevent such destruction. The East and West had a joint interest and stake in the prevention of war. It was the realisation of this joint interest that provided restraint and contributed to détente.

Some students of international affairs have claimed that this realisation did not influence American and Soviet decision-makers until 1962, when the Cuban Missile Crisis brought the world to the brink of nuclear war. To some extent this is true. However, the evidence suggests that many influential men reached this realisation in the mid-1950s. In keeping with previous Soviet statements on the devastating result of a war, Khrushchev stated unequivocally at the Twentieth Party Congress: 'There are only two ways: either peaceful coexistence or the most destructive war in history. There is no third way.'[67] In October 1954, Eisenhower stated: 'Since the advent of nuclear weapons, it seems clear that there is no longer any alternative to peace.'[68] In 1955, Eisenhower confessed that the threat of the H-bomb was 'so serious that we cannot pretend to be intelligent human beings unless we pursue with all our thought, all our souls . . . some way of solving this problem . . .'.[69]

Even within the United States military establishment there was an increasing realisation that a general war could not be won. In January 1955, the retired heroic fighter of communism, General MacArthur, declared: the 'very success of invention . . . has destroyed the possibility of war being a medium of practical settlement of international differences. The enormous destruction to both sides of closely matched opponents makes it impossible for the winner to translate it into anything but his own disaster'.[70] Eisenhower acknowledged this observation in his radio and television address upon opening his presidential campaign on 19 September 1956:

Humanity has now achieved, for the first time in its history, the power to end its history. This truth must guide our every deed . . . the only way to win World War III is to prevent it.[71]

Albert Einstein had stated: 'The unleashed power of the atom has changed everything save our modes of thinking, and thus we drift toward unparalleled catastrophe.'[72] By 1955, many leaders seemed bent on disproving this prophecy.

In short, the growing realisation that war would prove disastrous for both sides, and hence must be avoided, injected a common purpose into a relationship traditionally dictated by divergent interests. The testing of the hydrogen bomb raised fear and tension but, at the same time, had a sobering effect on those elements pushing for a solution through the application of force. The decline of force as an option in settling differences eventually led the powers to the negotiating table which, in itself, was a significant contribution to détente. Both sides practised almost complete restraint when the possibility of direct confrontation was likely; the United States decided against coming to Hungary's aid during the Soviet invasion in November 1956 and the Soviet Union reluctantly respected United States interests in other parts of the world. The threat of war simply worked to shift the conflict to other levels that were less potentially dangerous and explosive.

The 'spirit of Geneva' represented and affirmed the common commitment to avoid conflict. This would prove to be its most enduring accomplishment.

The fourth factor contributing to the 'spirit of Geneva' was the settlement or subordination of issues producing tension.

For instance, the settlement of the Korean War in July 1953 represented an important event in East–West relations. While the settlement only confirmed an old stalemate at a cost of hundreds of thousands of lives, and while conflict continued throughout Southeast Asia, the settlement displayed the triumph of negotiations and the limited objectives of both sides. In other words, it was more important for both sides to end the conflict than to 'win' the war.

Another settlement contributing to the 'spirit of Geneva' was the signing of the Austrian Treaty in May 1955. This mutual agreement to withdraw troops was viewed as the first step in settling the status of occupied countries. In fact, many claimed that it was this act that clinched the agreement to meet at Geneva in July.[73]

Despite the settlement of these two important issues, most major issues still remained unsolved. By 1955, a settlement on the reunification of Germany was no closer than it had been ten years before. In fact, new barriers to reunification had been imposed by the efforts of both sides to integrate the occupied sections into their relative security systems. With the exception of Austria, Eastern Europe was still firmly within the Soviet grip as assured by the Warsaw Pact. Likewise, NATO and the Marshall plan guaranteed continued American influence over West European affairs. Both sides continued to stock their arsenals and, with few exceptions, disarmament proposals continued to be designed more for propaganda purposes than for serious negotiation. Finally, the superpowers increased their efforts at expanding their influence and ideology into other areas of the world.

Despite the lack of progress in solving these divisive issues, their importance was subordinated in the months leading up to Geneva. The major reason for this downgrading was the general fear of war. For instance, the United States was prepared continually to demand the liberation of Eastern Europe, but was not prepared to fight for it. Likewise, the Soviet Union was willing to push the Berlin issue to the brink of war, but never over it. Issues of the greatest political, military, economic and ideological importance increasingly became subordinated to the cause of peace as the threat of nuclear destruction grew. This downgrading of issues was revealed in the comments of the Soviet and American leaders before Geneva. On 11 May 1955, when asked what he thought would be the most important thing to discuss at the Four-Power conference, Eisenhower, bypassing all the individual issues, replied: 'To see whether there is any opportunity to relieve the tensions in the world.'[74] On 13 June 1955, *Pravda* declared that the Soviet government 'considers the task of the four-power conference to be the easing of international tension and the strengthening of trust among states'. The two sides appeared to be pursuing détente for détente's sake and their efforts met with success.

By 1955, the stalemate had progressed to the point where both sides were willing to try something new. While divisive issues were discussed at Geneva, the success of the spirit achieved seemed to outweigh the failure of making any progress on the issues. For a time, their importance had been subordinated, augmenting the hope that meaningful progress in other areas could be made.

The fifth factor contributing to détente in 1955 was the consolidation of the Eastern and Western security systems. The inclusion of West Germany in NATO and the establishment of the Warsaw Pact in May 1955 provided a significant measure of security and confidence, allowing both sides to approach negotiations with their boundaries firmly drawn. Both Eisenhower and Khrushchev recorded in their memoirs that the completed security arrangements were significant in their decisions to go to Geneva.

Both leaders had worried that an easing of tension might threaten ties with allies, since it was tension in the face of the enemy's threat that provided the impetus and legitimacy for allied relationships. The consolidation of the Eastern and Western security systems solidified allied commitments.

While the security arrangements crystallised the division of Europe and therefore defined the future boundaries and limitations of negotiations, they provided the stability and predictability necessary for the pursuit of détente. These security guarantees gave both sides the confidence to explore new roads to peace.

The final factor contributing to détente was the liberalisation of domestic and foreign policies on both sides. In the Soviet Union, the process of domestic and foreign liberalisation began after the death of Stalin and reached its climax following Khrushchev's speech to the Twentieth Party Congress.

Khrushchev's declaration of 'independent roads to socialism' was, by far, the most significant aspect of this liberalisation programme. In fact, the Soviet leadership displayed a growing willingness to be tolerant of East European self-assertion up to the day before Soviet tanks rolled into Hungary. The Soviet declaration of 30 October, on the sanctity of independence and non-interference, represented an unprecedented attempt to make liberalisation work.

Furthermore, the conciliatory actions of the new Soviet leadership leading to Khrushchev's declaration of peaceful coexistence represented the most notable liberalisation of Soviet foreign policy in the decade. These policies contributed to and characterised the 'spirit of Geneva'.

In the United States, liberalisation or 'de-McCarthyisation' did not occur until the end of 1954. The waning of McCarthyism coupled with the election of a Democratic congress represented a shift to the left in public opinion. Having established his credentials as a trustworthy hardliner, Eisenhower was able to ride the crest of this wave and experiment with new turns in foreign policy. The political reaction to the excesses of McCarthyism, coupled with pressure from the European Allies to recognise Soviet peace overtures, led to a liberalisation of United States domestic and foreign policy.

From the early months of 1953 to the final months of 1956, these factors contributed to an easing of tension, thereby bringing about the first détente in the contemporary US–Soviet relationship. Either directly or indirectly, they worked together to generate feelings of hope, confidence, and a desire for peace – or what was to become known as the 'spirit' of Geneva.

In October–November 1956, however, the tides turned. The events in Hungary and the Middle East swept away the 'spirit of Geneva', and the cold war feelings of fear, hate and distrust re-emerged. It became increasingly clear that the 'spirit' did not represent a new US–Soviet relationship but merely an oasis in the middle of the old one.

Six factors appear to have contributed to the crises of 1956 and the re-emergence of the cold war. First, liberalisation in the domestic and foreign policies of the superpowers progressed too quickly and too far beyond the practical limits of détente. In other words, the price of liberalisation was eventually viewed as being too high. This was especially true in the Soviet Union where Khrushchev's policies of liberalisation opened the 'Pandora's box' of East European nationalism. Khrushchev's declaration of 'independent roads to socialism' not only encouraged the East Europeans to diverge from the path of Soviet leadership, but his de-Stalinisation programmes seemed to highlight the potential fallibility of that path. As liberalisation in the East European satellites progressed, the voices of dissent and independence grew louder. When the explosion of nationalism occurred in Hungary, the Soviet Union attempted to mollify the situation by reasserting the Soviet commitment to 'independent roads to socialism' and offering to renegotiate the presence of Soviet troops. However, Hungarian nationalism flared out of control. Because Hungary was perceived as a vital part of the Soviet security system, further liberalisation was perceived as inimical to the primary interests of Soviet security. Soviet troops moved in and the limits of liberalisation were spelled out.

It is not clear to what extent liberalisation encouraged domestic dissent in the Soviet Union. However, following the events in Hungary, police controls were tightened everywhere and Khrushchev suffered a temporary but significant decline in influence. His policy of peaceful coexistence coupled with his withdrawal of human and financial resources from the military sector left him open to the charge that liberalisation of Soviet foreign policy was endangering Soviet security interests.

If liberalisation went too far in the Soviet Union, the post-McCarthy liberal reaction also pushed to the limits in the United States. In the months following Geneva, the American people became increasingly aware that the 'spirit of Geneva' was more 'spirit' than substance. The Soviet invasion of Hungary confirmed this realisation and caused an immediate reversal of the 'liberal' trend. The progressive face of liberalisation was replaced by the image of appeasement and naïveté. What the public had seen and disliked on the 'right' in the excesses of McCarthyism, they now saw on the 'left' in the failure of détente. In response, a practical, cautious and conservative course was charted for the future.

In short, the liberalisation that had initially contributed to détente eventually brought about its downfall. Up to a point, liberalisation had worked to diminish international tension. However, when liberalisation surpassed the practical limits of the superpower relationship and began to threaten stability and security, it augmented international tension.

The second factor that contributed to the fall of détente is closely related to, and followed the same course as, the first. The lessening of ideological warfare which had initially contributed to the 'spirit of Geneva' eventually backfired and led to the creation of new tension. Before the 'spirit of Geneva', ideological warfare had played a significant role in the internal and external security of both superpowers. In the Soviet Union, where ideological fundamentalism had performed the essential functions of maintaining order and control domestically and within the alliance, security and stability were threatened. The Soviet leadership blamed the rise of dissidence on the influx of ideological pollution from the West. Accordingly, *Pravda* credited the events in Hungary to the influence of 'American agents'. Such events exemplified a fundamental dilemma in the process of détente for the Soviet Union. On one hand, détente involved the establishment of freer contacts with the West and the reduction of ideological vigilance. On the other hand, these steps served to inhibit Soviet influence and control, ignite the flames of silenced frustration and unrest, and hence, threaten Soviet security.

At the same time, the United States felt betrayed by the events in Hungary. After all, American ideological warfare had been reduced in reaction to Soviet 'liberalisation' in Eastern Europe. When the Soviet Union invaded Hungary, Americans felt their silence and co-operation had been purchased by a policy of deception. Their reaction was one of outrage, not strictly at their own naïveté but at the 'unscrupulous' nature of the Soviet régime. This raised hatred, fear and reawakened deep-seated ideological passions.

In short, as the application of ideological warfare declined, the function that it had served went unfulfilled. Eventually this decline facilitated the violation of vital security interests and new tension was produced.

The third factor contributing to the fall of détente was the re-emergence of issues that had been subordinated during the 'spirit of Geneva'. Once again, however, it was the unrealistic downgrading of important issues that eventually sowed the seeds of tension.

The major cause of the subordination of issues had been the rise of the threat of war. Additionally, however, issues had been downgraded artificially in the hope of creating a new relationship. When no progress was achieved at the Geneva conferences in July and October 1955, it became increasingly clear that the 'spirit of Geneva' was based simply on 'atmospherics'. Without any real progress on the issues, a new relationship could not be created. As the 'atmospherics' of Geneva faded away, the unresolved issues re-emerged.

A fourth factor contributing to the fall of détente was the growing differences within the new alliance organisations. While the consolidation of NATO and the Warsaw Pact gave leaders the confidence in their security to pursue détente, the failure of these new security organisations to deal with the easing of tension eventually led to feelings of insecurity. This failure was exhibited in the crises of October–November 1956, and the insecurity created led to a new rise in tension.

A fifth factor contributing to the new rise in tension may have indirectly involved the declining influence of the threat of war. While the testing of the hydrogen bomb had initially created genuine alarm on both sides about the prospect of a nuclear war, three years had passed in relative peace and calm. From the end of the Korean War to the beginning of the crises in 1956, no major superpower confrontation had taken place. The expectation of nuclear war had declined and the nuclear impasse had set the tone for the 'spirit of Geneva'.

While this impasse provided the backbone for peace, the longer it was maintained, the less urgent and credible the nuclear threat became, thereby causing the moratorium on opportunism to become less effective. There was an increasing temptation to explore and test the boundaries of the superpower relationship in order to enhance national security and maximise unilateral advantages.

Both superpowers risked the game of nuclear brinkmanship during the crises of 1956. The Soviet Union took the risk of invading Hungary and threatened to become involved in the Middle East to protect and advance its interests. The United States considered retaliatory action in Hungary and threatened retaliatory action should the Soviet Union become involved in the Suez Crisis.

The final factor contributing to the fall of détente involves the politics of living with its failure. The new political leadership in the Soviet Union and the United States, which had been primarily responsible for ushering in the 'spirit of Geneva' now had to deal with the domestic political consequences of its failure. Having initiated the peace efforts at Geneva, Khrushchev and Eisenhower were identified with and held accountable for the success and failure of those efforts.

As the Geneva Conference had drawn near, optimistic political rhetoric worked to widen the base of support, thereby allowing negotiations to be conducted from a position of national unity. After years of maintaining a simple anti-Soviet or anti-American policy, the leaders had to 'sell' the new détente relationship. Unfortunately, optimistic rhetoric and political salesmanship, especially in the United States, raised hopes beyond the realistic potential of the US–Soviet relationship. The widespread hunger for peace only served to augment these hopes. The natural conclusion was disappointment and disillusionment. When the crises of October–November 1956 brought about this conclusion, the tide of public opinion turned quickly against détente.

With the people looking for scapegoats, the leaders could not afford politically to salvage détente and chose to re-assert their hardline credentials. In the United States, Eisenhower blamed the failure of the 'spirit of Geneva' on Soviet cheating, thereby exonerating the Administration from the charge of naïveté. In the

Soviet Union, Khrushchev credited the failure of détente to the re-emergence of the capitalist warmongers in the United States, thereby suggesting that failure was not inherent in the pursuit of détente itself but in elements beyond the control of the Kremlin.

In short, the politics of dealing with this reaction involved reasserting the untrustworthiness and threat of the adversary nation with renewed vigour. As the leaders who had initiated the process of détente turned against it, the new threat became all the more convincing.

THE LEGACY OF THE 'SPIRIT OF GENEVA'

Despite the decline of détente in 1956, the 'spirit of Geneva' did leave a legacy to the future of US–Soviet relations. First, the period opened up the lines of communication which had been frozen by the cold war. As Eisenhower recalled in his memoirs:

> The cordial atmosphere of the talks, dubbed the 'spirit of Geneva', never faded entirely. Indeed, the way was opened for some increase in intercourse between East and West . . . there began, between the United States and Russia, exchanges of trade exhibitions, scientists, musicians, and other performers; visits were made by Mikoyan and Suslov to the United States, and returned by Vice President Nixon and my brother Milton, to the Soviet Union and Poland. These were small beginnings, but they could not have transpired in the atmosphere prevailing before Geneva.[75]

Second, following the failure of the Foreign Ministers' Conference of late-October 1955, Dulles made a claim that was to be echoed by historians thereafter: 'The greatest surviving element of the spirit of Geneva was a confirmation of the joint commitment to avoid nuclear war.'[76] Despite the many problems that lay ahead, most people seemed to feel that somehow, the world had become slightly safer. While the 'spirit of Geneva' was shortlived, these two legacies endured.

4　The 'Spirit of Camp David'

... the stay in the U.S.A. of the head of the Soviet Government is regarded all over the world as the greatest event of our day ...[1]
Izvestia

Khrushchev's historic 'maiden' visit to the United States in September 1959 symbolised the second US–Soviet détente. The visit marked the first time any Soviet leader had ventured forth on to American soil, and was highlighted by a series of meetings between Eisenhower and Khrushchev in the tranquil setting of Camp David. Appropriately called the 'spirit of Camp David', this brief period and the months that followed represented a 'calm' in the midst of a storm of crises that pushed the US–Soviet relationship to the brink of military confrontation.

The primary characteristic of détente during this period, however, was its superficiality. While a significant easing of tension did take place in response to the Khrushchev visit, the informal summit produced absolutely nothing substantial. Within months, the Camp David détente was shown to be even more dependent on atmospherics than its predecessor, the Geneva détente. In part created and greatly maintained by the press, the 'spirit of Camp David' could not withstand the force of real events. The fragile structure of the Camp David détente was entirely destroyed by the decision to abort the Paris summit meeting in May 1960.

The superficial nature of the 'spirit of Camp David' is especially relevant to the study of détente because it raises several questions. For instance, how can a significant easing of tension take place independent of any substantive progress? How can a period of détente arise and survive merely on images and atmospherics? As the cold war drama of the 1950s unfolds, it becomes apparent that such antithetical and impersonal factors as an abundance of crises

63

can lay the foundation for détente. In the search for stability among the crises of the cold war, the superpowers welcomed the 'spirit of Camp David' as a possible means to peace.

THE SETTING 1957–MAY 1959

The period beginning in 1957 and lasting throughout the first half of 1959 was one of open hostility. The collective crises of October–November 1956 had thrust the United States and the Soviet Union back into the grip of the cold war or, at least, back into the familiar pattern of mutual suspicion, vilification and fear. In his inaugural address on 21 January 1957, President Eisenhower christened his second term in office with a renewed but familiar attack on the evils of communism:

> . . . Rarely has this earth known such a peril as today. . . . The divisive force is international communism and the power that it controls. . .
> The designs of that power, dark in purpose, are clear in practice. It strives to seal forever the fate of those it has enslaved. It strives to break the ties that unite the free. And it strives to capture – to exploit for its own greater power – all forces of change in the world, especially the needs of the hungry and the hopes of the oppressed.[2]

On 2 February, *Izvestia* boldly asserted, 'Everyone who observes American political life these days is very much reminded of the worst period of the "cold war".' To some extent, the 'old days' had returned and more dangerous ones were yet to come.

During this period, several problems contingent on the US–Soviet relationship served to exacerbate tension. First among these was the growth of superpower competition in the Middle East. Despite its strategic importance, both from a geo-political and economic point of view, the region had played only a limited role in the cold war. While the renewal of Soviet pressure on Turkey, the civil war in Greece and the waning of British power had brought the United States into the Mediterranean after the war, the Soviet Union was not yet prepared to play a world role. In fact, the American government had hoped that Britain would maintain strategic responsibility for the region.[3] Nonetheless, with British and French influence on the decline and the renewal of the Arab–Israeli conflict, the United States played an increasingly active role in maintaining a balance of forces and in protecting its economic interests. To protect the Middle East from Soviet influence, Dulles supported the idea of a Middle East pact with Egypt at the centre. When Nasser refused to participate, the United States and Britain turned to Iraq and in April 1955, the Baghdad Pact was signed. While the West viewed the rise of Egyptian nationalism and neutralism as potentially dangerous, Nasser perceived the creation of the Baghdad Pact as a direct threat to Arab independence. During the summer of 1955, Egypt and the Soviet Union concluded a secret arms deal using Czechoslovakia as a front. When the deal became public in September, the West was shocked. The United States offered to consider financing the Aswan Dam in an attempt to woo the Egyptians. Nasser had been looking to the West for both economic and military assistance but was unwilling to retreat from a growing friendship with the Soviet Union whose motives were less suspect. In the summer of 1956, Dulles withdrew the offer and unknowingly precipitated the Suez Crisis.

If the signing of the Baghdad Pact and the conclusion of the Czechoslovak arms deal introduced the cold war to the Middle East, the Suez Crisis set the stage for greater conflict. By undermining the British and French positions in the region, the crisis created a vacuum – one that invited superpower intervention. For this reason, Eisenhower's first move of 1957 was the proclamation of a new policy authorising the deployment of American armed forces 'to secure and protect the territorial integrity and political independence' of Middle East nations threatened by 'international communism'.[4]

The 'Eisenhower Doctrine' received its first test in April 1957 when trouble arose in Jordan. Challenged by anti-Royalist rebels backed by Egypt and Syria, King Hussein claimed that the independence and integrity of Jordan was threatened by 'international communism'. When Eisenhower sent the Sixth Fleet to the Eastern Mediterranean, Egypt and Syria decided against aiding the rebels and the crisis quickly passed.

A second test of the Eisenhower Doctrine came in August when it looked as if Syria was in danger of becoming a Soviet satellite. Soviet influence had been growing in Syrian political circles, and on 13 August, top ranking Syrian officers were purged and replaced by young leftist officers. These developments alarmed Syria's neighbours as well as the American State Department. A Deputy Undersecretary was sent on a fact-finding tour and reported that Syria's neighbours were correct in their assessment – Syria was on the verge of succumbing to 'international communism'. Washington stepped up the transfer of arms to Middle Eastern countries and Turkey built up forces on the Syrian border. Moscow promised and delivered diplomatic and military support to leftist groups within Syria and in mid-October, Turkish and Syrian border guards exchanged fire. Suddenly, however, Moscow's aggressive support waned, and confrontation was avoided. Four months later, to the Soviet government's dismay, the troops Nasser had sent to Syria in aid of Moscow's cause aided those Syrian groups favouring a political merger with Egypt. Staunchly anti-communist, these groups succeeded in forming the United Arab Republic, effectively destroying Moscow's main channel into the Middle East.

In short, the Jordanian and Syrian crises attested to the growing superpower conflict in the Middle East and the American government's determination to halt the spread of 'international communism' with active force. It is difficult to say to what extent the Eisenhower Administration's perception of the Soviet threat in the Middle East was real or imagined. On the one hand, Khrushchev had launched a new foreign policy in 1955 which was designed to extend Soviet influence throughout the newly developing countries of Africa and Asia. On the other hand, Soviet activity in the Middle East had been minimal before the signing of the Baghdad Pact – a move viewed by Moscow as an American attempt to extend NATO throughout the Middle East. In fact, Soviet movements in the Middle East throughout the 1950s appear to have been more a reaction to American policies than ambitious initiatives of their own. In this way, the 'Soviet threat' probably became a self-fulfilling prophecy for the American government. While the quick and decisive application of the 'Eisenhower Doctrine' continued to achieve short term goals, it oversaw a decline in the potential position of the United States *vis-à-vis* the Soviet Union. American intervention was deeply resented and contributed to the image of the Soviet Union as the protector of Arab independence. Soviet technological successes in late 1957 only served to augment Moscow's image in the region.

While the Soviet Union strengthened its position in the Middle

East, serious problems confronted the Soviet leadership domestically and within the Soviet bloc. Throughout the first half of 1957,
tremors of political unrest continued to shake the foundations of
Soviet hegemony in Eastern Europe. Tension in Hungary continued to run high. While outwardly reconciled, Poland was still
seething. Despite Tito's support for the aims of the Soviet
intervention in Hungary,[5] the whole situation had uncovered
some of the fundamental differences that still remained between
the Soviet and Yugoslav governments. Furthermore, Soviet
leaders expected trouble in East Germany that might create the
conditions for a total revolt within the Eastern bloc.

It was characteristic of the cold war that such 'internal
problems' were credited not to 'internal causes' but to the
clandestine activities of the opposing side. The Soviet press was
full of articles accusing America of practising widespread espion-
age and subversion. This propaganda campaign portraying a
bellicose, aggressive America helped to draw the socialist camp
together in the face of rising tension. As historian David Dallin
observed: '. . . this verbal and literary sabre-rattling, the deliberate exaggeration of American aggressiveness . . . a score of
conferences, and numerous visits of the highest Soviet leaders to
the capitals of the 'camp', served to combat the centrifugal forces
and provide an antidote to the poison of national independence'.[6]
In reality, there was no direct threat from the West. American
support for nationalism in Eastern Europe continued to be strictly
verbal. As the year progressed, the challenge of Eastern European
nationalism posed less and less of a threat to Soviet control.

Beyond the problem of nationalism, a further factor promoted
instability and effectively brought all Soviet initiatives in the
international arena to a standstill. After the events in Hungary
exposed the failure of Khrushchev's policies of liberalisation and
the fragility of the 'Soviet empire', Khrushchev's position became
increasingly insecure. In mid-June, he returned home from a visit
to Finland to find a majority of the Presidium demanding his
resignation. To the consternation of those present, Khrushchev
refused to resign, claiming that he had been elected by the Central
Committee and could be ousted only by that body. Marshal
Zhukov dispatched 300 army planes to all corners of the country
to pick up Central Committee members and bring them to
Moscow. In the end, it was the 'plotters' who were thrown out of
the Presidium. Several months later, Khrushchev became Prime

Minister as well as First Secretary. Such was the fate of 'collective leadership'. By the end of summer 1957, Khrushchev had survived the power struggle, disposed of his opponents and gained firm control.[7]

While the first part of this period was characterised by an aggressive American policy and a disorientated Soviet policy, a sudden change occurred in August 1957 which illuminated the second major problem contingent to the US–Soviet relationship. This change resulted in a sudden acceleration of the nuclear arms race and a perceived shift in the balance of power. On 26 August, the Soviet Union launched the first intercontinental ballistic missile (ICBM), instantly demonstrating a major Soviet lead in rocket technology. More significantly, this stunning technological feat was the harbinger of an even greater feat when, in October, the Soviet Union launched the first man-made satellite (Sputnik). While the initial impact of these accomplishments was greater in psychological terms than in strategic terms, the implications for the future of warfare, national security and the strategic balance were undeniable.

In the Soviet Union, no time was lost in exploiting this psychological advantage. On 27 August, the day following the launching of the ICBM, a TASS communiqué boasted, 'It is possible to direct rockets to any part of the globe.'[8] The message was clear; the Soviet Union had seized the initiative in the arms race and was prepared to squeeze every possible political advantage out of its current position.

The successful launching of Sputnik in October was immediately declared 'a major victory for socialism in the competition with capitalism'.[9] The Soviet Union had not only achieved an area of superiority but had beaten the Americans at their own technological game.

In the following weeks, Khrushchev's comments began to reflect an overwhelming confidence in Soviet strategic superiority. In an interview with United Press Correspondent Henry Shapiro on 19 November, Khrushchev claimed Soviet rocket technology had made all types of Western bombers obsolete and explained what this would mean to America if nuclear war were not averted:

The United States . . . will experience the most devastating war ever known by mankind; it will rage not only in Europe and

Asia, but, with no less fury, in the United States . . . with the deployment of military technology, the United States is just as vulnerable as all other countries.[10]

Most significantly, Khrushchev suggested that mankind could survive a nuclear war; 'The losses will be very heavy, mankind will suffer very much, but man will not disappear from the face of the earth and society will live and develop.'[11] This statement represented an alarming departure from Khrushchev's previous claims that nuclear war meant complete destruction and hence was unthinkable. Khrushchev was sending a clear and calculated message to the West. Given its new strategic status, the Soviet Union was prepared to risk nuclear conflict if it was not treated with a level of respect commensurate with its great power. One year later, Khrushchev was to make it clear that this new respect included the immediate resolution of the Berlin question on terms favourable to the Eastern bloc.

Khrushchev also used the prestige resulting from the recent Soviet successes to reassert Soviet leadership within the socialist camp. The Fortieth Anniversary celebration of the Bolshevik Revolution held in Moscow in November assumed the dimensions and importance of a worldwide Congress of Communist Parties, the first since 1935. Sixty-four Communist parties paid reverence to the Soviet Union by sending their highest leaders. Basking in the glory of the recent Soviet achievements, Khrushchev accomplished a significant acknowledgement of Soviet leadership. With the notable exception of Yugoslavia, the twelve ruling Communist parties signed a Declaration attesting to the solidarity of 'the invincible camp of Socialist countries headed by the Soviet Union'.[12] This Declaration marked the end of a year of crisis and the triumph of Moscow over the 'revisionists'. Tito's refusal to sign this Declaration signalled an end to the *rapprochement* between the Soviet Union and Yugoslavia. As Adam Ulam observed: 'Tito was no longer seen as a reliable antidote to nationalism but as a virus that might induce it.'[13]

Significantly, Mao Tse-tung spoke of the necessity for strong Soviet leadership, and summarised the optimism and unity of those present in the wake of the Soviet achievements:

. . . the international situation has now reached a new turning point. There are two winds in the world today; the East wind and the West wind. . . I think the characteristic of the situation today is the East wind prevailing over the West wind.[14]

In the United States, the impact of the Soviet technological successes was tremendous. In Eric Goldman's words, '. . . a sense of alarm, exasperation, humiliation, and confusion mounted'.[15] The launching of the ICBM in August and the subsequent launchings of Sputnik I and II in the autumn of 1957 were a direct challenge to America's supposedly unchallengable resource – technological know-how. It was this resource upon which Americans had most relied for their national security. Suddenly, Americans were struck with a new sense of vulnerability.

Americans were also shaken by the political and ideological implications of the Soviet achievements. As Walter Lafeber pointed out:

The newly emerging nations could view Russia as a people which in 1917 had been generations behind other industrialized nations, but which through harsh regimentation, had assumed first place in the race for control of outer space. They could also interpret the launching as a dramatic swing in the balance of military power towards Moscow . . . (Moreover) the Soviet gross national product . . . had increased on the average of 7.1 percent annually between 1950 and 1958, nearly 50 percent greater than the American rate.[16]

The true significance of the Soviet accomplishments was revealed in November 1957 when the findings of the Gaither Committee were leaked to the press. Secretly entrusted with the responsibility of drawing a comparative analysis of American military strengths and weaknesses, the Committee concluded that by the 1960s, the Soviet Union would deploy a first-strike ICBM force capable of destroying the United States Strategic Air Command. Anything short of converting the entire foundation of the United States strategic force to ICBMs would eventually leave the United States vulnerable to attack and destruction by the Soviet Union.

This 'leaked' information violently shook the confidence of Americans. As Alastair Cooke observed:

. . . it can no longer be taken for granted that the United States is militarily and technologically the leading world power. The trauma of this recognition is evident in every influential station of American life, among the Senators who investigated the state of missile research, among educators, scientists, businessmen, and now among the Chiefs of Staff. . .[17]

While the Soviet Union's feats were impressive, the impact on American confidence was far greater than these Soviet achievements warranted. Rocket technology was still so underdeveloped that the Soviet leaders decided to forego building a first-generation ICBM complex in favour of a second or third generation model. This meant, for the next few years, that the Soviet government would attempt to exploit a false lead. Khrushchev's exaggerated claims, coupled with the overblown American reaction to the ICBM and Sputnik launchings, reinforced the myth of Soviet superiority. Khrushchev strengthened the credibility of this myth by having Soviet radio and newspapers quote back to the West the West's own exaggerated view of Soviet missile capacity. In short, this image of Western vulnerability and Soviet strength was made credible by the Soviet Union's willingness to exploit it and the West's willingness to believe it.

This image, however, proved to be a mixed blessing. While the exaggeration of Soviet strength promoted Soviet propaganda and augmented its diplomatic clout, it also fed America's self-perception of vulnerability, thereby producing a militaristic response:

> Americans were extremely disturbed. Strategic Air Force units were dispersed and placed on alert, short range Jupiter missiles installed in Turkey and Italy to offset the long-range Soviet weapons, money poured into missile and bomber programs, and 'gaps' were suddenly discovered in everything from missile production to the teaching of arithmetic at the preschool level.[18]

Therefore, the successful propagation of Soviet missile strength proved to be a two-edged sword. The United States government felt compelled to reply to the Soviet challenge with a far greater response than was required, for reasons of both domestic and international politics.

The overall effect of the Soviet achievements on superpower relations was an acceleration of the arms race and a perceived shift in the balance of power. These developments ushered in a period of great uncertainty that was to promote tension for the next six years. This period began with a concerted attempt by Khrushchev, Gromyko and Bulganin to dissuade the United States and its allies from introducing tactical nuclear weapons to Europe. The aim was to impress the West with the Soviet Union's peaceful intentions in the hope of persuading the NATO ministers to cancel the missile plan. Khrushchev issued statements calling for a summit conference, but Eisenhower refused to negotiate with Khrushchev from a position of strategic vulnerability. In his speech to the Supreme Soviet on 27 December, Gromyko warned, 'The arms race has never been so dangerous as it is today.'[19] Despite these Soviet overtures and warnings, the NATO ministers approved the United States plan for the deployment of missiles in Western Europe in the final days of 1957.

Khrushchev's New Year's toast to 'America, the wonderful American people and President Eisenhower', predicted, somewhat optimistically, that 1958 would 'bring a weakening of international tension'.[20] Indeed, on 27 January, the Bilateral Exchange Agreement was signed by the Soviet and American governments representing the first major agreement of its kind. The agreement (which had its genesis in American medical aid during a Soviet poliomyelitis epidemic in 1956) called for exchanges in cultural, technical, educational, agricultural, industrial, scientific and medical fields. Despite this hopeful interlude on the lower levels of the superpower relationship, however, East/West relations failed to improve. Khrushchev's repeated calls for a summit meeting were viewed as a means by which the Soviet Union could capitalise diplomatically on its recent successes, while at the same time putting the brakes on the growth of tension in the West brought by these successes. Despite the decision of the NATO council to deploy missiles in Europe, the Soviet government continued to push for the prevention of such an arrangement. One attempt involved the propagation of the Rapacki plan which called for a nuclear-free zone in Central Europe (Poland, Czechoslovakia, and East and West Germany) in which the production and stockpiling of atomic weapons would be prohibited. The Soviet government immediately called for a summit meeting to discuss it, but the United States declined for several reasons. First, after the recent Soviet achievements, the United States feared it would be negotiating from a relatively weaker position than before. Therefore, the American reaction was to increase vigilance and support a more adequate and unified defence within the Alliance. On 5 January 1958, *The Sunday Times* held that 'the West finds itself in a position when it would like to make progress in disarmament yet must redouble its efforts to catch up with Russian nuclear advantages. (Therefore) the United States, for the time being, does not want to go beyond a Foreign Ministers Conference'. In a speech to the National Press Club on 16 January, Dulles claimed that Khrushchev's calls for a summit meeting were designed to lull the West into a false sense of security thereby weakening popular support for necessary arms programmes.[21]

Second, some Western leaders feared that a summit meeting would raise undue hopes and only end in disillusionment. The public desire for peace was so great, and the likelihood of any real progress toward that goal so remote, that any high level talks would probably result in failure. In his National Press Club address, Dulles claimed:

> There are, I know, many who feel that the cold war could be ended and the need for sacrificial effort removed by the stroke of a pen at the summit. This is the kind of illusion that has plagued mankind for a long time. Actually peace has never been achieved that way, and there could be no greater folly for us than to act on the belief that all our danger could be ended by peaceful platitudes proclaimed from the summit by Heads of Government.[22]

Despite public pressure. Eisenhower rejected Soviet appeals for a summit conference. In his State of the Union message on 9 January, he disputed the sincerity of Soviet peace overtures claiming, 'The Soviets are, in short, waging total cold war.'[23]

Third, the Eisenhower Administration was pursuing a variety of other measures aimed at bolstering Western security and did not wish to engage in serious high level discussions until these modifications were added to the West's negotiating hand. For instance, Dulles was busy setting up a string of American foreign bases to 'contain communism'. There was little reason, therefore, to hold a conference which might involve dismantling what Dulles was attempting to build.[24]

Finally, the Soviet Union's new-found global power was

making itself felt in the Middle East, or so it was thought in Washington. Iraq, which had become the vital link in the chain of Western security throughout the Middle East, served not only as the anchor of the Baghdad Pact but also the supplier and protector of Western oil supplies. On 14 July 1958, the pro-Western anti-Soviet government of Nuri-as-Said was overthrown. Suddenly, the cornerstone of Western security in the Middle East had been removed, leaving what the Soviet press tauntingly called, 'The Baghdad Pact without Baghdad.'

Eisenhower felt the need to make some display of force in the region. In response to an urgent appeal for assistance from Lebanon, where pro-Nasser Moslems were fighting Christians, Eisenhower sent 14 000 American Marines wading ashore among public bathers in Lebanon. At the same time, British parachutists landed in Jordan at the request of King Hussein. The operation was successful in terms of its limited objectives – preventing Nasser's revolution from 'swallowing up' Lebanon and Jordan. Nasser's reluctance to counter Western military intervention with force suggested that he had accepted the realities of power politics, and the American willingness to apply it. As Eisenhower claimed, one result of the American action was a 'definite change in Nasser's attitude toward the United States'.[25]

Another result, Eisenhower claimed, was a demonstration – particularly to the communists – of 'the ability of the United States to react swiftly with conventional armed forces to meet small-scale, or 'brush-fire' situations'.[26] However, behind these claims of success there was the realisation that such military responses were limited to 'putting out brush-fires' and could not achieve long-term solutions. The Lebanon crisis is significant in terms of superpower relations because it represented an attempt by the United States to reassert its power – however crudely – in the face of a perceived Soviet threat in the Middle East. Rather than threatening the United States into submission, Khrushchev's boasting had contributed to the American need to take some action, in one form or another, to make its presence and power felt.

The United States gambled and won. The Soviet government made its usual protests, issued warnings, and renewed calls for a summit conference but otherwise took no direct action. In fact, Khrushchev got himself into trouble on 19 July when he called for a summit conference of the 'Big Four' plus India to discuss, among other things, the crises in the Middle and Far East. The fact that India had been mentioned in the place of China deeply insulted the Chinese. Luckily for Khrushchev, the United States rejected this suggestion. In its place, the West suggested that a conference be held within the framework of the United Nations. Khrushchev accepted this idea on 23 July. Nonetheless, Khrushchev was forced to travel to Peking on 31 July to placate the Chinese.

The meeting in Peking highlighted the confrontation between the Soviet Union's Eastern interests and its Western interests. Khrushchev had felt that the Lebanon Crisis presented the perfect opportunity to exhibit the necessity of holding a summit meeting.[27] When he expressed his willingness to travel to the United States for a summit meeting without China but with India, and then agreed to a conference within the context of the Security Council, where he would sit at the same table as Chiang Kai-shek's ambassador, the Chinese reacted strongly. Not only was Khrushchev willing to travel to the leading 'capitalist/imperialist' country and negotiate East–West peace without China, he was willing to pursue peace with China's major adversary. During his Peking visit, Khrushchev weighed the benefits of China's goodwill and immediately lost his enthusiasm for a summit meeting.

This sudden reversal by Khrushchev was indicative of yet another problem contingent to the superpower relationship during this period; namely the rise of China and the resulting Sino-Soviet split. While the Sino-Soviet dispute did not become apparent until after the turn of the decade, the seeds of contention were already firmly rooted in 1958. In *The Sino-Soviet Conflict 1959–1961*, Donald Zagoria traces the origins of the Sino-Soviet split from the Twentieth Party Congress in February 1956, at which Khrushchev denounced Stalin, set a new pattern for intra-bloc relations, and introduced a new global strategy based on peaceful coexistence.[28] These changes not only took the Chinese by surprise but threatened the very principles upon which their form of socialism was based. Concurrently, as Klaus Mehnert points out, Khrushchev's denunciation of Stalin undermined the Stalinist myth and with it the moral and psychological basis for Moscow's claim to leadership.[29]

These concerns were accentuated in the latter half of 1957 when Chinese domestic politics took a sudden turn to the left. After letting 'a hundred flowers bloom', Mao clamped down on his opponents, condemned all forms of revisionism, and raised internal vigilance against the 'bourgeois imperialists' to a new height. Domestically, this swing to the left was expressed in the establishment of communes, a means by which China was to leap over the intermediate stages of socialism directly into communism – a stage the Soviet Union had yet to achieve. The Great Leap Forward not only implicitly challenged the Soviet Union to a contest of economics and ideology, but also involved a contest of power; namely, competition for the leadership of the communist movements throughout the developing countries of Asia, Africa and Latin America.

Externally, Mao's new policy involved a staunch anti-revisionist approach to intra-bloc relations and a particularly aggressive foreign policy. As Khrushchev shifted his policy of peaceful coexistence from that of a tactical expedient to a fundamental principle of Soviet foreign policy, the Chinese leadership felt that the Soviet government was restricting itself too much – as was revealed in the polemics on détente between 1958 and 1960.

When Khrushchev failed to counter Western actions in Lebanon and tried to establish Middle East negotiations without the Chinese, Mao evidently decided to force Khrushchev's hand. On 23 August, less than three weeks after Khrushchev's return from Peking, the Chinese renewed their drive against Formosa. The island of Quemoy was bombarded daily. Just as it looked as if the island was going to fall to the Communists, American airborne supplies reinforced the defences of the island. In a series of messages exchanged between Moscow and Washington, Khrushchev claimed that Soviet military forces would go to the aid of Communist China if necessary. Despite his doubts about the importance of the island, Eisenhower felt compelled to warn the Communists that the United States would intervene to counter an assault 'perhaps using nuclear weapons'.[30] As a result of these exchanges, talks between the ambassadors of the United States and China were scheduled to resume in Warsaw, the bombardment of Quemoy was eased and international tension declined. For Khrushchev, the Chinese bombardment came as an unwelcome surprise at a time of high international tension. Having previously discouraged Mao from pressing the Taiwan Straits issue too far, Khrushchev was probably incensed at Peking's actions.[31] As Jan Kalicki observes, 'PRC actions in August and September represented a tacit declaration of independence from Soviet control, as well as an effort to embarrass the Russians into supporting Chinese demands.'[32] Not only did Khrushchev fail to back up the Chinese with Soviet strategic power until after the threat of war had passed; he also applied pressure on Peking to back down.[33] When, in 1963, the flood of Chinese accusations finally flowed forth, this act was portrayed as nothing less than betrayal.[34]

In the Quemoy crisis, the Soviet Union was not alone in having to deal with an incident created by a troublesome ally. As Eisenhower recalled:

> Chiang Kai-shek had helped complicate the problem. Ignoring our military advice, he had for many months been adding personnel to the Quemoy and Matsu garrisons, moving them forward, nearer to the mainland. By the summer of 1958, a hundred thousand men, a third of his total ground forces, were stationed on those two island groups. . . . It seemed likely that his heavy deployment to these forward positions was designed to convince us that he was as committed to the defence of the offshore islands as he was to that of Formosa.[35]

Eisenhower was highly sceptical about the importance of Quemoy and felt the crisis involved an unnecessary risk of nuclear conflict.[36] With the force of public opinion becoming more significant, it was important to demonstrate that the United States did not approve of the use of force in taking the mainland. Nonetheless, in this crisis, the course of events had determined United States policy, not Eisenhower.

In short, the Quemoy crisis was not only significant because of its contribution to the Sino-Soviet split, but because it revealed two new developments in superpower politics. First, there was a growing realisation that each superpower maintained some degree of responsibility for the action of its allies. Second, despite their unparalleled military strength, the superpowers were becoming increasingly 'muscle-bound' as smaller powers attempted to play the superpowers off to their own ends.[37] The rise of new nation-states and the economic and political rejuvenation of the superpowers' allies meant that the allegiance and co-operation of these states would have to be purchased at a price.

With the Quemoy crisis finally winding down in October, there was little time before the last and most dangerous crisis of 1958 took place. It involved the most salient issue in the US–Soviet relationship, the future of Germany.

The continued four-power occupation of Berlin served as a painful reminder of the limited progress that had been made in solving this fundamental problem of the cold war. For Khrushchev, the continued occupation of Berlin was an embarrassment and a symbol of political impotence, especially in light of the overwhelming conventional superiority of Warsaw Pact forces in the area. In 1958, new uncertainties had entered the European scene with de Gaulle's return to power in France and the decision of the British to base their European strategy on nuclear weapons. Having failed to achieve any solutions in the Middle East and the Taiwan Straits by way of Soviet 'missile' diplomacy, it is likely that Khrushchev felt the pressure to attempt a solution in Berlin. The warning signs first appeared on 10 November when, during a visit to Poland, Khrushchev declared that the status of Berlin must be changed.

These threats were replaced by an ultimatum on 27 November. In official notes to the United States, Britain and France, Khrushchev declared his intention to correct the 'abnormal' situation in Berlin. In the thirteen years since the war, he claimed, two German states had emerged instead of one. The Soviet Union had recognised this sad fact, but the West continued four-power occupation of Berlin. Therefore, in six months, the Soviet Union would terminate its occupation agreement. If a negotiated settlement had not been reached by that time, the United States, France and Britain would be forced to negotiate their rights of access to West Berlin with East Germany. Furthermore, the Soviet Union recognised the right of the East German government to bar Western access to Berlin and warned that any attack on East Germany would be considered as an attack on the Warsaw Pact. In short, the West would have to give up occupation rights in West Berlin, recognise the German Democratic Republic, or run the risk of nuclear conflict with the Soviet Union and its satellites.

The reasons behind Khrushchev's sudden ultimatum have been the subject of great historical debate. In his memoirs, Khrushchev claimed that the Soviet moves were designed to settle the legal status of the two Germanies, thereby providing stability to the German Democratic Republic.[38] More specifically, however, it seems likely that the main Soviet objective was to secure an agreement neutralising Germany. This objective was revealed in the Soviet note: 'the best way to solve the Berlin question . . . would mean the withdrawal of the Federal Republic of Germany from NATO, with the simultaneous withdrawal of the German Democratic Republic from the Warsaw Treaty Organization.'[39]

If the previous plan of neutralising Germany did not work, Khrushchev may have hoped to gain recognition of the German Democratic Republic as well as close off West Berlin, an open wound in the side of East Germany.[40] Recognition would facilitate the reduction of Soviet military commitments and augment the policy of 'peaceful coexistence'. Ending the division of Berlin would not only increase the status of East Germany as an independent state, but would also serve to stop the 'bleeding' of hundreds of thousands of East Germans into the West.

A third reason for issuing the Berlin Ultimatum was probably the need of Khrushchev and the Soviet leadership to score a success in foreign policy. One year had passed since the Great Soviet technological victories and the Fortieth Anniversary celebrations. Yet, these events had failed to bring the Soviet leaders the type of diplomatic leverage they had envisioned. Throughout this year of crisis, the United States had dominated each successive event with determined action while the Soviet Union had simply engaged in issuing empty threats. In Berlin, the Soviet leaders held an overwhelming tactical advantage and felt certain that disunity in the Western camp would prohibit any effective response. Such a success would greatly enhance the prestige of the Moscow leadership and demonstrate the efficacy of their new 'missile-backed' diplomacy.

Finally, Khrushchev probably felt compelled to press the Berlin issue as a sign of Soviet virility to the Chinese. In response to China's criticism that the Soviet Union was buying peace at the expense of the Communist revolution, Khrushchev may have wanted to show the more forceful side of his policy of peaceful coexistence. Conversely, Khrushchev may have accepted the tenuous nature of the Sino-Soviet relationship and wanted to push the Berlin issue before the concept of the 'unshakeable unity of the Socialist' camp ceased to carry conviction.[41]

Whatever the reasons for the Berlin Ultimatum, it displayed Soviet impatience with the negotiating process. Only days before, the superpowers had come together at the Conference on Measures to Prevent Surprise Attack. Khrushchev's ill-timed ultimatum doomed it to failure, just as the United States had sabotaged the Geneva Nuclear Test-Ban Conference three months earlier. The Ultimatum may have been, in part, a product of Soviet frustration with the lack of progress in negotiations.

The Berlin Ultimatum immediately produced a crisis of major proportions. The West was keenly aware of Khrushchev's ability to carry out his threats in Berlin and the pressure on him to do so. Dulles branded the Soviet ultimatum as another exercise in Soviet blackmail.[42] The official United States response was registered on 31 December 1958, when the Eisenhower Administration sent a reply to the Soviet Union:

> If Berlin has become a focus of international tension, it is because the Soviet Government has deliberately threatened to disturb the existing arrangements at present in force there . . .
> The Government of the United States could not embark on discussions with the Soviet Union upon these questions under menace or ultimatum.[43]

The first three months of 1959 were dominated by the Berlin Crisis. While New Year's Day brought such significant events as the official formation of the European Economic Community and the overthrow of the Batista régime in Cuba by Fidel Castro, the attention of Western leaders was focussed on Berlin. On 9 January, in his State of the Union Message, Eisenhower stated:

> We have learned the bitter lesson that international agreements, historically considered by us as sacred, are regarded in Communist doctrine and in practice to be mere scraps of paper. The most recent proof of their disdain of international obligations, solemnly undertaken, is their announced intention to abandon their responsibilities respecting Berlin.[44]

While de Gaulle stood firmly with Adenauer in opposing negotiated compromises on Berlin, British Prime Minister Macmillan was anxious to explore whether a solution could be found through diplomatic means. After receiving cautious 'blessings' from Eisenhower, de Gaulle and Adenauer, Macmillan made a historic visit to the Soviet Union. While the talks were held in a congenial atmosphere, so little progress was made that Khrushchev snubbed the Prime Minister by failing to accompany him throughout the remainder of his visit. He claimed that he had a toothache. Whether Khrushchev was upset at having failed to 'separate Britain from her allies',[45] or whether he was attempting to play the visit down, his 'toothache' indirectly served the cause of Western unity. By accentuating Macmillan's tough stand, the incident contributed to Eisenhower's, de Gaulle's and Adenauer's faith in Macmillan's initiative. In the end, Khrushchev accepted Macmillan's proposal for a foreign ministers' conference during May in the hope that it would lead to a summit meeting. This agreement had the significant effect of easing pressure on the six months deadline. As Macmillan recorded in his memoirs, 'the chief practical result was the postponement, if not the solution, of the Berlin crisis.'[46] Concurrently, Macmillan's visit had the equally important effect of softening Western attitudes.

About the same time, Soviet domestic and intra-bloc politics were focused on the Special Twenty-First Party Congress. Amid great fanfare, Khrushchev launched his Seven Year Economic Plan designed to enable the Soviet Union to overtake the United States in consumer and producer commodities. This ambitious goal required the transfer of resources from the military sector into the consumer sector. In his foreign policy message, Khrushchev stressed, with renewed emphasis, the absolute inadmissibility of war in the nuclear age, and called for détente in US–Soviet relations. He also made another peace offer that was completely overlooked in the West. In one of the few underlined sentences in the official text, Khrushchev stated: 'One can and must construct in the Far East and the whole Pacific Ocean area a zone of peace, and, first of all, a zone free of atomic weapons.'[47] This statement represented the first indication of the Soviet intention to keep nuclear weapons out of the hands of the Chinese. Six months later they were secretly to denounce their nuclear agreement with Peking.

Khrushchev's language at the Special Twenty-First Party Congress contrasted sharply with his previous statements. During the Congress, Soviet Deputy Premier Anastas I. Mikoyan was sent on an unofficial visit to the United States to explore the possibilities of further co-operation. Despite the Berlin Ultimatum, both sides had agreed on 29 December 1958 to exchange 'exhibitions' demonstrating the continued interest in maintaining contacts despite the wider political picture.

Renewing his calls for a summit meeting, Khrushchev softened his stance on Berlin at the beginning of March. Hints were dropped about an unofficial visit by Eisenhower to the Soviet Union – a suggestion the White House quickly rejected. Khrushchev's sudden change of heart was viewed suspiciously in the West. Harrison Salisbury suggested in the *New York Times* that Khrushchev had purposely manufactured the Berlin Crisis in the hope of bringing about a summit meeting.[48]

In the weeks leading up to the foreign ministers' conference, Khrushchev continued his peace efforts and even observed a pre-conference easing of tension: 'Everybody has sensed a definite warming up of the international atmosphere and the hope has risen that the statesmen will be able to reach agreement and peace can be guaranteed.'[49]

The American pre-conference mood was not so optimistic. On 16 April, Dulles was forced to resign due to severe illness. While he was replaced by a veteran diplomat, Deputy Secretary Herter, the sudden change meant that the American approach would be one of calculated conservatism. Beyond this, Dulles' age-old policy of 'anti-communism' had assumed a certain aimless quality and nothing had emerged to take its place. Due to this lack of direction and confidence, as well as the change in leadership, the Americans approached the foreign ministers' conference with nothing new to offer.

The foreign ministers of the 'Big Four', along with representatives of the two German states, met in Geneva in the summer of 1959. The positions of the Western allies ranged from Britain's conciliatory approach to France and West Germany's hard line stance. In the middle was the United States presenting sterile proposals for a limited, temporary agreement. At the same time, the Soviet Union was unyielding on the concept of 'two German states', and it soon became evident that Gromyko had been instructed to 'hold out' for a summit at which wider issues could be discussed.

On 14 May, Dulles died and the West called for a temporary adjournment. The second stage (13 July–5 August) of the conference produced nothing.

During this time, however, the first American exhibition opened in Moscow with a historic visit by Vice President Nixon. While his visit was primarily ceremonial, Nixon held informal discussions with Khrushchev – the most famous of which took place in the kitchen of a model American display home. As Nixon recalled in his memoirs, the 'kitchen debate' was a polite but heated exchange, involving the relative merits of the Soviet and American systems, that revealed an extremely defensive quality in the Soviet character.[50] Indeed, in the months leading up to the Nixon visit, the Soviet press had derided the American displays as objects of propaganda. For example, commenting on the American home exhibit, TASS jeered:

> In reality, this can no more be called a typical American worker's home than, say, the Taj Mahal can be called a typical home of a Bombay textile worker or Buckingham Palace a typical British miner's home. . . . It is hard to imagine who is supposed to be fooled by all of this.[51]

Given the remarkably high standard of living in the United States, the exchange of exhibitions raised a more general problem for the Soviet leaders. How could the two countries expand their peaceful relations through increased contacts without Soviet citizens becoming 'ideologically poisoned' by Western culture? Khrushchev had revealed his answer to this question at the Special Twenty-First Congress the previous January. He stated that there was a need to 'intensify the ideological and educational work of the party, raising the level of communist consciousness of the working people, particularly in the rising generation, training it in the communist attitude toward work and in Soviet patriotism and internationalism'.[52] The view that peaceful coexistence somehow involved an intensification of the ideological struggle was either misunderstood or seen as inimical to the pursuit of peace in the United States. This issue was to remain a stumbling block to détente.

Nonetheless, the same month Nixon was in Moscow holding 'friendly' kitchen debates, the United States Congress declared 'Captive Nations Week' remembering the 'captive status' of the Soviet satellites in Eastern Europe. The Soviet Union viewed this as an American attempt to stir up the forces of Eastern European nationalism during Nixon's visit. While 'Captive Nations Week' was largely produced for domestic consumption, the Soviet government viewed the Congressional act as inconsistent with the American calls for peace.[53] These misunderstandings were continually to confuse and complicate the peace process.

HIGH DÉTENTE: AUGUST 1959–APRIL 1960

Suddenly, with no apparent warning, the political atmosphere began to change. This change was precipitated by a bold step taken by Eisenhower. Immediately following Nixon's trip to Moscow, First Deputy Premier Kozlov reciprocated by travelling to New York to open the Soviet exhibit. It was during this week that Eisenhower issued his surprise invitation encouraging Khrushchev to visit the United States. According to Eisenhower, the failure of the Foreign Ministers' Conference in Geneva necessitated a fresh approach to the Berlin question. The invitation was viewed as 'a device to break the stalemate'. Khrushchev accepted the invitation and, in return, offered one to Eisenhower. On 3 August, the visits were officially announced.

Despite the boldness of Eisenhower's initiative, the Administration made it clear that the Soviet leader's visit to the United States would be conducted on an informal basis. Having experienced the disillusionment and disappointed expectations of the 'spirit of Geneva', Eisenhower was cautious in his stated expectations for the visit. On 10 September, in a 'Report to the American People', Eisenhower stated:

> . . . my invitation to Mr. Khrushchev does not . . . suggest any purpose of reaching definitive negotiation. . .
>
> It is my profound hope that some real progress will be forthcoming, even though no one would be so bold as to predict such an outcome.[54]

Being the first US–Soviet meeting of its kind, Eisenhower was careful to inform Americans and their Allies that there would be no sell-out in the interests of superpower relations. He continued:

> Neither America nor her allies will mistake good manners and candor for weakness; no principle or fundamental interest will be placed upon any auction block. This is well understood here and abroad.[55]

The mere fact that Eisenhower had to state this point revealed the extent of his sensitivity to the problem of images and expectations surrounding the visits.

In the Soviet Union, there were no such reservations. The

Soviet press billed the visit as a great event beyond all other events and a testimony to the success of Soviet policy:

> . . . the stay in the USA of the head of the Soviet Government is regarded all over the world as the greatest event of our day . . . this news testifies to how high the international prestige of our homeland . . . has risen.[56]

Furthermore, the Soviet press practised no restraint in airing expectations for the visit. On 18 September, *Pravda* optimistically claimed: 'Given a mutual desire to mitigate international tension, urgent disputed problems are wholly solvable.'[57] It became obvious that Eisenhower's 'informal, non-summit' invitation was being interpreted and displayed in the Soviet Union as the summit meeting Khrushchev had so persistently demanded.

The diverging US–Soviet views and expectations of the September visit were symptomatic of the bilateral relationship on the whole. Little had happened in the previous months suggesting the possibility of any reconciliation between the superpowers. In fact, tension had been exacerbated by the Berlin crisis, and the two countries were no closer to solving their conflicts than they had been the year before. Nonetheless, on 15 September, Khrushchev arrived in Washington D.C. to begin his historic visit to the United States.

Accompanied by United Nations Ambassador Henry Cabot Lodge, Khrushchev travelled throughout America – from Washington D.C. and New York to Los Angeles, San Francisco, rural Iowa and Pittsburgh. His 'informal' visit was designed to include an overview of American life. He met with businessmen, labour leaders, farmers, workers, entertainers and many others. Throughout the journey, Khrushchev was extremely jovial and optimistic. Speaking at the Soviet Embassy in Washington he declared: 'The ice of the "cold war" has not only cracked but has begun to break up.'[58] *Izvestia* observed, '. . . love for peace in America has now become more profound, more serious and . . . more responsible'.[59]

The highlight and litmus test of the visit came, however, at the conclusion of Eisenhower's and Khrushchev's talks at Camp David. On the surface, it appeared that nothing substantial had emerged from the discussions other than a joint commitment to expand relations and continue talking about conflicting issues.

However, the United States gained one concession that went unreported on Khrushchev's request. Khrushchev promised Eisenhower he would not set a time limit on the Berlin question, thereby agreeing not to conclude a separate peace agreement with East Germany. In this sense, the meetings at Camp David accomplished exactly what Eisenhower had set out to do – break the deadlock. Nonetheless, the Soviet assessment of the meeting was entirely positive. *Pravda* declared: 'The proclamation by the leaders of the USSR and USA of the principle that disputed questions should be settled by peaceful means through negotiations launches a new stage in Soviet-American relations, opens up favourable prospects for a *rapprochement* between our two peoples and is a step toward the relaxation of international tension as a whole. . .'.[60]

For Khrushchev, the significance of Camp David was partly personal. Speaking upon his return to Moscow, he shared the realisation that Eisenhower, the head of the most 'aggressive imperialist power', did not want war:

> I can tell you in all frankness, dear comrades, that as a result of my talks and discussions of concrete questions with the United States President, I have gained the impression that he sincerely wishes to see the end of the cold war, to create normal relations between our countries and to help improve relations among all countries.[61]

Compared to the generally optimistic Soviet attitude, the American appraisal was cautious. The White House and the State Department assessed the visit as a 'successful experiment', but warned that the only true gain was to lessen the pressure on Berlin.[62] Eisenhower cautiously called the event a 'beginning', but he still refused to commit himself to a summit meeting.[63] There were several reasons for this American reserve. First, nothing tangible had been achieved. While the image of Eisenhower hosting Khrushchev for friendly talks at Camp David had a powerful impact on domestic and foreign opinion, there was a certain artificiality about the entire occasion. With the exception of the exchange of exhibits, no major events had preceded the visit suggesting an improvement in US–Soviet relations. Indeed, the Berlin crisis had, if anything, signified a worsening of relations. When Khrushchev eventually withdrew his ultimatum, tension was eased but only because a serious confrontation had been averted. Eisenhower had issued the invitation in an attempt to break the deadlock. He made it clear that the visit would not involve a summit meeting because conditions were still not right.

Second, the Western experience with the 'spirit of Geneva' in 1955 encouraged American leaders and observers to be more cautious in their assessment of the new peace initiative. Not only was there a scarcity of tangible accomplishments backing up the new initiative, but the West was in a relatively weaker position than before. The myth of the 'missile gap' was growing, and Western security appeared threatened. Therefore, once again, policy makers had to guide their actions through two conflicting goals – lessening tension with the Soviet Union and maintaining domestic and allied vigilance against the Soviet Union. In his 16 November address before the National Foreign Trade Council, Secretary Herter expressed his concern: 'Nothing could be more fatal than to confuse relaxation of tension with relaxation of ourselves, and one of the most serious dangers ahead is that people will be tempted to do exactly that.'[64]

A third reason for American reserve in assessing the Khrushchev visit was based in the delicate dynamics of the Atlantic Alliance. In both Bonn and Paris, the 'spirit of Camp David' was viewed with suspicion. Adenauer was fearful that the American government, spurred on by the British government, would be willing to grant concessions concerning Germany in the interest of superpower relations. The situation with France was more complicated and directly related to the return of Charles de Gaulle.

In the late spring of 1958, a French government crisis over the Algerian conflict led to de Gaulle's return to power. The vision that he had long held for restoring France's grandeur was now given a political means. The dual hegemony practised by the superpowers in Europe however presented a fundamental obstacle. Through NATO, the United States controlled the defences of Europe and therefore, in de Gaulle's view, held the destiny of France in its hands. Given his view of the nation-states and belief that ultimately, the United States would only act in its own interests, he sought 'independence' through a gradual withdrawal from the integrated structure of NATO.[65] In March 1959, de Gaulle withdrew the French Mediterranean fleet from NATO and three months later prohibited nuclear stockpiling on French soil unless control of the weapons was shared. Despite the expense, he augmented the programme begun by his predecessors for a national nuclear deterrent force. He also declined signing the test-ban proposals on the grounds that they represented a ploy by the superpowers to maintain their monopoly. While remaining fundamentally loyal to the alliance, he aimed primarily to reassert French independence[66] – a process that was to culminate in France's withdrawal from the integrated structure of NATO in 1966.

Politically, he sought to 'create among Europeans, from the Atlantic to the Urals, new relationships, new ties, a new atmosphere'.[67] He had a vision of Europe, with France in the lead, as a 'third force' that could collaborate with both East and West or act as an arbiter between the camps.[68] This first demanded a reduction of American and British influence in Europe and the establishment of a new relationship with the Federal Republic of Germany.[69] De Gaulle's attempts to woo Adenauer met with some success but were impaired when the West German Parliament amended the Franco-German Friendship Treaty of 1963 to reaffirm Atlantic orthodoxy. In the European Community, de Gaulle vetoed Britain's application for membership probably due to his fear that Britain's 'special relationship' with the United States would make it America's 'trojan horse' in Europe. After all, Gaullism was based on the premise that certain European and, more specifically, Franco-German interests were different from those of the Atlantic community.

While de Gaulle's eventual attempts to establish a new relationship with the Soviet Union and Eastern Europe failed, the entire Gaullist programme was highly unsettling to the Alliance and Western security. In the autumn of 1959, this entire process was in its initial stages and the Eisenhower Administration was careful in reports on Camp David not to encourage its development. In fact, it was largely on de Gaulle's account that the summit meeting was delayed until May 1960. Despite the willingness of Eisenhower and Macmillan to hold a summit meeting before the end of the year, de Gaulle called for a delay until spring, thereby pushing the summit into the United States presidential election year and limiting Eisenhower's freedom of action. Furthermore, French pride could be appeased by inviting Khrushchev to visit France before the Paris summit.

The Soviet government was upset by the French delay and was

doing everything possible to bring about an immediate summit meeting – such as limiting anti-American, anti-Western statements in the Soviet press. The major reason for Soviet impatience was the splintering of the Sino-Soviet relationship. Time was running out and the split was becoming more and more apparent, thereby weakening the Soviet bargaining position. Like the French, the Chinese government viewed Khrushchev's American tour with suspicion and despair.[70] With the Soviet Union reneging on the Chinese nuclear development programme, and with Khrushchev's pursuit of peaceful coexistence with the leading 'imperialist' power, it was becoming clear that Chinese interests were being sacrificed to the interests of superpower relations.

Khrushchev's tour of America served to exacerbate and illuminate Sino-Soviet differences. The 'superpowers only' meeting at Camp David promoted the belief in China that the Soviet Union was engaging in a conspiracy with the United States to dominate the world and prevent China from becoming a nuclear power. When the Soviet government expressed its desire to offer the West a 'nuclear-free' China in exchange for a 'nuclear-free' neutralised Germany, the Chinese rejected the proposal and opted for their own nuclear capability. As Adam Ulam pointed out, the Soviet decision to withdraw the promise of nuclear aid was the most bitterly resented decision thus far in the Sino-Soviet relationship. Chinese bitterness was later reflected in their accusation that 'the real aim of the Soviet leaders is to find a compromise with the United States in order to seek monetary ease and to maintain a monopoly of nuclear weapons and to lord it over the socialist camp'.[71]

The second reason Khrushchev's visit widened the Sino-Soviet schism revolves around the way the Camp David meetings accentuated the differences in strategy and ideology. The meetings suggested that Khrushchev had totally rejected Peking's line about putting forth Soviet strength rather than negotiating from it. The Chinese leadership scoffed at the naïve idea that one could lie down with imperialist lions. When it became clear that the Soviet leaders were not going to use their new found influence (via Sputnik) to force concessions from the West, the Chinese claimed the Soviet government had grown soft on the Communist revolution. The ideological differences in foreign affairs were compounded by the divergent approaches to communism within each society. To the Soviet government, the 'Great Leap Forward' revealed the intention of the Chinese to liberate themselves from economic and technological dependence on the Soviet Union. The rhetoric surrounding the 'Great Leap' was also inherently insulting. The suggestion that the Chinese were ideologically purer and capable of surpassing the Soviet Union on the road to communism caused irritation in the Kremlin. Khrushchev's visit to America represented an ideological 'parting of the ways' between the Soviet and Chinese Communist parties.

Finally, the discussions at Camp David augmented the Sino-Soviet conflict by demonstrating to Khrushchev just how difficult an ally China could be. Both Eisenhower and Herter made it clear to Khrushchev that whether he liked it or not the Soviet Union would have to 'accept a great degree of responsibility' for Chinese actions. As Alastair Buchan pointed out, 'it was an essential characteristic of this period of extreme bipolarity that each superpower did in fact hold the other responsible for the acts of its allies'.[72]

The risks involved in accounting for the Chinese had surfaced during the Quemoy crisis one year before. Khrushchev had not favoured risking nuclear war over a few small islands off the Chinese mainland. To complicate matters, the Chinese were engaging in further offensives beyond their borders. In July–August 1959, the Chinese crossed the disputed Sino-Indian border claiming over 50 000 square miles and creating a *fait accompli*. The Chinese dispute with India was especially awkward for the Soviet leaders, who had worked so hard to establish good relations with the Indians. For the first time, the Soviet government refused to take sides with a Communist ally – an observation bitterly noted in Peking.

Despite efforts to maintain the façade of unity with the Chinese, the Soviet Union placed a high priority on détente with the United States. From the Kremlin's view, there was more to be gained by pursuing peaceful coexistence with the West.

In mid-December, a TASS report stated, 'The forces of peace and sane thinking are growing in the United States as 1959 comes to a close.' There are 'grounds for hoping for further thawing in the cold war and a happy era in Soviet–American relations'.[73] Hopes were high for the new decade.

The months leading up to the summit meeting in May 1960 constituted a 'waiting period' in US–Soviet relations. Both superpowers carefully guarded their words and actions so as not to disturb the ambiguous spirit binding them together.

In his January address to the Supreme Soviet, Khrushchev welcomed the New Year with an optimistic appraisal of the international environment. This set the stage for Khrushchev's proposal involving a unilateral reduction of Soviet troops by 1.2 million men.

The United States response was, as usual, cautiously optimistic. In the Administration's view, a troop reduction would unquestionably aid the relaxation of tension, but there was no way of verifying Soviet compliance with such a reduction.[74] US–Soviet disarmament talks had always been hampered by the problem of verification and compliance.

In February, a Declaration of the Warsaw Pact observed that tension was slowly being reduced and the threat of war declining. At about the same time, however, Khrushchev dropped some comments on the necessity of solving the Berlin question at the summit. If no solution was forthcoming, he warned that the Soviet government would be forced to apply other measures. In a news conference on 8 February, Herter carefully stated that a new ultimatum would violate 'not the spirit of Camp David, but the spirit of the agreement made at Camp David'.[75] Backing down, Khrushchev issued an appeal that 'no one makes statements that might trouble the atmosphere'.[76] With the summit conference still several weeks away, both sides felt compelled to practise restraint in the interests of peaceful and productive negotiations. This joint commitment, however, proved to be shortlived.

THE AFTERMATH: APRIL 1960 UNTIL JULY 1960

In early April, without warning, the political atmosphere took a radical turn for the worse. Perhaps the growing realisation that the forthcoming Paris summit was unlikely to produce desired results led to this sudden shift in directions. Whatever the reason, the superpowers dropped their 'moratorium' on words and deeds violating the 'spirit of Camp David' and engaged in some pre-summit posturing.

Issuing the near equivalent of a new ultimatum on Berlin, Khrushchev demanded that the West accept the Soviet position in Paris or else face the prospects of a separate Soviet-East

German Treaty. On 20 April 1960, Under-Secretary of State Dillon attacked Khrushchev's position and observed that 'the so-called German Democratic Republic (East Germany) is one of the outstanding myths in a vast Communist web of prodigious mythology'.[77] Demanding concessions on Eastern Europe, Korea and the United Nations, Dillon countered Khrushchev's posturing and claimed that by issuing his recent threats, Khrushchev 'is skating on very thin ice'.

Speaking five days later in Baku, Khrushchev hardened his position on Berlin and confirmed that an unproductive summit along Soviet lines would automatically lead to a separate peace treaty with the German Democratic Republic.[78] He also interpreted Dillon's statements as a shift in the American position and warned 'such hotheads that when they start invoking force and not right and justice, it is but natural that his force will be countered with the force of the other side'.[79]

Anxious to escape the appearance of attending the summit under a Soviet ultimatum, Eisenhower dismissed Khrushchev's comments as the 'same old stuff'.[80] He then proceeded to diminish the importance of the Paris summit as well as the hopes and expectations surrounding it.

The opportunities for making peace at the Paris summit were never tested, however, because a series of events in the month of May led to the summit's abortion. On 1 May, an American spy plane on a reconnaissance mission over the Soviet Union went missing. On 5 May, Khrushchev suddenly announced that the Soviet military had shot down the American spy plane and that it had been violating Soviet air space. Despite United States attempts to deny this, Khrushchev produced film from the plane as well as the pilot who had parachuted to safety.

In a speech to the Supreme Soviet on 6 May, Khrushchev continued to express his desire for peace but harshly criticised the United States for violating the process on the eve of the summit.[81]

In a note to British Prime Minister Macmillan on 9 May, Khrushchev claimed that while certain parties had raised difficulties, the Soviet government still hoped for fruitful negotiations. This was to be the last sign of Khrushchev's desire and willingness to pursue fruitful negotiations at the Paris summit.

The first obvious sign of a change in Soviet intentions came with their announcement that secrecy would be banned at the summit. This suggested that the summit was to be used strictly as a propaganda ploy with little hope of conducting serious negotiations.[82] Next, the Kremlin cancelled Soviet Chief Air Marshal Vershinin's visit to the United States in protest against the U-2 incident. Third, optimism about the summit was suddenly replaced by 'fury and indignation' in the Soviet press over 'American aggression'. When Eisenhower finally took full responsibility for the incident, and admitted that he had full knowledge of the flights, the Soviet leaders were more irate than ever.

When Khrushchev arrived in Paris for the summit, he immediately met separately with de Gaulle and Macmillan, thereby snubbing Eisenhower. Instead of a meeting, Khrushchev sent Eisenhower a note demanding that he (a) denounce U-2 flights as acts of inadmissible provocation; (b) renounce future flights; and (c) punish those responsible. While de Gaulle and Macmillan attempted to persuade Khrushchev to soften his position, these demands and Eisenhower's refusal to meet them caused the summit to collapse. The summit ended before it had even begun.

Despite widespread disappointment, the official American response was calm, practical and rational. It is interesting to note that this calm reaction was directly related to the fact that the Eisenhower Administration had constantly downgraded expectations for the summit.

On the other hand, the Soviet reaction displayed grossly disappointed expectations. In an unprecedented personal attack on President Eisenhower, and in reply to concerns over his Camp David assessment about the President's peaceful intentions, Khrushchev stated, 'The road to hell is paved with good intentions. And that's where Eisenhower will land. The whole world knows the President has two functions – one to play golf, the other to carry out his Presidential duties, the latter being the subsidiary one.'[83] The Soviet press also joined in claiming that Eisenhower 'showed himself to be one of the masters and apostles of hypocrisy and dispelled the last illusions regarding his role in the shameful farce of trying to justify United States policy'.[84]

These personal attacks on Eisenhower were simply a taste of things to come. Khrushchev launched a wild and belligerent verbal attack on the United States and its allies, rattling sabres and threatening a storm of missiles if Western spying continued. In reality, however, the shift in Khrushchev's approach was more one of style than substance. He did not proceed to solve the Berlin problem unilaterally, nor did he give up the idea of peaceful coexistence.[85] Nonetheless, Khrushchev's new terminology and techniques gave the impression war was being planned. Numerous diplomatic protests were issued covering a variety of problems. Demands and short-term ultimatums were issued and often accompanied by threats of military retaliation.

The Soviet approach had changed so radically that Western leaders were perplexed as to Khrushchev's motives and goals. Khrushchev continued his missile rattling throughout the end of Eisenhower's term of office. A local crisis in the Congo in July was blown into a superpower conflict as both sides sought to maximise their advantages at the risk of war. As Eisenhower sadly remembered, 'The peaceful line was gone; in its place was a Kremlin attitude reminiscent of the days of Stalin. . . . For whatever reason, it was obvious the Chairman had concluded that his policy of conciliation had not paid off.'[86] By the summer of 1960, the 'spirit of Camp David' was dead and a new round of the cold war under way.

FACTORS CONTRIBUTING TO, AND DETRACTING FROM, DÉTENTE

Seven factors contributed to an easing of tension during this period, thereby producing the 'spirit of Camp David'. First, Khrushchev's retreat from his Berlin Ultimatum in the spring of 1959 set the stage of the events surrounding the Camp David talks. In a perverse way, the Berlin Ultimatum contributed to détente by raising tension to such a high pitch that an automatic relaxation of tension occurred in the wake of the crisis. Instead of pushing the issue to the brink of conflict, Khrushchev expressed his willingness to back down in favour of a foreign ministers' conference. In the absence of progress, these moves raised the hope that progress was being made. The aftermath of the Berlin Crisis produced the setting and the tone for the months to come.

Second, a relaxation of international tension occurred because both superpowers leaders 'willed' it to happen. In other words, the mutual desire to ease tension automatically contributed to an easing of tension. One of the ironies of the cold war was that two world leaders could scarcely have held a stronger desire for peace than Eisenhower and Khrushchev. However, their international positions were inherently conflicting and required that peace be achieved on their own terms. Therefore, the peace process was constantly hampered by the 'necessities' of power management. After the intense and anxious moments of the Berlin Crisis, some of the 'necessities' and considerations were temporarily cast aside. Khrushchev's retreat from the six month deadline brought relief in Western quarters and the realisation that something must be done to settle the issue before Khrushchev attempted another unilateral move. Eisenhower's invitation of late July 1959 was specifically designed to find, at least, a temporary settlement to the Berlin question.

On a similar score, Khrushchev was under increasing pressure to settle the Berlin question. Having backed down on the six month deadline, Khrushchev was more anxious than ever for a summit meeting or some spectacle indicating progress.

The meeting at Camp David represented the manifestation of these desires. In an age when traditional diplomatic means seemed to be failing miserably, the idea of two leaders sitting down to discuss problems was viewed as the most potentially successful means to peace. The spectacle of the two masters of the world's destiny meeting to work out problems of peace had a considerable impact on observers throughout the world, raising hopes and contributing to an easing of tension. In the view of foreign and domestic opinion, the mere suggestion that the two great adversaries would visit each other's country was ample proof of a new spirit.

A third factor contributing to détente was the 'perceived' shift and reinstatement of relative power positions in 1959. While perceptions are always ambiguous, especially when related to shifts in the balance of power, it is apparent that détente was jointly pursued only after Khrushchev's inability to exploit the new Soviet 'missile-lead' had contributed to the rebuilding of United States self-confidence.

The months of August to December 1957 had witnessed the most visible and dramatic shift in the power balance in the 1950s. By the end of this period, the Soviet leaders had regained control over their rebellious satellites, seized the initiative in the arms race, scored their most impressive economic growth-rate to date, and celebrated their Fortieth Anniversary with most of the world's communist parties pledging their total support to the leadership of Moscow. Conversely, the United States was experiencing economic recession and had suffered a loss of confidence and prestige due to Moscow's impressive gains. It was bad enough to have let United States strategic superiority slip away, but the Soviet lead in rocket technology was politically unbearable. Given the perceived magnitude of this shift, Eisenhower could not strategically or politically afford to make peace with the Soviet Union on these terms. Only after missiles had been placed in Europe to 'redress' the balance, and the United States had accelerated its missile-oriented scientific and educational programmes, was Eisenhower in a position to bargain. Furthermore, American sensitivity to the perceived power shift undoubtedly contributed to the more forceful application of the Eisenhower Doctrine between 1957 and 1959. The lack of an effective Soviet response to these American displays of force no doubt helped to reassert the image of American power. Khrushchev's retreat on the Berlin Ultimatum augmented this process.

Despite the Soviet achievements of 1957, Khrushchev was unable to exploit this new found status with any significant degree of success. With this new respect and power, Khrushchev had hoped to settle a number of international issues, including Berlin and the wider German question. When these goals failed to materialise, the significance of the 'power shift' of 1957 was diminished.

In short, by late 1959, the shift in the balance of power had either been partially rectified or else shown to be overstated. This relative equalisation process allowed the superpower leaders to meet with a similar degree of confidence in their power positions. This perception of relative equilibrium contributed to an easing of tension.

Fourth, the post-Geneva legacy of cultural, social and scientific exchanges contributed to the 'spirit of Camp David'. Significantly, Eisenhower used the occasion of Kozlov's visit to the Soviet exhibition in Washington to issue his invitation to Khrushchev. After all, despite the problems plaguing the overall relationship, progress was being made in the area of East–West contacts. The signing of the Bilateral Exchange Agreement during a period of high tension (January 1959) demonstrated the desire of the superpowers to maintain mutually advantageous contacts despite the political environment. Negotiations to expand such relations continued throughout this period without interruption from the crises plaguing the wider relationship.

Within weeks of Khrushchev's tension-producing ultimatum on Berlin, Soviet and American negotiators agreed on the exchange of national exhibits in each other's capital city. When Vice President Nixon visited Moscow and First Deputy Premier Kozlov visited Washington in order to open up the exhibits, the stage was set for an exchange of the Heads of State. The symbolism of the two great adversaries in world politics meeting for informal talks at Camp David cannot be overstated. The legacy of cultural, scientific and social exchange played a vital role in initiating this historic visit and the 'spirit' it produced.

Fifth, the growth of mass communications and superpower competition for the sympathies of the newly emerging nation-states placed an increased importance on the image of peacemaking, thereby encouraging such experiments as the meeting at Camp David. With the growing fear of nuclear war throughout the world, Eisenhower and Khrushchev could not afford to ignore the calls for a resolution of the cold war. For this reason, Khrushchev's carefully orchestrated campaign for a summit meeting met with widespread approval. In both camps, the cold war was taking its toll economically, politically and psychologically. The acceleration of the arms race was exacerbating this burden. The aspiration for peace was high, and there was a general feeling that all potential avenues for peace should be explored. As one observer noted: 'Summit meetings became ingrained in world diplomacy when people, weary of war and crying for quick solutions, demanded them.'[87]

Sixth, the proliferation in the 1950s of superpower competition on a global scale ironically expanded the area of common superpower interests. For instance, such events as the Quemoy Crisis in 1958 demonstrated how the superpower contest could be manipulated by smaller powers to obtain their own ends. Therefore, the superpowers gained a joint interest in preventing events from getting out of control. In the case of Quemoy, both superpowers agreed that the issue was not worth the risk of a nuclear war and worked to diffuse the crisis. Because the superpowers increasingly held each other responsible for the actions of their allies, there was a growing tendency to temper or restrict any actions which might lead to war.

The crises in the late 1950s provided both the need and opportunity for some form of crisis control. The dramatic increase in the number of diplomatic notes between Washington and

Moscow suggested that the superpowers increasingly perceived themselves as the Joint guardians of world peace and order.[88] The Eisenhower/Khrushchev meeting at Camp David reinforced this view. While Eisenhower attempted to play down the bilateral meeting, the absence of the Western allied leaders was conspicuous. Future agreements (i.e. the hotline agreement) would increasingly demonstrate that the fate of the world was in the hands of the superpowers.

While the superpowers were only partially cognisant of their mutual areas of interest, the unwritten commitment to avoid nuclear war, or even a direct clash of arms, tempered provocative behaviour and contributed to the relaxation of tension. As superpower competition became global, the need for direct communication, caution and restraint became greater.

Finally, economic considerations encouraged both sides to seek détente as a means to ease the growing burden of the arms race. The introduction of rocket technology to the cold war by the Soviet Union in 1957 opened up a whole new area of competition in the arms race and augmented its intensity. The cost of this competition was high. Immediately following the Soviet technological successes, Khrushchev began his peace offensive, tempering all provocative comments and pushing for a summit meeting. While this peace offensive was primarily designed to weaken Western resolve in placing short-range missiles in Europe, it was also designed to facilitate the success of Khrushchev's Seven-Year Plan. With the ambitious goal of overtaking the United States economically, Khrushchev wished to transfer human and material resources from the unproductive military realm to the productive consumer-oriented investment realm. He planned to accomplish this goal by cutting the armed forces and saving on defence funds by exploiting a fictitious missile lead. The support for his policies of peaceful coexistence depended greatly upon the perceived threat from the West. Economic considerations provided part of the impetus for Khrushchev's energetic pursuit of a summit conference.

Economic considerations were also a factor in Eisenhower's decision to try a new approach with Khrushchev. The upsurge in the arms race, necessitating a dramatic American response at great expense, was upsetting to Eisenhower's plans. In the campaign of 1956, Eisenhower had promised to cut taxes and balance the budget. The recession of 1957 made this all the more essential in the eyes of Eisenhower and a significant proportion of the electorate. The Soviet technological and economic successes of late 1957 complicated this plan, and exposed Eisenhower to criticism from all sides. On one hand, he was criticised for letting the United States' technological lead slip away while on the other, he was criticised for mishandling the economy. Eisenhower probably hoped that his invitation to Khrushchev might provide a new environment for alleviating the pressure of the arms race.

The factors leading to the decline of the Camp David détente go deeper than the U-2 incident and the aborted summit meeting in Paris. These events were the manifestation of two underlying limitations of the 'spirit of Camp David'. One was its superficiality: while a significant easing of tension did take place, it was based almost entirely on 'atmospherics'. With its original foundations built in the 'shadows' of the Berlin Crisis, the Camp David détente was doomed to instability. Few events had taken place suggesting that progress was possible in superpower relations. When, through the means of personal diplomacy, Eisenhower and Khrushchev attempted to build détente at Camp David, nothing substantial was achieved. This lack of substance led to the adaptation of the word 'spirit' to describe the collection of hopes, aspirations and dreams surrounding the meetings. Unfortunately, these hopes, aspirations and dreams only served to obscure what was not there. Neither side had subordinated issues over which there was conflict nor shown a willingness to make concessions on vital questions. The arms race was out of control, and the ideological contest had taken on global dimensions. The leaders of both superpowers were under domestic political pressure to 'hold the line' or seek unilateral advantages at the risk of conflict. Given these realities, any perception of détente at this time was the product of wishful thinking.

Moreover, the Camp David détente declined because it was based, almost entirely, on personal diplomacy. When Eisenhower and Khrushchev 'willed' an easing of tension, the process of détente was augmented; when they withdrew their support, the process ground to a halt. This factor was especially apparent in Khrushchev's actions from April 1960 to the end of Eisenhower's term. It is likely that in April, Khrushchev realised that he was not going to get his way concerning the Berlin issue and that the likelihood of progress at the summit was limited.[89] American policy statements had confirmed his doubts that no concessions would be made in an election year. Unlike Eisenhower, Khrushchev had practised no restraint in his declared expectations for the 'spirit of Camp David' and the Paris summit. As the summit neared and the prospects of fulfilling these expectations waned, Khrushchev probably chose to abort rather than fail. The intensity of his attacks on Eisenhower and the United States throughout the remainder of 1960 reflected his disappointment. Within the Moscow leadership, the decision was less personal. Berlin was an issue of the highest priority, and the pursuit of détente had failed to resolve it. When Eisenhower continued to show immobility on Berlin, the value of détente declined.[90]

The Soviet assessment of United States policies and intentions was not accurate. At Camp David, Eisenhower aimed not at a settlement, but at a promise from Khrushchev to refrain from acting unilaterally on Berlin. It is likely that Eisenhower approached the summit conference in Paris with the same limited objectives in mind.

Given the factors militating against a successful summit, it seems likely that the pre-summit posturing by both superpowers was designed to score propaganda points on its predicted failure. The U-2 incident provided the Soviet leadership with the most convincing excuse to abort the summit. The incident, however, was also a source of embarrassment for the Soviet Union because it demonstrated Soviet vulnerability. Furthermore, it served to weaken Khrushchev's domestic position because he had partly based his détente policies on the 'good intentions' of the Americans. When he awkwardly attempted to use the incident politically, Khrushchev inadvertently generated support for his right-wing opponents, who were critical of his peacemaking with the capitalists. Indeed, the majority of Western observers credited Khrushchev's new attitude to his weakening position in the Kremlin. Both Macmillan and de Gaulle expressed the opinion that Khrushchev had used the incident as an excuse to cancel Eisenhower's visit to the Soviet Union which had become a political liability for him.[91] At a Central Committee meeting on the eve of the summit, several of Khrushchev's closest advisers and supporters had been displaced from leading positions in the Kremlin.[92] It was likely that with the limited prospects of making progress at the summit, many Party members were reassessing the costs and benefits of Khrushchev's détente with the West and his split with China. The U-2 incident served to confirm doubts about Khrushchev's policies.[93]

In short, it became increasingly clear that détente could not deliver what it had 'appeared' to promise. In fact, in the case of Khrushchev, détente had become a political liability. As a lame-duck president in an election year, Eisenhower was not able to take any progressive steps aimed at breaking the deadlock in East–West relations. The mutual 'will' for détente upon which the 'spirit of Camp David' had partly rested, was no longer present.

Eisenhower and Khrushchev had been able to build a period of relaxation out of the rubble of the Berlin Crisis. Camp David created a break in the cold war in which tension was reduced by will, desire and expectation rather than concrete achievements. However, as the fragility and superficiality of this détente became apparent, its worth was called into question. At the first major test, it collapsed like a house of cards.

Because the 'spirit of Camp David' had its foundation in images, it is legitimate to ask whether it represented a real period of détente. The answer must be affirmative. A significant relaxation of tension did occur and whether it was based on firm foundations or an ambiguous spirit is not immediately relevant. Whether it was a substantial peace effort or simply a phrase coined by politicians and journalists, it was perceived as a significant step toward peace. For a while, at least, tension was eased. People were more optimistic, less fearful and full of expectation. The likelihood of war appeared to have declined.

THE LEGACY OF DÉTENTE

The question of substance does become relevant, however, when the legacy of détente is assessed. Despite its transparency, a four-part legacy appears to have emerged out of the 'spirit of Camp David'. First, the superpowers reaffirmed their commitment to avoid nuclear war. While the Berlin Crisis represented the most dangerous problem of the late 1950s, its peaceful resolution demonstrated the superpower commitment not to venture over the brink.

Secondly, this period introduced embryonic methods of crisis management. The increase in communication between Washington and Moscow served to promote superpower 'consultation' on several issues. The bilateral meeting at Camp David provided the opportunity for 'exclusive' superpower discussions, for the first time in the history of the US–Soviet relationship, on matters of mutual concern. This signified a recognition of joint responsibility in the management of world peace.

Third, the 'spirit of Camp David' had the effect of revealing both the assets and liabilities of personal diplomacy. Personal diplomacy was seen to have both potential and limits. It was viewed as a useful instrument, especially in times of crisis, but it was also shown not to be the panacea of all international problems. The limited number of summits in the 1960s was in part a consequence of this realisation.

Conversely, the value of traditional diplomacy was recognised and revived, with relative success; later events in the 1960s were to provide confirmation of this.

Finally, the post-Geneva legacy of cultural, social and scientific exchanges was augmented during this period. Despite the wild fluctuations in tension, these relations expanded dramatically. As previously mentioned, the agreement to exchange national exhibits was signed at the height of the Berlin Crisis. This led to the exchange of top-level invitations resulting in the 'spirit of Camp David'.

Despite its superficiality, the 'spirit of Camp David' provides insights into the nature of détente. These will be discussed in the concluding chapter.

5   The Post-Missile Crisis Détente

... the first step has been taken on the road of getting the nuclear genie back into its bottle.[1]   *New York Times*

The icy barriers of the "cold war" have been breached and discernible prospects for easing international tension have appeared.[2]   *Izvestia*

The signing of the Test-Ban Treaty in the summer of 1963 marked the beginning of a new era in US–Soviet détente. In contrast to the 'atmospherics' of the 1950s, détente in the 1960s was built on substantive accomplishments. The Test-Ban Treaty, the Hotline Agreement and the Non-Proliferation Treaty provided notable and enduring monuments to détente during this tumultuous decade. Recognising the dangers arising from superpower tension, the architects of détente in the 1960s attempted to introduce an element of restraint through the negotiation of mutually advantageous agreements. These agreements were to provide the framework for peaceful competition and, eventually, co-operation.

The substantive nature of the Post-Missile Crisis détente was best exemplified by the course of US–Soviet relations throughout the 1960s. While détente emerged in 1963 following the Cuban Missile Crisis of late 1962, it cannot be said to have ended at any specific time. Unlike the 'spirit of Geneva' and 'spirit of Camp David', periods which are said to have ended abruptly with the events in Budapest and Paris, the Post-Missile Crisis détente was more stable and enduring. Agreements were achieved without the flash and fanfare of summitry, in a spirit of sobriety and pragmatism. For example, as the United States escalated its involvement in Vietnam, thereby inhibiting high-level exchanges and achievements, negotiations continued at lower levels. When the Soviet Union invaded Czechoslovakia, the process was merely interrupted, not terminated. At the height of United States involvement in Vietnam, and in the aftermath of the Soviet invasion of Czechoslovakia, the Non-Proliferation Treaty was ratified (5 March 1970) because, despite these crises, the treaty was seen as a means of setting certain limits on the continuing superpower conflict. Compared to the 1950s, the characteristics of détente had changed as radically as the styles.

THE SETTING: 1961–62

As John F. Kennedy took the Presidential oath in January 1961, Khrushchev issued an inauguration day note expressing the hope that 'by joint efforts we shall be able to attain a radical improvement of relations between our countries'.[3] A few days later as a gesture of goodwill, the Soviet government released two captured American fliers. It had already agreed three weeks earlier to drop the Gary Powers/U-2 case in the United Nations. Unfortunately, these acts were not harbingers of the coming months in US–Soviet relations.

On the American side, the new Administration was decidedly cautious; its popular mandate had been based on the promise of standing up to the Soviet communists and 'getting America going again'. On 6 January 1961, William Stringer of the *Christian Science Monitor* observed that the American mood was exceptionally anti-communist and that 'nobody expects that future Soviet–American relations will be anything less than cagey and catch-as-catch-can'.[4] John Hightower of the *New York Herald Tribune* observed four days later that Kennedy was committed to earning his hardline credentials by building up United States defences and seizing the initiative in the cold war.[5] These priorities were reflected in Kennedy's Inauguration Address and first 'State of the Union' report. In the former he charted an activist course for American foreign policy, especially in the Third World, and promised to 'bear any burden, oppose any foe' in the pursuit of American interests. In the latter, Kennedy dwelt on the growing dangers in a world where the tides were flowing contrary to United States interests and called for a massive increase in American military strength.[6] While these grim warnings were at least partially designed to generate legislative support for Kennedy's military proposals, they had the obvious side effect of creating additional concern and fear throughout the nation. This was evident as 'right-wing' organisations reached their peak in membership and contributions in 1961.[7] As Kennedy pioneered the 'New Frontier', tension was on the rise.

On the Soviet side, Khrushchev seemed more interested in winning quick unilateral concessions from the new and inexperienced American leader than in pursuing a peace based on mutually advantageous agreements. In early January, Khrushchev let the United States Embassy in Moscow know that 1961 was the last opportunity for a *modus vivendi* between the United States and the Soviet Union. The Soviet leadership criticised Kennedy's State of the Union speech in February for invoking 'irksome echoes of the cold war'[8] and by the following month, Western journalists were noting Soviet disillusionment with the new administration.[9] While it was suggested that Khrushchev's impatience was rooted in his own domestic, economic and political problems as well as the growing Sino-Soviet split,[10] one thing was clear: the immediate future of US–Soviet relations did not look promising.

In March 1961, Kennedy began to seize the initiative in foreign relations by creating the Peace Corps, declaring the 'Alliance for Progress' with Latin American countries and promising future initiatives in US–Soviet relations. Nonetheless, pessimism was growing as the British, Soviet and American governments resumed test-ban talks in Geneva on 21 March. The announcement, one week later, of Kennedy's programme to rapidly increase United States military potential only served to worsen the prevailing mood.

It was in this atmosphere that the first major crisis of the new Administration occurred. On 17 April, a disorganised and ill-equipped army of Cuban exiles stormed the island of Cuba in an attempt to generate an insurrection against Castro. Within hours, the army was defeated by Castro's forces. The attempted invasion immediately became an international incident because the American CIA had trained and supported the exiles. American–Cuban relations had been steadily worsening since Castro's seizure of power and were exacerbated by Castro's policies and growing contacts with Moscow. To the United States, the thought of Castro peddling Moscow's influence in its own backyard was unbearable. In order to rectify the situation, Kennedy approved the ill-fated invasion plans designed under Eisenhower. When the Bay of Pigs invasion failed, the repercussions were significant.

For the Soviet leadership, the Bay of Pigs fiasco provided proof that the new President was both inexperienced and weak. Moscow also seized the opportunity to score points through propaganda. On one hand, the United States was portrayed as a bullying neighbour trying to place a small helpless power in the 'chains of American slavery'.[11] On the other hand, the United States was portrayed as a weak and awkward monster unable to wage an effective campaign in defence of its interests. The day following the invasion, Khrushchev warned Kennedy that the Soviet Union would render the Cuban people and their Government all necessary assistance in beating back the armed attack on Cuba.[12] A second message came four days later, lecturing Kennedy on morality and justice in international relations. Finally, a week later, *Pravda* launched a series of *ad hominem* attacks on Kennedy, reminiscent of Khrushchev's unprecedented abuse of Eisenhower following the U-2 incident. If there was anything left of the honeymoon that supposedly accompanies the coming to power of a new administration, it was definitely over by the end of April. On 20 April, *Pravda* criticised 'the hypocrisy of Kennedy's former pledges and assurances', claiming that 'the new master of the White House preferred to follow in the footsteps of his bankrupt predecessors'.[13]

By shaking American confidence and bolstering Soviet confidence, the Bay of Pigs incident had an unsettling effect on superpower relations. It evidently convinced Khrushchev that the time was right to push for a resolution of the nagging and embarrassing Berlin question. New 'threats' began to emerge out of Berlin and Moscow and when Khrushchev proposed summit talks, the United States accepted. Throughout the month of May, a flourish of diplomatic activity led to the convening of the Geneva Conference on Laos and the arrangement of the Kennedy–Khrushchev meeting in Vienna in June.

On 3 June, the Vienna summit convened in an atmosphere of mutual suspicion and curiosity. It was, most of all, an opportunity for each leader to size the other up. While the discussions were conducted in a civil manner, they were characterised more by statements of position than any real search for accommodation. Kennedy had come to Vienna, partly out of the need to demonstrate his and America's determination to stand firm. He did not wish Khrushchev to evaluate his competence and resolve on the basis of the Bay of Pigs fiasco. Conversely, Khrushchev had come to Geneva in the hope of gaining concessions from the young President on Berlin, a German peace treaty, disarmament and a test-ban. Khrushchev's intentions and expectations were revealed by the fact that his proposals were nothing more than reproductions of those the Eisenhower Administration had previously rejected. Given these factors, the likelihood of progress was limited.

In one area, however, some progress was made. Both leaders agreed that Laos should not become a major area of confrontation between them. This downgrading of the superpower conflict in Laos aided the negotiation process in Geneva, thereby facilitating the eventual signing of a fourteen nation Geneva accord one year later.

While, on the whole, the Vienna Conference produced no agreements, the more intangible benefits justified its occurrence. First, the meeting provided an opportunity for Kennedy and Khrushchev to meet and develop a personal basis of communication that was to prove valuable in future crises. To Khrushchev's dismay and discomfort, Kennedy spent an inordinate amount of time discussing the dangers of nuclear 'miscalculation' and the need for open communication and mutual restraint. It is possible that Khrushchev had this discussion in mind when he decided to back down during the Cuban Missile Crisis.

Second, the Vienna summit exemplified the limitations of summitry. Both leaders accepted the invitation and approached the meeting with very limited expectations. The press and the public shared these limited expectations. The aborted Paris summit thirteen months earlier had taken the magic out of summit meetings. When the subject of further summits was raised at Vienna, Kennedy reasserted his commitment to negotiation through traditional diplomatic channels. He was so sensitive about the dangerous mirages surrounding summits that he took every opportunity to stress that no progress, other than establishing a basis for communication, had been made in Vienna. As Presidential assistant Theodore Sorensen recalled:

> ... he wanted no newsman or citizen to be under any impression that the complacency he had battled so long could be tolerated any longer, or that there were any easy, magic ways

to deflect the Soviet drive. He wanted Congress, dawdling on his foreign aid and related programs, awakened to support his next moves. He wanted no one to think that the surface cordiality in Vienna justified any notion of a new 'Spirit of Geneva, 1955' or 'Spirit of Camp David, 1959'.[14]

Despite all of this, a large price was paid for the lack of progress at Vienna. A new and more dangerous crisis arose out of the stalemated discussions on Berlin. During their talks, Khrushchev had abruptly stated that unless the Western Powers were willing to settle the Berlin question, the USSR would have no other choice than to sign a separate peace treaty with East Germany. The treaty would acknowledge the postwar division of Germany and settle the outstanding issues left over from World War II. Furthermore, the West would lose its occupation rights in Berlin. He claimed that nothing could stop the settlement and stated that, within six months, it would have to be completed. Kennedy replied that, unlike Laos, Berlin was at the top of the list of American and Western interests. He assured Khrushchev that the West was committed to maintaining its rights and responsibilities to the German people – especially those in Berlin. If the United States wanted to make war over the issue, Khrushchev stated, so be it. Unless an interim agreement was arranged, the decision to sign a peace treaty by December was absolutely final. Kennedy observed, 'If that is true, it will be a cold winter.'[15]

With this introduction to the crisis, the summer of 1961 proved to be even hotter. Khrushchev restated the deadline in separate speeches on 15 June and 21 June. The time-frame had been set and it was up to the West to respond. Khrushchev had stated that the United States would have to be the first to initiate military action over Berlin. He knew that harrassment of Western access rights could proceed without the United States starting a nuclear war.

Khrushchev's assessment was fundamentally correct. American strategy and deterrence was based on a nuclear response with all of its consequences. On 26 July, Kennedy announced his plan to rectify the situation. He called for a $3.25 billion increase in defence spending and asked Congress for the authority to increase the armed forces by an additional 217 000 men. Furthermore, he called for the reactivation of old conventional equipment, as well as announcing new plans for civil defence. His speech represented not only a symbolic commitment to the security of Berlin, but a real commitment to the vigilant maintenance of Western security. By July, Kennedy had succeeded in either 'waking up' Americans to the danger in the international arena, or else scaring the public into supporting his policies. By late July, *U.S. News and World Report* revealed that public opinion was three-to-one in favour of a showdown with Khrushchev over Berlin.[16] International tension was quickly reaching the crisis point.

The Soviet response was twofold. Initially, Khrushchev sent notes to the Western Allies calling for talks. This proposal was reiterated during the meeting of First Secretaries of the Warsaw Pact in Moscow (3–5 August) and reaffirmed a few days later in an important radio and television address by Khrushchev. When the West failed to respond to these overtures, the Soviet leadership engineered a second and more spectacular response. On 13 August, Berlin was suddenly sealed off and the army proceeded to build a wall separating the Eastern sector of Berlin from the Western sector. The initial Allied reaction was one of disbelief and confusion. Only by the end of the week did Kennedy issue a token protest by sending Vice President Lyndon Johnson to Berlin as well as 1500 more combat troops.

The building of the Berlin Wall in August 1961 represented the first major climax in the prolonged Berlin Crisis of 1961–2. It is significant to the course of superpower relations because it had the immediate after-effect of defusing the larger crisis at hand. Westerners have often interpreted the incident as a provocative act, and many have criticised Kennedy for not responding to the provocation. However, the building of the wall solved part of the problem that had been pushing Soviet and East German leaders to a radical and dangerous conclusion of the Berlin question. The problem involved the fact that the very life-blood of East Germany had been flowing out of East Berlin and into West Berlin daily for years through emigration. As the educated and talented fled communist rule for a better life style in the West, the Eastern economy sank deeper and deeper into crisis. Because of this and the concerns of security and prestige, the Berlin problem had become an unbearable thorn in the side of the communists.[17] When it became apparent in June that a new crisis was in the making, the steady stream of emigrants turned into a flood. In the first twelve days of July, over 8000 persons fled to West Berlin and by the 13 July, they were arriving at a rate of 1000 per day. One month later, when the wall was erected, the flow virtually stopped. Within the next month, Khrushchev let it be known through a variety of channels that he was no longer insisting on the year-end deadline for an agreement. For the moment, the crisis had been defused.

At the same time, however, the wall served the purposes of détente; it was a statement in brick and mortar by the Soviet Union and the German Democratic Republic that a *modus vivendi* could be arrived at only on the basis of acceptance of the divisions and differences separating East and West; and the West's tacit acceptance of the wall brought that *modus vivendi* nearer.

Just as the Berlin Crisis was temporarily winding down, a new move succeeded in keeping tension high. On 31 August, after having respected the mutual ban on the testing of nuclear weapons with the United States for over three years, Khrushchev announced the Soviet intention to resume nuclear testing. Sorensen reported that no Soviet announcement angered Kennedy more than Khrushchev's decision to break the moratorium.[18] Kennedy had placed great hope in the test-ban negotiations that had been pursued, at various intervals, over the past few years. However, the reality of the situation was that both sides felt some necessity to test their new weapon systems. Khrushchev simply gave in first. Kennedy followed suit six months later.

These decisions were significant because they exemplify the high level of superpower tension during this period. They reflect a declining faith in the peace process via negotiation, a consensus that superpower conflict and competition would continue long into the future, and an insecurity worthy of incurring the risks of a new arms race. One month before there was any hint of Khrushchev's desire to resume nuclear testing, a Gallup Poll revealed that Americans favoured unilateral resumption of testing by a margin of two-to-one.[19] The events of 1961 had re-awakened Americans. The price of this growing vigilance was heightened international tension.

On the Soviet side, the embarrassing inability to bluff the West out of Berlin no doubt lent support to the cries of the military for a resumption of nuclear testing. Throughout 1961, Kennedy had announced significant increases in United States military spending, and his July proposals reportedly sent Khrushchev into a 'foot-stamping, bellowing rage'.[20] The Soviet announcement of 31

August reflected further considerations of prestige. The August meeting of Warsaw Pact First Secretaries, as well as the forthcoming Twenty-Second Communist Party Congress, no doubt weighed in the decision to resume testing.

Having raised the level of international tension, both leaders spent the autumn months trying to regain the peace initiative. In competition for the sympathies of the Third World, Kennedy challenged Khrushchev to a 'peace race'. Conversely, Khrushchev carried his campaign to the United Nations on 25 September where he presented his proposals for 'General and Complete Disarmament'. Kennedy replied the following day by creating the United States Disarmament and Arms Control Agency. During his speech to the Twenty-second Communist Party Congress in October 1961, Khrushchev formally announced his intention to drop the year-end deadline on Berlin. Despite this show of 'goodwill', the Soviet communist party members were preoccupied with another issue at the Twenty-Second Congress. In an attempt to frighten the rebellious Chinese and bring them back under the leadership of Moscow, the Soviet government launched a series of harsh verbal attacks on the Albanian communists who had been supported by the Chinese communists in their differences with Moscow. Unfortunately for the Soviet leaders, the attacks had the opposite effect. The Chinese supported the Albanians by walking out of the meeting. This example of the growing Sino-Soviet split might have proved significant in superpower relations had Kennedy not been blinded by a monolithic view of communism. He viewed the dispute as being 'over means, not ends. A dispute over how to bury the West is no grounds for Western rejoicing'.[21]

If this was a time of missed opportunities, it was also a time when some of the opportunities seized might have best been missed. In December, Kennedy increased the number of United States advisers in Vietnam.

Of all the events during this period of growing tension, the continuing Berlin Crisis remained the most serious. Border harrassment began again in late October resulting in a series of 'check-point' crises. In early 1962, the provocations became more intense and more frequent. February saw Soviet attempts to reserve certain altitudes as air corridors. When Western planes refused to respect these demands, Soviet fighters harrassed them. As harrassment continued, the United States announced that Air

Force fighters would escort planes if their safety required it. In mid-March, despite Soviet hints of a new deadline, Soviet statements took on a more conciliatory tone and harrassment died down once again. In April, Gromyko announced that he saw a 'glimmer of hope' for a Berlin agreement and in May, the release of some East German troops was announced.

In the meantime, an interesting phenomenon was occurring in superpower relations. While contributing to tension in Berlin, both superpowers made attempts to relieve tension in other areas of their relationship. It was as if both superpowers recognised the need to control the growing dangers inherent in the Berlin Crisis yet were unwilling to back down on the Berlin issue itself. Therefore, the crisis developed a life of its own while the superpowers tried to lessen tension in other spheres. In this atmosphere, the United States began diplomatic probes of the Soviet Union and the Soviet leadership did the same. In January, two American college students were released from East Germany, and Moscow indicated a willingness to exchange U-2 pilot Gary Powers for a Soviet agent. Also in January, the Soviet government issued a surprise informal invitation to Robert Kennedy (the President's brother and attorney general) to visit Moscow.

When the three-year-old test-ban talks stalemated and adjourned in late January, Khrushchev proposed that the world leaders open a full-scale disarmament conference. A seventeen-nation United Nations disarmament conference was opened in Geneva the following month. Kennedy responded to Khrushchev's initiative by calling for a joint US–Soviet space venture following John Glenn's successful orbit of the earth.

It would be a mistake to think that these gestures were motivated by a desire for détente. There is little evidence to suggest that such a desire was predominant in the thinking of either Kennedy or Khrushchev at the time. In fact, many of the initiatives were launched exclusively for reasons of propaganda. Nonetheless, both leaders were aware that the constant provocations feeding tension in Berlin could lead to a major confrontation, and peaceful co-operation in other areas demonstrated the mutual desire to avoid such an outcome. For this reason, superpower relations had the appearance of getting both better and worse at the same time. From the Western point of view, this observation was noted in the headlines of the day. The *New York*

Times observed that the 'Kremlin Blows Hot and Cold'[22] while the *Guardian* noted 'The Soviet See-saw'.[23]

As tension began to ease in Berlin once again, it resurfaced in other areas. In early March, Kennedy fulfilled the predictions of political observers by announcing the resumption of United States nuclear tests. On 4 May, the Kennedy Administration attempted to strengthen the United States deterrent by its declaration of the 'Flexible Response' Doctrine. Eleven days later, Kennedy sent 5000 Marines to Thailand in response to the perceived communist expansion in Laos. This show of determination helped to speed up the negotiations in Geneva and on 23 June 1962, a fourteen-nation accord was signed declaring Laos neutral. While this accord helped to remove one source of conflict between the superpowers, the cold war raged on.

On 10 July, the Berlin Crisis threatened to raise its ugly head once again. In a speech to a Communist-front peace conference, Khrushchev declared that the Soviet Union would accept the replacement of 'occupation forces' in Berlin with neutral or United Nations troops. A quick rejection from the State Department set the stage for a new ultimatum.

Within the next week, full-scale harrassment started yet again. Soviet jet fighters flew within yards of Western transport planes, and in one case, actually 'buzzed' the wings of a civilian charter plane en route to Berlin. Access land routes were also subject to constant harrassment.

Tension within the city reached the breaking point in the latter part of August when Communist guards shot a young East German as he was trying to escape and left him lying without medical attention for a prolonged period. In the following days, massive crowds of angry West Berliners raged throughout the city. Thousands waited outside crossing points in order to storm Soviet vehicles. Then suddenly, as quickly as it all began, Khrushchev temporarily defused the crisis.

On 11 September, Khrushchev announced that no action would be taken on the East German treaty until after the United States November elections. However, the delay did little to comfort American officials. Writing from Washington at the end of September, James Reston noted:

the growing conviction here is that the Soviet Union will sign a peace treaty with the Communist East German régime, probably in mid-November. . . . There is a greater sense of anxiety in Washington over Berlin than at any time since November 1958 . . .[24]

Little did these Washington officials know that a much larger and more dangerous crisis was in the making several thousand miles away.

Since the Bay of Pigs invasion, Cuba had moved closer to the Soviet Union. In the interests of tying Cuban security to Soviet strategic interests, Castro eagerly responded to Khrushchev's overtures for extensive economic, political and military relations between the two countries. During the summer of 1962, Castro's brother, Raul Castro, travelled to Moscow to discuss these possibilities. While the exact content of these talks is unknown, they contributed to an agreement where the Soviet Union would place nuclear missiles on Cuban soil aimed directly at American cities.

The course of events stemming from this agreement are well known. Throughout August, September and October 1962, the Soviet Union transported and assembled a missile system in Cuba. While United States intelligence reports revealed some evidence of this activity, it was not until 14 October that an American U-2 spotted and confirmed a missile site in Cuba. Over the following thirteen days, the greatest and most dangerous crisis in postwar superpower relations occurred. Kennedy demanded immediate withdrawal of the missiles, leading the Soviet government initially to deny their very existence. As the evidence mounted, the Soviet leadership claimed that the missiles were purely 'defensive' in nature and ignored Kennedy's demands. Rejecting the suggestion by half of his advisory team to bomb the sites, Kennedy opted for a naval blockade on 22 October. The opportunities for superpower conflict reached a head as Soviet vessels were stopped by American warships on the open seas. An unwelcome addition to this confusion had come two days earlier when China launched an offensive against India. The world looked on with the fearful knowledge that one spark could ignite the fuse of nuclear war. Suddenly, however, on 28 October, after an exchange of notes, Khrushchev backed down and agreed to withdraw the missiles. By late November, both sides had stepped back from the brink of war and had taken their weapons with them.

If tension could be measured, the Cuban Missile Crisis would probably top the scale. Therefore, it is difficult to overstate the significance of this crisis to superpower relations and the development of détente. In order to understand its contribution and significance to these areas of inquiry, two questions must be discussed. First, why and how did a crisis of such magnitude occur and, second, how did it influence the events that followed? The answer to the first question lies in those considerations motivating Khrushchev to place missiles in Cuba. While it is only possible to speculate, several factors appear to have motivated his decision. First, since the 'missile gap' had been shown to be a myth and it was clear that the Soviet strategic arsenal was significantly inferior to the American arsenal, there were obvious strategic benefits supporting such a move. The placement of Soviet missiles in Cuba was a quick, cheap, cost-effective move designed to help correct the strategic imbalance. Second, Khrushchev may have sought to create a new and powerful bargaining chip that could be used or traded for any variety of Western concessions. Anatol Rapoport, a fervent proponent of this view, contends that Khrushchev's tremendous need for a success as well as the Soviet failure to camouflage the construction of the missile sites provides proof of the intention to exploit the situation politically rather than militarily. Rapoport hypothesises that Khrushchev wished to swap the missiles for the dismantling of some United States bases encircling the socialist camp, the neutralisation of West Berlin, or a firm promise to deny nuclear weapons to West Germany.[25] Charles Bohlen submits that Khrushchev was in desperate need of achieving a Berlin settlement on Soviet terms.[26] William Griffith agrees with this assessment.[27] The Cuban missiles would provide him with the means to achieve such a development. British Prime Minister Macmillan claimed that the Cuban incident was designed to give the Soviet leaders a success they could not earn in Berlin and thereby test American credibility for future moves.[28] However, as Khrushchev recorded in his memoirs, Soviet credibility was also at stake in terms of protecting Moscow's only communist ally and foothold in the Americas. Khrushchev believed that the missiles would deter another American invasion of Cuba in addition to providing an important symbol of Soviet strength.[29]

Other motives for Khrushchev's decision to place missiles in Cuba are suggested by Roger Hilsman in *To Move a Nation*. As the

State Department's intelligence chief, Hilsman observed the severity of the Sino-Soviet split, and credits Khrushchev's Cuban actions partly to the need to respond to Chinese criticism and maintain Soviet leadership of the socialist camp. A success in Cuba 'via' the Cuban missiles would serve to answer the Chinese charges that the Soviet leaders were growing 'soft' in their competition with the capitalists. Furthermore, Hilsman contends the cost-efficient 'Cuban solution' was the best Soviet option in the light of the 'impossible combination of demands on their limited resources made by defense, their space program, their people's appetite for consumers' goods, and the drain of foreign aid needed to support their foreign policy'.[30]

Finally, the Soviet action in Cuba has been traced to the adventurism and dramatics in Khrushchev's personality and style of leadership. He was a gambler and since the chips were down, he was ready to take a chance. His impatience, however, led him into a situation where a miscalculation of his adversary's will led to a damaging defeat based on his adversary's geo-political advantage. The speed with which Khrushchev volunteered to withdraw the missiles suggests that he had not purposely brought the world to the brink of nuclear war in the hope of winning a showdown with Kennedy.

The aforementioned considerations lead to at least one significant conclusion. The motivations behind the Cuban Missile Crisis were probably no different than those behind many of the other confrontations during this period. As Roger Hilsman pointed out, given the right formula, any of the Kennedy–Khrushchev crises could have exploded into a major confrontation. The components of conflict were constantly present, and any attempt to shift the balance of power dramatically increased tension and the risk of war. Therefore, the 'how and why' of the Cuban Missile Crisis became applicable to the entire sphere of superpower relations. Given that any crisis could lead to armed conflict, and given that the probable consequences of such conflict were so potentially dangerous, the superpowers began to realise that they could no longer risk miscalculation. Kennedy's and Khrushchev's correspondence in the resolution of the crisis attested to that fact.

'HIGH DÉTENTE': 1963–64

The first signs of the thaw in US–Soviet relations came with the first signs of winter. This was not surprising, however, given the intensity of the Cuban episode in the autumn months. Not unlike the period following the Berlin Ultimatum of 1958, this period witnessed an automatic relaxation of tension, by virtue of the fact that the previous events in Cuba had caused tension to rise so high. However, unlike the thaw in 1959, the United States seized the initiative. Just as the Soviet government had gained its impetus from the successful Sputnik tests, the American government gained new confidence from its success in the Cuban Crisis. The American leadership now saw a chance to negotiate peace on the basis of a favourable status quo. Max Frankel observed in the *New York Times* on 1 November 1962 that American leaders viewed the Cuban Missile Crisis as a watershed event, where at long last the United States had regained the momentum and the initiative.[31]

In the beginning of November, Kennedy announced the completion of the United States nuclear testing programme and urged the Soviet Union to join the United States in banning all atmospheric tests. Observing that both countries had collectively exploded about 170 bombs since the resumption of testing, *The Times* claimed that 'both countries should be ready for a respite, if not for a test ban'.[32] When Kennedy labelled this climactic period a turning point in history, the press picked up on the theme. *The Times* speculated that Kennedy was busily preparing for a summit,[33] while the *Sunday Telegraph* reported the unprecedented amount of 'diplomatic flurry' based on the Anglo-American commitment that 'any détente which results must on no account be allowed to slacken'.[34] On 23 November an article in the *New York Herald Tribune* suggested that great decisions to end the cold war were being made in Washington and Moscow,[35] and on 28 November conservative columnist Joseph Alsop claimed the contemporary situation strongly favoured East-West negotiations.[36] While these expressions of high hopes and expectations seemed to reflect just one more incident of the press creating atmospherics, this time the optimism was justified. The Soviet leaders let it be known through a variety of channels that they were ready for serious negotiations. In late November, an article in *Izvestia* by Nikolai Polyanov claimed the resolution of the

Cuban crisis could represent 'the beginning of the end of other controversial problems and this opportunity must not be lost'.[37] Furthermore, the article called for a speedy agreement on several issues, most importantly, the nuclear test-ban question. As Soviet–American priorities continued to converge, Khrushchev and his deputies stressed the renewed need for 'mutual concession and compromise' leading Secretary of State Rusk to concede that the post-Cuban situation provided 'possibilities of real opportunity'.[38] At the turn of the new year, Khrushchev wrote to Kennedy expressing his expectation that both superpowers will engage in 'an energetic effort to adjust the urgent problems that could give rise to new crises . . .'.[39] In return, Kennedy reported to Khrushchev that

> the American people look forward to the coming year with the deepest desire that the cause of peace be advanced. For our part, I assure you that no opportunity will be missed to promote world peace and understanding. . .[40]

In short, the first contribution of the Cuban Missile Crisis to the following period of détente was made by default. The high tension created by the crisis led to a post-crisis honeymoon in which the necessary lines of communication were established and a dialogue was begun.

The chilling experience of the Cuban Missile Crisis had done more to create a united concern about the necessity of solving problems than any amount of negotiation could ever have done. However, despite this unified concern, real progress was delayed for several months. This delay can be partially credited to the differences remaining, but another factor was probably important. While the Cuban Missile Crisis had exacerbated an already widening Sino-Soviet split (the Chinese labelled the Soviet backdown 'a Munich, pure and simple'), the Soviet leaders were still preoccupied with achieving some sort of reconciliation within the socialist family. After criticising Albania for being lured off the proper ideological path, Khrushchev called for a halt to polemics and throughout the first half of 1963, attempted to mollify the Chinese. In February, *Pravda* published an invitation from the Soviet Communist Party to the Chinese, encouraging them to meet and discuss their ideological differences.[41] Soon thereafter, Khrushchev affectionately embraced the Chinese ambassador at a reception announcing that they would bury capitalism together.[42] The Chinese responded to these conciliatory steps by publishing recent Soviet criticisms of Chinese ideology[43] and rejecting the Soviet invitation. When, in late March, the Soviet government sent the Chinese Communists another invitation for 'ideological talks' in mid-May, the Chinese reluctantly accepted but stated that they would not come until mid-June.

On 14 June 1963 before the talks were to convene, the Chinese issued a scathing 25-point indictment of Khrushchev and the Soviet Communist Party. When the Chinese attempted to distribute the indictment in the Soviet Union, Soviet patience ran out. Three months earlier, Seymour Topping observed in the *New York Times* that the Soviet government had shifted to a tougher line with the West in the hope of achieving a reconciliation with the Chinese.[44] When this reconciliation proved impossible, the Soviet government shifted right back. On 14 July 1963, Khrushchev issued his scathing reply to the Chinese, and nuclear test-ban talks were resumed with the West on the following day.

The summer of 1963 soon proved to be the most productive and progressive period yet in US–Soviet relations. The substantive phase of the Post-Missile Crisis détente was initiated by President Kennedy's historic speech at American University on 10 June 1963. In sharp contrast to the cold war rhetoric that had characterised the first half of his term in office, Kennedy issued a dramatic appeal for an end to the cold war. He asked each American to examine 'his own attitude toward the possibilities of peace, toward the Soviet Union, toward the course of the cold war, and toward freedom and peace . . .'.[45] Significantly, Kennedy issued his appeal without creating illusions about the nature of peace or the challenges ahead. He acknowledged that the Soviet Union would remain a threat for many years to come but claimed, 'We can seek a relaxation of tensions without relaxing our guard.'[46] He defined peace as a 'process' involving a 'series of concrete actions and effective agreements . . . the sum of many acts'. He warned against holding the illusion that peace could be achieved by some 'grand or magic formula to be adopted by one or two powers . . .', an obvious allusion to the previously held views surrounding summitry. In many ways, the speech was a master-piece. It inspired hope without creating illusions. It advocated pragmatism and caution while, at the same time, called for positive action in the pursuit of peace.

Khrushchev, having been repeatedly frustrated in his attempts to appease the Chinese Communists and mend the Sino-Soviet split, had already taken Kennedy's cue. He and Kennedy agreed through correspondence to resume nuclear test-ban talks on 15 July. The first sign of progress, however, came as early as 20 June when both sides agreed on the establishment of a 'hotline' between Washington and Moscow. The Hotline Agreement signified a joint acknowledgement of the potential danger of superpower conflict and the need to control crises before they got out of hand. The agreement also displayed a joint sense of responsibility for the future of the world . . . a relationship that was to be viewed with increasing unease among the allies. Predicting this problem, Kennedy had promised in his American University speech that 'the United States will make no deal with the Soviet Union at the expense of other nations and peoples, not merely because they are our partners but also because their interests and ours converge'. Kennedy then travelled to Europe to reassert this point. It was with this in mind that Kennedy rejected the idea of a summit meeting and opted for a special negotiating team.

In mid-July, special negotiators Averell Harriman and Lord Hailsham left for Moscow to begin the test-ban talks. After ten days of intense negotiations, a limited but historically significant agreement was reached. On 5 August 1963, the Partial Test-Ban Treaty was signed between the United States, the Soviet Union and Great Britain. At long last, a first step had been taken in an effort to control the arms race and to place a cap on the development of nuclear weapons.

The overall response was immediately one of euphoria. Tad Szulc of the *New York Times* declared, 'the first step has been taken on the road of getting the nuclear genie back into its bottle'.[47] The *Daily Telegraph* stated, 'With the signing of the Test-Ban treaty there unfolded before us the distant but glorious vision of Russia and the West working together in accord to preserve the peace of the world.'[48]

The Soviet reaction was also optimistic. *Izvestia* declared, 'The icy barriers of the "cold war" have been breached and discernible prospects for easing international tension have appeared.'[49]

The official United States blessing was registered as the Senate voted overwhelmingly to ratify the treaty. Kennedy's successful handling of the Cuban Missile Crisis had paid handsome dividends in terms of earning him the necessary credentials to pursue such an agreement.

During late August and throughout the autumn months, détente continued to progress. Khrushchev confirmed the Soviet split with China by paying an extended visit to Yugoslavia. In September, Kennedy advocated further international and super-power co-operation in his speech to the United Nations, and suggested that the United States and the Soviet Union engage in a joint effort to reach the moon. In October, Kennedy authorised controversial negotiations for the sale of United States grain to the Soviet Union – a move Richard Nixon called 'harmful to the cause of freedom'.[50] Additionally, Defense Secretary Gilpatric suggested that some United States troops might soon be withdrawn from West Germany.[51]

Suddenly the criticism began to emerge in the United States that maybe things were happening a bit too quickly. Kennedy was especially sensitive to these attacks from the right as the election year drew near. Speaking at the University of Maine on 19 October, Kennedy attempted to project his sober and balanced view of the situation:

> A pause in the cold war is not a lasting peace . . . and a détente does not equal disarmament. The United States must continue to seek a relaxation of tensions, but we have no cause to relax our vigilance.[52]

Kennedy's harder position did not go unnoticed. In *The Sunday Times*, Henry Brandon noted that Kennedy was increasingly being forced to 'realise how fragile the policy of the détente was and how risky, politically, if given too much emphasis'.[53] Going beyond the issue of Kennedy's political vulnerability, Max Frankel outlined the strategic dilemma détente posed for the West:

> There is real concern here now about the decay of the vigilance so carefully developed in the non-Communist world and about the erosion of barricades erected against the spread of Soviet influence . . . no one expected quite so many difficulties to develop from the first few hesitant steps toward a détente.[54]

The immense complexities involved in the pursuit of détente were not overlooked by Kennedy. He proceeded with renewed caution but with no less commitment. He went ahead and approved the grain deal while encouraging negotiations in more and more areas. Despite the various interruptions in addition to dilemmas and difficulties involved, the landmark achievements of the summer of 1963 inspired hope and the view that similar achievements were possible. As Ted Sorensen recalled, 'The breathing spell had become a pause, the pause was becoming a détente and no one could foresee what further changes lay ahead.'[55] In this atmosphere of hope and anticipation, Kennedy was assassinated on 22 November 1963.

While Kennedy's assassination was a national tragedy, it surprisingly failed to interrupt the progress of détente. The groundwork had been set and Khrushchev seemed committed to keeping the moment alive. After all, the Cuban Missile Crisis had shown the failure of his more 'adventuristic' policies, and he had staked his split with the Chinese on the supremacy of peaceful coexistence. In the interest of the Soviet consumer sector, as well as his commitment to détente, Khrushchev announced a dramatic 4.5 per cent defence budget cut in December.[56] As the New Year approached, Khrushchev wrote to the new United States President, Lyndon Johnson, and expressed his wish for the continued development of détente.

Johnson's reply to Khrushchev was unequivocal. He stated, 'The American people and their Government have set the strengthening of peace as their highest purpose in the New Year.'[57] The new Administration's verbal commitment was immediately backed up with action as Secretary of Defense McNamara announced a 2 per cent cut in the United States defence budget. In concert with the cut in defence, Johnson announced the immediate unleashing of a 'peace offensive' designed to probe the various opportunities at hand. He ordered a 25 per cent reduction in the procurement of enriched uranium with the promise of slowing down the development of strategic weapons. Less than two weeks later, Khrushchev announced his decision to discontinue the construction of two new atomic reactors for the production of plutonium, to substantially reduce the production of U-235 for nuclear weapons, and to allocate more fissionable material for peaceful uses.

The development of these steps signalled a new experiment in the pursuit of détente. Both sides seemed interested in trying to build momentum through the achievement of a series of minor steps that required little sacrifice but, nonetheless, suggested movement.

The emphasis on movement had the immediate effect of creating optimism and hope. In early January, Walter Lippmann proclaimed in the *New York Herald Tribune*, 'The essence of the matter is that the Soviet Union and the United States are no longer on a collision course, as they were before the Cuban missile confrontation . . . there is a new relationship between the two adversary powers.'[58]

The movement continued and the minor concessions took on different forms. There was a minor but promising change in the cold war vocabulary. In President Johnson's words, the restraint in vilification served to 'cool the waters'.

In February, the fourth in a series of two year agreements on scientific and cultural exchange was signed. Furthermore, Khrushchev and Johnson continued exchange of personal correspondence on a variety of issues. On 20 April this exchange resulted in a further reduction in the production of fuel for nuclear and thermonuclear weapons. Two days later, James Reston of the *New York Times* enumerated the accomplishments to date:

> Johnson and Khrushchev have made modest reductions in their military budgets, the Soviets have continued the withdrawal of their troops from Cuba, the President has restrained those in his Administration who wanted to expand the war in Southeast Asia to North Vietnam, the Russians have turned over the United States fliers who strayed into Communist East Germany, and the President has taken new precautions against any future violations of East German or Soviet air space.[59]

In June 1964, after thirty years of sporadic negotiations, the Soviet Union and the United States agreed on consular practices and rights. The signing of the Consular Convention represented the first contemporary bilateral treaty between Washington and Moscow. For the United States, it signified the Soviet intention to 'play by the rules' of established international customs, practices and norms. After failing miserably throughout the 1950s, the traditional means of diplomacy appeared to be bearing fruit.

While the superpowers had been pursuing détente, a relaxation of tension was also occurring at another level. West Germany and Rumania had boldly established a trade mission in October 1963 opening a small hole in the Iron Curtain. When West Germany negotiated and established a similar trade mission in Budapest on 15 July 1964 and Bulgaria on 19 October 1964, this hole appeared to be growing wider. Because the general relaxation between the East and the West was still directly tied to and limited by superpower détente, this break in the Iron Curtain did not proceed much further. Nonetheless, it may have contributed to some developments in such countries as France and Czechoslovakia that were eventually to have significant repercussions on détente. For instance, while the French government had been demonstrating an inclination toward an independent foreign policy since the election of Charles de Gaulle, the Soviet–American détente of the mid-1960s provided the opportunity to experiment with those inclinations. In March 1966, the French announced their decision to withdraw from NATO. Two years later in Czechoslovakia, internal 'democratisation' (as the Czechs described it) achieved new heights – a situation that was viewed by the Soviet Union as threatening and led to the invasion of 1968.[60] These and other examples demonstrated the difficulties involved when a general relaxation of tension contributes to the disintegration of those strategic power bases upon which national security is thought to rest.

In August, an event occurred that was to influence the progress of détente throughout the remainder of the decade. In response to an alleged attack on the United States Destroyer Maddox in the Gulf of Tonkin, Johnson ordered the Navy to retaliate against North Vietnam. Up to this time, United States involvement in the Vietnam conflict had been limited even though it had been growing. Through the Tonkin Gulf Resolution, passed by Congress on 7 August 1964, Johnson was given the power and authority to provide America's South Vietnamese allies with all necessary protection and assistance. Little did the administration know at this time the extent to which the Vietnam conflict would affect and influence the future course of American domestic policy, foreign policy and détente.

Ironically, the initial impact on US–Soviet relations was negligible because of the Peoples' Republic of China's backing of the North Vietnamese. While Americans still tended to view Communism in monolithic terms, China's aggressive opposition to détente, coupled with its contribution to the North Vietnamese war effort, made China appear especially menacing, threatening and dangerous. This assessment led Secretary of State Rusk to make the extraordinary claim in mid-August that Communist China had become the main threat to world peace. This subordination of the Soviet threat was both purposeful and significant. Within a couple of weeks, the common Soviet-American concern about China led one writer in the *New York Times* to observe the 'strange alliance between the United States and the USSR, even while the cold war continues'.[61]

On the Soviet side, Khrushchev's action, or inaction, seemed to justify this American view. Despite the Kremlin's support of North Vietnam, Khrushchev showed great reluctance to make a local war in Southeast Asia a major issue in US–Soviet relations. Under Khrushchev's theory of a peaceful coexistence, small local wars involved the risk of escalating into larger, more uncontrollable conflicts and China seemed to be willing to take such a risk. On 11 August, Mao had raised the Sino-Soviet conflict to a furious pitch by demanding the return of all 600 000 square miles of territory which he claimed Tsarist and Soviet Russia had appropriated. This claim went far beyond ideological concerns and raised the disturbing spectre of a border conflict with the Chinese. These fears were compounded two months later when the Chinese tested their first nuclear device. Such was the state of the world and the US–Soviet relationship in October 1964, when an event within the Kremlin caused the process of détente to wind down.

THE AFTERMATH: LATE 1964–68

On 15 October 1964, Khrushchev was suddenly removed from the seat of Soviet power. While Khrushchev's 'resignation' came as a surprise to the West, it had been long expected in domestic political circles. His policies had increasingly disturbed elements in the Kremlin upon whom he counted for support. First, Khrushchev's cutbacks in defence and the heavy industry sectors had antagonised the hardliners. His reductions in the armed forces had caused resentment among army leaders whose support was vital. Second, Khrushchev's policy of building bridges with the greatest capitalist country, the United States, offended the ideological purists and propagandists. Third, the growing *rapprochement* in diplomacy and trade between Eastern Europe and

Western Europe worried Soviet strategists, as well as those East European leaders whose positions were threatened by liberalisation. Finally, ideologists and strategic planners were greatly concerned by the loss of Russia's revolutionary face to China in competition for the loyalties and the leadership of the world communist movement. Khrushchev was blamed for the extent of the split with China as well as the decline of Soviet influence in other areas of the world.

A variety of domestic considerations also contributed to Khrushchev's fall.[62] First, his hasty and ill-considered reorganisation of the Soviet agricultural system had produced only misery. His reorganisation of the industrial and educational system also proved to be misguided and unpopular. Most significantly however, Khrushchev's mania for reorganisation[63] led him to introduce two intra-party structural changes which had the effect of striking directly at the positions of those party members upon whom his authority depended. Unlike the 'conspiracy' to unseat him in 1957, the fall of Khrushchev in October 1964 was the result of widespread discontent.

By arranging for the vacationing Khrushchev to stay on 'permanent' vacation, the team of Brezhnev and Kosygin seized power and set about the task of righting the listing Soviet ship. Their explanation for the sudden change of leadership provided a glimpse into the new direction they would take and how it would affect détente. Through the issuance of 'Twenty-Nine Points', Khrushchev was criticised for blundering incompetence in the Cuban affair, fostering a 'cult of personality' based on the Stalin model, overemphasising consumerism to the detriment of heavy industry and defence while at the same time pursuing 'false policies', causing disruption in Eastern Europe and engaging in nepotism. In short, these criticisms were partly aimed at Khrushchev's détente policies with the West and the results they had produced.

One of the first problems the new leadership dealt with was the embarrassing presence of the United States in Vietnam and the even more embarrassing Soviet inaction. While Western information is limited, there is evidence that in late October or early November, the Soviet government approached Ho Chi Minh with an offer of expanded Soviet military assistance.[64]

Another indication of a shift in directions came with Chinese

Communist Premier Chou En-lai's surprise visit to Moscow in November for the 'October Revolution' celebrations. While high level discussions produced little, if nothing, the meetings probably signified an attempt by the new leadership to inform the Chinese of their intention to pursue a more 'revolutionary' course. Ironically, this meeting eventually appeared to augment the tension it was designed to diminish. Now that the Chinese had exercised their independent bid for the leadership of the communist bloc, the new Soviet claim represented a bold challenge. In addition, this new Soviet commitment to 'revolutionary' causes had implications for Chinese designs on Southeast Asia. The Soviet leadership had decided to play a more active role in Southeast Asia and, as it turned out, throughout the world.

In the coming months, almost all of Khrushchev's policies were reversed. First, the relationship that had been slowly developing between Moscow and Bonn was immediately turned around. A new friendship with France was sought, partly as a means to isolate the Germans. Second, the new government decided to tighten the Soviet grip on Eastern Europe, in the hope of closing some of the newly opened doors with the West. In Brezhnev's first major address, he announced his commitment to 'overcome the difficulties' that had arisen within the communist movement due to 'polycentrism'. Brezhnev set his first example by purposely moving away from the 'revisionist' Yugoslavians whom Khrushchev had been courting.

Third, Khrushchev's policy of levelling-off and cutting military expenditure was abandoned in favour of a modernisation programme aimed at achieving parity with the United States. Military expenditures were increased, thereby reasserting the dominance of the military–industrial sector of the Soviet economy over the consumer sector.

Fourth, the Soviet leadership no longer made a distinction between 'wars of national liberation' which were viewed as righteous, and 'local wars' which were condemned as dangerous. Soviet aid was stepped up to augment the 'world-revolutionary process' in which Moscow would play a dominant role.

Fifth, changes were made in relation to China. Accepting the realisation that China had become a threat to Soviet security, a strategy was devised to 'isolate and encircle' China by establishing positions in the Western Pacific (via North Korea and a new commercial intercourse agreement with Japan) and Southeast Asia (by establishing closer ties with Vietnam, India and Pakistan).

Sixth, Khrushchev's contention that thermonuclear war must be avoided because there would be no winners was revised to suggest that winning might be possible. The short push-button war scenario was replaced by the prolonged conflict scenario which envisioned the application of a wide range of weapons.[65]

Finally, and most significantly, the new Soviet leadership began to back away from Khrushchev's détente with the United States. Soviet propaganda began to speak of the 'imperialist and aggressive' nature of American foreign policy with increased frequency, and the applied meaning of 'peaceful coexistence' underwent a change. Instead of providing the atmosphere in which progressive agreements could be achieved between the superpowers, peaceful coexistence came more to represent a tactical phase in which to wage an unrelenting ideological struggle against the forces of capitalist imperialism. Within a few months, it became apparent that the fall of Khrushchev marked the conclusion of the Post-Missile Crisis honeymoon in US–Soviet relations.

Winning re-election by one of the largest margins in history, Johnson pressed on with his détente campaign but to no avail. His New Year proposals for an exchange of visits were ignored in Moscow. The Soviet leaders not only seemed intent on focusing on their internal problems but also wished to avoid 'blessing' America's provocative actions in Vietnam by engaging in acts of friendship with the United States. When Johnson continued to press for an exchange of visits, TASS pointedly replied that American officials 'are stubbornly continuing to entertain the illusion . . . that it is possible to hope for an improvement of Soviet–American relations and at the same time to continue aggressive actions against the Soviet Union's friends and allies'.[66] Five days later, the *New York Herald Tribune* sadly proclaimed, 'the atmosphere is no longer there'.[67]

While the fall of Khrushchev signified an end to the US–Soviet honeymoon, an even more significant phenomenon followed this event. That phenomenon was that very little happened at all. Throughout 1965, 1966 and 1967, the US–Soviet relationship seemed to lay dormant especially in terms of conflict. Given the changes in direction brought on by the new Soviet leadership, it is surprising that the cold war did not forge on with renewed velocity. Instead, a consistent but low level of tension seemed to characterise the superpower relationship. This phenomenon is especially instructive and significant in terms of détente because, unlike the aftermath of previous periods in which tension had been eased, there was no violent backlash. In fact, these years in which tension was neither visibly raised nor eased produced a couple of significant agreements in 1967 and 1968 which were to strengthen US–Soviet relations as well as the cause of peace.

The causes behind this phenomenon lie in the legacy left by the Post-Missile Crisis 'honeymoon', as well as the specific foreign and domestic problems plaguing each superpower during this period. A discussion of those specific problems will help to put the period into perspective.

In the mid-sixties, two themes dominated United States foreign and domestic politics – both of which contributed significantly to the stalemate of détente with the Soviet Union. The first and most dominant theme in foreign policy (with profound implications for domestic policy) was the escalation of United States involvement in the Vietnam War. The year 1965 brought the introduction of United States combat troops into Vietnam as well as extensive bombing in the North. This growing commitment demanded high levels of input and was soon causing a serious drain on America's economic and human resources. Due to the elusive nature of the war and the questionable aspect of America's participation in it, the public did not rally around the government as it had in past wars. As United States involvement grew, so did the domestic opposition to it. In January 1966, the tremendous cost of involvement was revealed as Johnson asked Congress for an additional $12.8 billion for the war effort. In May, the war expanded into Cambodia and Johnson sent additional troops to Thailand. By the end of 1966, United States involvement in the war was escalating at an alarming rate.

The domestic consequences of the war were both compounded and exacerbated by social upheaval and change. The civil rights movement illustrated part of what was wrong with America, and the United States role in Vietnam tended to confirm those claims. As public awareness of these problems increased dramatically through the revolution of television news media, there was a declining consensus about the nature, content and reality of the 'American Dream'. The specific problems caused by these events led Americans to be introspective.

Secondly, Johnson's solution to the Vietnam problem was to pour enough men and materials into the conflict in order to win it quickly. This meant escalation, which involved putting the force of America's energy behind the war effort. Likewise, Johnson's solution to America's domestic problems was legislation, and lots of it. Throughout 1965, 1966 and 1967, the Johnson Administration pushed through its 'Great Society' programmes, setting legislative records in Congress. These programmes were all focused on domestic needs, involving questions of health care, welfare, social security, civil rights, and so on. Once again, the result was an introspective focus. The energies of the American government were entirely consumed with the goal of winning the Vietnam War and in solving a series of domestic crises. Unlike the early sixties, the Soviet threat had fallen down the list of American concerns. A similar phenomenon was occurring in the Soviet Union.

When the new Soviet leadership came to power in October 1964, it inherited a series of problems which have been previously mentioned. Brezhnev and Kosygin's solution to these problems involved closing the outer doors, and rearranging the house from within. For instance, in order to tighten the Soviet grip on Eastern Europe, contacts with the West, and especially the United States, had to be restricted. This process was started by the Soviet Union backing off the active pursuit of détente which had led to breaks in the Iron Curtain. In 1966, Brezhnev attempted to diminish the American presence in Europe through his proposals for a European security system – excluding the United States altogether.

A second example lies in the problems plaguing the Soviet economy. Contrary to Khrushchev's bold claims that the Soviet economy would surpass the American economy in the 1960s, it was, in reality, falling farther behind. Faced with a declining economy and committed to the goal of building the Soviet defence capability, the new leadership inherited a situation that demanded 'breathing time' – a prolonged period of peace and stability. The United States preoccupation with Vietnam and numerous domestic problems enabled the Soviet leaders to concentrate more on solving their own economic and political problems. As the new leadership consolidated its political position, the Soviet economy regained much of its forward momentum. By 1967, the Soviet economy had grown to almost half of the United States economy.

On the military level, the Soviet government used this 'breathing time' to build Soviet defences. It had become clear by 1965 that the Soviet Union was far behind the United States in its defence capabilities. Khrushchev's premature globalism had convinced the United States of the necessity of engaging in a massive strategic build-up. In 1965, Secretary of Defence McNamara confidently observed that United States supremacy was secure:

> . . . we have a superiority of approximately 3 or 4 to 1. . . . In qualitative terms, it's impossible to come up with a precise evaluation but it far exceeds 3 or 4 to 1. . . . The programs we have under way are more than adequate to assure our superiority in the years ahead.[68]

In reality, the latter half of the 1960s brought about a steady erosion of United States strategic supremacy. By 1967, Soviet defence spending had crossed the $50 billion mark, and by 1968 the Soviet Union had some 900 operational ICBMs as opposed to America's 1054. While the United States still maintained superiority in strategic bombers and submarine launched missiles, the strategic relationship was nearing rough parity. Each side possessed the means to completely destroy the other as a viable society, with neither side possessing a clear-cut first strike capability. While the United States had been preoccupied with building conventional forces for Vietnam, the Soviet Union had been building a strategic arsenal to equal its American adversary. Distracted by Vietnam, the United States had let McNamara's professed strategic advantage slip away.

In short, after the American successes and the Soviet failures of the early 1960s, the new leadership had sought retrenchment in order to correct the economic, political and strategic policies that had led them into such a bind. However, this withdrawal and inaction was only temporary as the Soviet leaders were increasingly tempted to exploit the United States preoccupation with Vietnam.

The first break in this Soviet-American calm[69] appeared in

June 1967. In mid-1966, the Twenty-Third Communist Party Congress had confirmed a number of new directions in post-Khrushchev foreign policy. One decision was to exercise greater influence in the Middle East by developing closer ties with militant, anti-Israeli elements and ruling circles in Moslem North Africa, from Algeria to the United Arab Republic and Syria. The United States focus on Vietnam had led to a deterioration of the United States position in the Middle East and opened up the opportunity for Soviet gains. Extensive military aid was granted to the militant Arabs and, in the spring of 1967, skirmishes broke out in disputed areas between Syria, Egypt and Israel. As the crisis gathered momentum, the Soviet government informed the Syrians that it had received reports of specific Israeli troop movements on Syria's borders – movements which suggested an impending attack.[70] Similar reports were given to the Egyptians.[71] There was little hard evidence to substantiate this claim but the Soviet action contributed significantly to tensions. Nasser ordered United Nations troops out of the Sinai and Gaza Strip and Arab and Israeli troops stood face to face once again. When Nasser closed the Tiran Straits to Israeli ships, the Israeli government pleaded for help. Totally immersed in the Vietnamese conflict, Washington was unprepared and very reluctant to provide any adequate response. On 5 June 1967, Israel suddenly launched an attack and for six days pushed the Arabs backwards, deep into their own territory. By way of the 'hotline' both the United States and the Soviet Union expressed their fear of escalation and agreed to work for a ceasefire.[72] In a few days a ceasefire was achieved but, given the staggering losses suffered by the Arabs (over 8000 square miles of territory), the humiliation was on the side of the Soviet Union. In Arab eyes, the Soviet government had failed them by providing sub-standard military equipment and by not providing military assistance at a strategic time. Given the Soviet government's general unwillingness to become involved militarily in a Middle East conflict, its rather strange warning to the Syrians seems to have been either designed to promote Arab preparedness or provide what limited assistance it could. Nonetheless, it had the unfortunate effect of fomenting a crisis which had far more profound effects than the Soviet leaders presumably had intended. To save what influence it could, the Soviet Union broke off diplomatic relations with Israel and called for a special session of the United Nations General Assembly to deal with the problems in the Middle East. Against United States opposition, the Soviet government mustered the necessary sixty-two votes required for a meeting. Immediately, word came from Moscow that Soviet Premier Kosygin would come to the United Nations himself to present the case. Because the meeting had all the makings of a Soviet propaganda effort, Johnson decided against attending. Nonetheless, Johnson invited the Soviet leader to the White House for a 'frank exchange of views' covering 'the Middle East, Vietnam, the Non-proliferation Treaty, and prospects for limiting the missile race'.[73] With the Chinese, the Arabs and the North Vietnamese looking on, Kosygin could not afford to accept the official White House invitation. However, he did express a willingness to meet elsewhere. On 23 June 1967, Johnson and Kosygin met in the small college town of Glassboro, New Jersey. To call this meeting a 'summit' would be an overstatement. Neither side came prepared with any significant new proposals nor had there been time for any expectations to rise. The leaders met briefly and little was accomplished. The Glassboro meeting confirmed the existing stalemate on the higher levels of US–Soviet relations. Significantly, however, progress was being made on other levels of the relationship. While the Soviet leadership could not afford the appearance of pursuing détente at a time when the United States was still increasing its involvement in Vietnam, it was interested in keeping the lines of communication and negotiation open.

The impetus for this continuing relationship was, in part, the community of interests shared by the United States and the Soviet Union during this period. For instance, when in 1966 Chinese radicalism and extremism exploded in the form of the Cultural Revolution, both superpowers were united in their opposition to this wild and potentially dangerous episode in Chinese history.

In the same year, the Soviet Union negotiated the Tashkent Agreements, thereby ending the Kashmir War between India and Pakistan. The United States welcomed these agreements, implicitly endorsing a US–Soviet community of interests in the subcontinent.

Most notably, the superpowers expressed their community of interests in the negotiation of the Non-proliferation Treaty. Sharing a common interest in preventing the development of nuclear arms in China and Germany, the superpowers set to work on an agreement designed to inhibit the proliferation of nuclear technology.

The co-operation behind the signing of the Non-Proliferation Treaty can be attributed to the legacy of the Post-Missile Crisis détente. When, on the surface, progress in US–Soviet relations appeared to freeze in October 1964, lower level contacts were maintained. Both powers participated in the Geneva disarmament talks which resumed on 27 July 1965. Both powers were parties to the sixty-three nation Demilitarisation of Space Treaty signed on 27 January 1967. Between 1964 and 1968, the superpowers exchanged numerous letters on the topic of the non-Proliferation and their common interests grew as China and France became members of the 'nuclear club'. After hammering out a number of difficulties involved with the NATO arrangement of 'nuclear sharing', an agreement was reached and the Non-Proliferation Treaty signed in the summer of 1968. The signing demonstrated how progress on mutually advantageous proposals could continue despite the overall status of superpower relations. Furthermore, the mutual commitment to open communication and crisis control was demonstrated when the superpowers used the 'hotline' during the 1967 Middle East War. As the Non-Proliferation Treaty was being completed, the superpowers agreed to begin Strategic Arms Limitation Talks (SALT). Unfortunately, this agreement was undermined by various events in Eastern Europe.

The Kremlin's attempts to reassert Soviet control over the East European satellites in the mid-sixties did not meet with total success. Despite the lull in superpower détente, European reconciliation had begun to take on a life of its own. The West Germans continued to increase contacts with Eastern bloc countries leading to the establishment of diplomatic relations with Rumania in January 1967. These moves were to establish a pattern for West German Chancellor Brandt's 'Ostpolitik' which will be discussed in the next chapter.

On all levels, Johnson had announced his intention to seek wider contacts with East European countries in the hope of establishing the basis for a settlement of the German question. Luckily for the Soviet government, Johnson did not have the time to make good his announced intentions. Nonetheless, the forces of liberalism and nationalism were moving forward under their own power.

In no country were these forces more potent than in Czechoslovakia. The old Stalinist régime of Antonin Novotny had been overthrown and the more liberal régime of Alexander Dubcek had taken its place. In response to public pressure, the Dubcek government had been granting concessions designed to liberalise or, as the reformists called it, 'democratise' Czechoslovak politics. As these concessions grew more numerous throughout the first half of 1968, conservatives in the Kremlin and the old-line East European Communist leaders grew worried. While the Czechs were careful not to make the mistake Hungary had made twelve years earlier of threatening to pull out of the Warsaw Pact, the seemingly uncontrollable forces of Czechoslovak liberalism and nationalism were viewed as a counter-revoltionary epidemic that threatened to spread. The Soviet leaders were faced with a dilemma. On one hand, if they invaded the country they would risk international condemnation as well as threatening the initiation of SALT. Furthermore, a visit to Moscow had just been arranged for Johnson and such a move would certainly interrupt it. On the other hand, if something was not done immediately, the consequences for Soviet security could be ruinous. When by late August the Czechoslovak government had failed to check the tide of 'democratisation', the USSR and four other Warsaw Pact countries invaded Czechoslovakia.

In terms of superpower relations, the Czechoslovak episode is highly significant for two reasons. First, while Johnson issued a strong warning about the consequences of any Soviet move against Rumania, the American response generally demonstrated an understanding of the needs of Soviet security in their spheres of influence and a commitment to the larger framework of détente. Johnson had to cancel his Moscow visit as well as the proposed SALT talks but made several attempts to rearrange these contacts two months later after the criticism had died down. In contrast to previous periods, the impact of such a provocative event had been tempered by a commitment to a greater priority.

Secondly, in the aftermath of the invasion the Soviet government attempted to apply the instruments of détente as a diversionary tactic. While, on one hand, Brezhnev had used the crisis to lay down his doctrine on the right and duty of intervention to 'protect' a socialist state from undue capitalist influence, he simultaneously launched a rhetorical peace drive. Instead of withdrawing indignantly in the spirit of 'we are madder at you than you are at us', the Soviet leadership immediately called for a summit and sent Ambassador Dobrynin to the White House, expressing the Soviet hope that the invasion would not interrupt the scheduled SALT talks. To a great extent the tactic worked. Official American criticism was limited, and Johnson responded favourably to the Soviet offers, after a suitable period of 'mourning' for Czechoslovakia. Unfortunately, by the time Johnson was ready to resume progress, the Soviet government had decided against dealing with the lame-duck President. On 5 November, Richard Nixon had been elected as President and the future course of American policy toward the Soviet Union would rest with him.

FACTORS CONTRIBUTING TO, AND DETRACTING FROM, DÉTENTE

The factors contributing to the Post-Missile Crisis détente can all be tied to one event . . . the Cuban Missile Crisis. The Cuban confrontation not only acted as a catalyst for détente; it contributed to the formation of new attitudes essential to détente's occurrence. In this way, the crisis created a lasting force in superpower relations, one that was to influence the course of superpower actions for many years to come.

First, as previously stated, an automatic relaxation of tension occurred in the wake of the crisis. As with the Berlin Crisis of 1958, tension had risen so high that any peaceful resolution of the crisis was bound to bring relief and hope. However, unlike the Berlin Crisis, the Cuban Crisis led to superpower confrontation on the high seas with both leaders perceived as having their fingers poised over the nuclear button. The expectation of war was great. When the crisis was peacefully resolved, relief was expressed throughout the capitals of the world, producing an atmosphere that was conducive to the progress of détente.

The impact of the Cuban Crisis, however, went much farther than simply creating an atmosphere for détente. The intensity of the event had been so great and the spectre of the nuclear holocaust perceived so broadly that it is safe to assume that profound lessons had been impressed upon the participants. Both countries emerged committed to the belief that since nuclear war could not be won such an event should never be allowed to develop again. While the superpowers had generally shared this view prior to the events of October 1962, the mere occurrence of the crisis pointed out the necessity of 'living by it'.

A further lesson emerging from this crisis was the necessity of respecting each other's vital interests. Kennedy's hard-line reaction convinced Khrushchev that any threat to vital American interests also represented a threat to world peace and stability. This is one reason why the American commitment to Berlin was not tested after the crisis to the degree it had been preceding it. Likewise, the low-key American response to the Soviet invasion of Czechoslovakia represented a tacit understanding and respect for Soviet vital interests. In this way, various issues that had caused tension in the first half of Kennedy's term were assigned a lower priority. Despite varying views on the question, it was realised that peace and stability rested with maintaining the status quo. This subordination of various issues and respect for the vital interests of the adversary helped to produce confidence in the sanctity of negotiated agreements. An extra measure of predictability was added to the unpredictable superpower relationship. With this predictability came a relaxation of tension.

Finally, the crisis convinced both governments of the necessity of constructing safeguards against a miscalculation of those vital interests. Miscalculation had produced a crisis of such intensity that the frightening scenario of 'nuclear destruction by accident' haunted both Kennedy and Khrushchev. The extent to which both leaders shared this concern was demonstrated in June 1963 when the 'hotline' was established. This mutual concern also led to a growing exchange of communication between the Kremlin and the White House. These measures helped to avert superpower confrontation in the Middle East in 1967, as well as establish a base for progress on several negotiated agreements.

A second factor contributing to the Post-Missile Crisis détente was the convergence of various superpower interests in the 1960s. After the Cuban Missile Crisis, the superpowers discovered that they shared a common interest and stake in the stability of the world. This realisation was exemplified by the extended period of stability following the crisis. It was as if something had put a moratorium on provocative actions. Kennedy's decision to clamp down on the activities of anti-Castro emigres provides but one example. Khrushchev's decision not to press the Berlin issue as fervently as he had done before provided another.

On another level, the events of the early sixties produced a second realisation – that despite stated revolutionary claims, the superpowers shared a joint stake in the existing distribution of power. Nothing did more to illustrate this fact than the rise of an aggressive Communist China. China threatened to upset the bipolar structure of the world by assuming leadership of the Third World and creating an independent revolutionary force in world politics. China's challenge to Soviet leadership of the world communist movement led the Soviet government to guard against the disruptive nature of Chinese policy by withdrawing nuclear assistance in 1960. When China and France developed independent nuclear capabilities in the 1960s, the superpowers worked together to limit the further expansion of membership in the 'nuclear' club of nations. As the dangers of nuclear confrontation grew, the superpowers were increasingly compelled to restrict their own actions and those of their allies so as not to create new crises. In the interests of maintaing peace, stability often took priority over change. For smaller states whose interests were often dictated by superpower decision making, the superpowers appeared to be building a 'condominium', or adversary partnership, in the interests of maintaining unchallenged military, strategic, and political superiority. This was the other side of the responsibility of 'world management'. Nonetheless, it became increasingly clear that the superpowers had found a common stake in the status quo. Out of this realisation came the groundwork for co-operation based on the principle of mutual advantage.

A third contributing factor to the Post-Missile Crisis détente was the dramatic shift in the power balance caused by the growing Sino-Soviet split. During this period, it was not only obvious that the Chinese had fallen out of the Soviet orbit; it became clear that they had taken other socialist countries with them. Furthermore, China's geo-political position represented a grave threat to Soviet security. What had once been a 'political blessing' in 1949 was quickly becoming a dangerous threat in the 1960s. In terms of détente, however, this shift in the power equation was to prove advantageous. Because the shift could not be readily measured in a zero-sum manner, it represented the introduction of a new element into the strategic equation – one that was initially to bring the superpowers closer together.

Because the Sino-Soviet split occurred gradually, Khrushchev was torn between the pursuit of peaceful coexistence with the West, and the appeasement of a rising China demanding change. Soviet policy in the early sixties reflected an attempt to have it both ways. Even in the aftermath of the Cuban Missile Crisis, the progress of détente was inhibited for several months by Soviet attempts to salvage the Sino-Soviet relationship. However, despite their fence-sitting, the Soviet leaders had made a subconscious decision on the future of Sino-Soviet relations when they chose to withdraw nuclear assistance from China. This action was not only an acknowledgement of the potential and threat of China but a blatant move demonstrating the Soviet desire to limit that potential and threat as well. The Crisis provided the Chinese with the opportunity by which to complete the Sino-Soviet divorce and make an independent bid for leadership of the socialist movement. As the schism deepened and took on permanence, the Soviet Union was faced with the spectre of confrontation on two fronts. Suddenly, an easing of tension became an essential priority in terms of Soviet national security. The timing of the landmark achievements of détente during the summer of 1963 leaves no doubt that the Sino-Soviet split was a primary force behind the development of détente.

On the American side, Kennedy and Johnson saw the split as a consequence of the Soviet decision to act responsibly in world affairs. Chinese calls for the initiation of revolutionary struggles throughout the world against the forces of capitalist imperialism did little to encourage American leaders to view the split as a golden opportunity to seek accommodation with China against the Soviet Union. The United States saw the split as an opportunity for superpower détente.

A fourth and final factor contributing to the Post-Missile Crisis détente involves the shift in confidence and initiative from the Soviet Union to the United States following the crisis. Kennedy's successful handling of the crisis had not only given the United States a renewed sense of confidence in meeting the Soviet threat but had also provided Kennedy with the necessary hardline credentials by which to seek détente. Throughout the 1950s, the American people had been told that the Soviet leaders had no respect for written agreements and could not be trusted. Therefore, despite claims to the contrary, American leaders did not anxiously seek agreements with their Soviet counterparts for fear of being credited with the sell-out of American security interests. The rise of Soviet power coupled with Sputnik successes in the latter half of the decade made the pursuit of such agreements politically unthinkable.

When Kennedy forced Khrushchev to back down in October 1962, Americans gained confidence in their ability to meet any Soviet threat. Furthermore, Khrushchev's withdrawal provided Americans with proof that when crises arose, the Soviet government would respond rationally. The rebirth of American confidence in the aftermath of the crisis coincided with the culmination of Kennedy's missile building plans. By 1963, America was strong, confident and ready to negotiate for peace.

On the Soviet side, the Cuban Missile Crisis represented the last in a series of adventuristic ploys by Khrushchev designed to shock concessions out of the West. Having failed to achieve results in Berlin or Cuba by these means, it became clear that Soviet interests would have to be realised by different means. These 'different means' involved the pursuit of détente. In addition, Soviet needs were accommodated by the pursuit of détente. The 'missile gap myth' had been exposed and the accelerated United States missile programme was leaving the Soviet Union far behind. The Soviet economy was lagging seriously and the East European satellites were threatened by the disunity within the socialist camp. Khrushchev's pursuit of détente represented an attempt to find an alternative to his bankrupt policies.

It is significant that the pursuit of détente from a position of weakness was not as great a problem for Khrushchev as it was for American leaders. He did not have to answer the expectations of the 'democratic' masses. However, Khrushchev was not free from scrutiny, as his 'forced resignation' in October 1964 demonstrates. Before the Cuban Missile Crisis, the Soviet leaders had seen the proper application of their supposed strength in terms of changing the status quo. Such was the nature of their political ideology or, at least, strategy. This application of superpower strength contributed greatly to tension. The realisation of Soviet weakness during the Cuban crisis brought about a new priority – the maintenance of the status quo. Because the United States viewed the proper application of its strength in terms of preserving the status quo, the rise of American confidence and the decline of Soviet strength complemented each other and contributed to the process of détente.

In late 1964, the process of détente was stalled. This paralysis was caused by two events. First, the overthrow of Khrushchev in October 1964 led to the introduction of new Soviet leaders who did not share Khrushchev's commitment to the active pursuit of détente. In fact, Brezhnev and Kosygin held the view that some essential Soviet interests were being sacrificed in Khrushchev's policy with the West.

Second, the war in Vietnam and the escalation of United States involvement in it arrested the progress of détente. For the Soviet government, the war was an embarrassment and a testimony to Soviet impotence. Khrushchev's continued pursuit of détente while the Americans were escalating their involvement in Southeast Asia only seemed to confirm Peking's criticism about the feebleness of Soviet commitment to the socialist cause. Immediately following Khrushchev's removal from office, the new leadership ceased all actions that could be interpreted as appeasing the West and proceeded to establish a more visible relationship with North Vietnam.

While Johnson continued to seek détente with the new Soviet leadership, the Vietnam War and related domestic problems consumed most of his time and effort. With the new Soviet government unwilling to pursue détente actively, there was little to encourage Johnson to upgrade an effort doomed to failure.

Despite the fact that these events served to halt the détente process, tension did not return to the level it had been preceding the Post-Missile Crisis détente. While the harsher rhetoric of the new Soviet leaders and the growing United States involvement in Vietnam caused tension to rise, a generally low level of tension was maintained throughout the following four years. As previously mentioned, this phenomenon can be credited to a variety of factors. First, both superpowers were preoccupied with pressing foreign and domestic problems, thereby distracting them from the mutual threat they posed to one another. The Johnson Administration was caught up in the Vietnam War and the numerous domestic crises plaguing the country. Administrative energies were spent on negotiating record levels of social legislation through Congress.

In the Soviet Union, Brezhnev and Kosygin were preoccupied with correcting the problems that had accumulated during

Khrushchev's reign. These included bolstering up a lagging defence posture, turning around a declining economy and reversing the dangerous trend of polycentrism among East European allies.

In short, these foreign and domestic problems led the super-powers to be introspective or tunnel-sighted in focus and deed during this period. Their needs were complementary and this helped to limit tension.

Next, the superpowers continued to subordinate those issues which had caused tension before détente. Despite the fact that they were no longer engaged in the active pursuit of détente, both Washington and Moscow continued to keep such provocative issues as Cuba and Berlin from arising.

THE LEGACY OF THE POST-MISSILE CRISIS DÉTENTE

Finally, a low level of tension was maintained between 1965 and 1968 because the Post-Missile Crisis détente had left a legacy of actions and commitments designed to control and limit those factors producing tension. The most significant legacy of détente from the 1950s was the common commitment to avoid nuclear war. While this legacy was strengthened even further by the Cuban Missile Crisis, the high pitch of the crisis also demonstrated that various instruments were needed to prevent nuclear war by miscalculation or miscommunication. The 'hotline' was installed to ensure the quick, efficient and accurate exchange of communication and consultation during a crisis. It was successfully used to avert superpower confrontation during the 1967 Middle East War. This represented a significant step in crisis control.

Open channels of communication were also established using different means. For instance, a constant exchange of notes between the White House and the Kremlin contributed to the achievement of various agreements involving the nuclear arms race. The Partial Test-Ban Treaty and the Non-Proliferation Treaty can be partly credited to this exchange of executive correspondence. The other factor contributing to these agreements represents one of the most important elements in the legacy of the Post-Missile Crisis détente – that is the re-emergence of traditional diplomacy via negotiation as a viable and workable means of achieving progress in superpower relations. After the aborted Paris summit in 1960, there was a conscious move away from summits. There had been too much opportunity to use summits for propaganda purposes, and the expectations created by their occurrence were always impossible to fulfil. When the magic was taken out of summits, the problem of 'atmospherics', to some extent, was taken out of détente. When Kennedy met Khrushchev in Vienna in 1961, every effort was made to portray the meeting simply as a frank exchange of views. The Johnson–Kosygin meeting at Glassboro was portrayed as a non-event. Important questions were relegated to special negotiating teams of diplomats committed to finding agreement on specific issues. Because these negotiations usually took place at lower levels and lasted for a period of months or even years, there was little problem with creating atmospherics or using the negotiations as high visibility platforms for propaganda and posturing. The power of this aspect of the Post-Missile Crisis legacy was demonstrated by the fact that these talks were, to a great extent, uninfluenced by the flow of US–Soviet relations. The goals and agreements that the participants were seeking were viewed as important unto themselves. The process was self-propelling. As one agreement was achieved, confidence was created by which to achieve another. Each agreement served to widen the base upon which to build the next one. Traditional means of diplomacy were at long last working in the US–Soviet relationship.

In conclusion, the Post-Missile Crisis détente provided a legacy that contributed to the maintenance of a relatively low level of tension in the following period. This legacy included the establishment of open lines of communication and methods of crisis control, the reintroduction of a traditional means of diplomacy in the pursuit of superpower agreements, the replacement of atmospherics with substantive agreements based on the principle of mutual advantage, the realisation of a mutual responsibility in the management of world peace, and a greater commitment to the avoidance of nuclear war. Furthermore, the landmark agreements produced during this period served to control the expansion of nuclear weapons as well as providing a precedent upon which to base future agreements. In short, the Post-Missile Crisis détente left a significant legacy to the following period. It is to this era we will now turn.

6 The Moscow Détente

After a period of confrontation, we are entering into an era of negotiations.[1]

Richard Nixon

Richard Nixon's declaration of an 'era of negotiations' upon assuming the duties and responsibilities of the Presidency turned out to be much more than just an empty political prediction. Out of this period emerged an unprecedented series of agreements spanning the entire sphere of US–Soviet and East–West political, strategic, economic, scientific, cultural and social relations. The accomplishments ranged from regulating superpower competition in the arms race to liberalising the flow of information and other contacts between East and West. Unfortunately, the full potential of these written agreements was not realised. Changing domestic political pressures and foreign policy considerations eventually inhibited implementation and restricted further progress. Nonetheless, the process of détente had achieved new heights.

These 'new heights' made the 'Moscow' détente sharply different from its predecessors. First, it lasted for almost four years, while previous periods had lasted no longer than fifteen months. A relaxation of tension based solely on 'atmospherics' could not have withstood this test of time. Second, the substantive nature of the achievements of this period was revealed in an unparalleled number of East–West agreements reflecting the desire of the participants to make more progress.

In assessing this fourth and final period of détente, two specific characteristics emerge. First, détente was characterised by a joint superpower commitment to define and regulate the relationship in an international environment where, despite the overwhelming strategic preponderance of the superpowers, decisions influencing the course of world events were increasingly being taken outside Washington and Moscow. The rising economic and political influence of Western Europe and Japan, coupled with the re-emergence of an independent China participating within the established international system, injected a new element into the power equation. The undying forces of nationalism and the newly emerging economic and political power of Middle East oil served to complicate this unpredictable arrangement. The rise of multipolarity threatened to upset the distribution of power, while the tendency toward polycentrism within alliances disrupted existing security systems. Even the one unchallenged area of superpower strength – the military area – was rendered less meaningful as the United States proved to be muscle-bound in its fight against Vietnamese communists. Given the growing inability to control events and the dynamic forces threatening to upset the power balance, the superpowers sought to establish a framework for competition in a rapidly changing world. It was hoped that the institutionalisation of détente would encourage restraint and guarantee a measure of predictability in a potentially explosive international environment.

The second major characteristic of the 'Moscow' détente in terms of superpower relations was the effort to employ the process of détente as a means to settle outstanding issues of joint concern. While there had been no pretence in the Post-Missile Crisis détente to go any farther than the introduction of an element of restraint into the superpower relationship, the Moscow détente sought to establish both a framework for competition and a basis for co-operation. As a result, it was characterised by a series of accords involving such varying subjects as Berlin, the environment, and a basic statement of principles.

The Moscow détente comprehends the Nixon–Brezhnev summit in May 1972 and the unprecedented number of superpower agreements emerging from it. The Moscow summit came to symbolise a seemingly new era in superpower relations – one based on negotiation, restraint and co-operation. This chapter will cover the course of US–Soviet relations from the beginning of 1969 to the end of 1976. This period provides a good framework through which to view the Moscow détente because it focuses on the men greatly responsible for inspiring it – Nixon, Kissinger and Brezhnev. In 1969, the firm leadership of Brezhnev and the election of Nixon with his appointment of Kissinger provided the personalities under which détente would take place.

THE SETTING: 1969 UNTIL LATE 1971

While Nixon christened his foreign policy an 'era of negotiations', the time for progress was still more than two years away. Similar pledges by Soviet leaders failed to surmount the barriers obstructing US–Soviet negotiations. While the Soviet invasion of Czechoslovakia in August 1968 proved to be only a temporary setback, it was not the only barrier preventing progress. American involvement in Vietnam continued to alienate the Soviet leaders and preoccupy the Americans. In early 1969, American combat deaths in Vietnam surpassed those suffered during the Korean War. With no end in sight, American impatience grew. Anti-war demonstrations waxed larger and more violent. Between 1969 and 1971, more and more American leaders were advocating complete withdrawal. The shootings of four students at Kent State University, Ohio on 4 May 1970 symbolised the hysteria and chaos the war had imposed on American society. As boycotts and walkouts by both sides continued to frustrate the Paris peace talks, Nixon moved unilaterally to scale down United States involvement in the war. By the end of his 'Vietnamisation' plan, American troop strength was to be scaled down from 530 000 in 1969 to 140 000 by the end of 1971. While this commitment to withdrawal might have served as a basis for co-operation in 1969, Nixon substituted United States air support for troops, and launched intensive bombing campaigns in Cambodia, Laos and North Vietnam. Because Soviet support of the North Vietnamese was partly motivated by the desire to have an ally on China's southern flank, respect for the North Vietnamese position was a fundamental part of Soviet foreign policy as long as United States involvement remained so high. It was not until the United States role in Vietnam had been reduced, and other factors began altering Soviet priorities, that Soviet leaders showed a willingness to overlook United States involvement in Vietnam. As Kissinger recalled, in the meantime, it was safer for the Soviet government to procrastinate on a Vietnam settlement.[2]

A second factor causing tension in the US–Soviet relationship was the volatile situation in the Middle East. Despite a Four-power agreement negotiated through the United Nations in 1969 to prohibit Middle Eastern problems from upsetting international security, an impending crisis threatened to pull the superpowers into the area. A massive build-up of armaments in the region was set against the backdrop of sporadic Arab–Israeli military exchanges. In 1970, the incidents threatened to develop into major international crises. Confrontation was narrowly averted by careful negotiation and mutual restraint.

Elsewhere throughout the world, superpower competition produced uncertainty and tension as both powers sought to deal effectively with the changing international scene. In Latin America, the Soviet government moved to establish diplomatic and commercial ties with the leftist governments of Chile and Peru. Growing Soviet naval activity in the Caribbean and the military conflict between Pakistan and India at the end of 1971 provided additional sources of superpower tension.

From the Soviet point of view, the United States was primarily responsible for a third factor promoting tension. American moves towards establishing friendly ties with China and two wayward Eastern European states appeared to the Soviet leaders as a strategy designed to alter the balance of power and encourage polycentrism within communist ranks. Having just been 'forced' to take distasteful and unpopular action in Czechoslovakia, the Soviet leaders were especially sensitive to the instability already threatening their security system. Nixon's visit to Rumania in the summer of 1969, in addition to increasing Western ties with Yugoslavia, was viewed as being primarily anti-Soviet in nature and design. Indeed, Nixon told Kissinger, 'By the time we get through with this trip they are going to be out of their minds that we are playing a Chinese game.'[3] Nixon's sarcastic comment about playing a 'Chinese' game turned out to be prophetic, as Chinese ping-pong served to usher in a new Sino-American relationship. Actually, there had been subtle moves toward China since Nixon's election. In July and December of 1969, Nixon liberalised Sino-American trade relations. Concurrently, the Sino-Soviet conflict was exacerbated by border disputes, and the world Communist conference held in Moscow in June was openly boycotted by China and its allies. Kosygin's visit to Peking the following year failed to produce a reconciliation and relations reached such a low point that it became increasingly difficult for the Soviet Union to ship supplies to North Vietnam through China, even though they were backing the same ally.

In response to these disputes, the Soviet government attempted to apply the threat of force. A co-ordinated campaign was started to raise the spectre of a Soviet pre-emptive strike on the Chinese nuclear force. This Soviet policy of intimidation only caused China to turn to the United States more quickly.[4]

In March 1971, the development that Soviet strategists feared most – Sino-American co-operation – started to become a reality. The Chinese invited American table tennis players to compete in China and Premier Chou En-lai credited the United States team with opening 'a new page in the relations of the Chinese and American people'.[5] The United States responded by lifting further the embargo on trade with China. Furthermore, curbs on the use of the dollar were lifted and both governments began discussing the possibilities of scientific exchanges. In relation to military issues, Nixon ordered a halt to spy flights over China and reversed a decision to station nuclear weapons near the mainland. Politically, the Nixon Administration reversed a long-standing United States policy and supported China's petition for membership in the United Nations. While this caused problems for Taiwan, the overall importance of normalising relations with China began to take priority.

After Kissinger's secret trip to Peking and the subsequent announcement in July 1971 that Nixon would pay an official visit to the People's Republic of China in 1972, the Soviet government made no secret of its distaste for the arrangement. On 1 August 1971, Moscow radio declared:

> In the confrontation with the Soviet Union, and this is the central aim of American policy, United States imperialism now seeks new partners: and Washington is trying to find such a partner in China.[6]

Between 1969 and the latter part of 1971, this issue, coupled with continuing American involvement in Vietnam and various cases of Soviet involvement throughout the world, caused tension between the superpowers and raised barriers to détente. However, the factors producing tension were somewhat neutralised by other factors.

The first and most visible factor promoting relaxation came in the form of European détente. While West Germany had been trying to 'build bridges' to Eastern Europe under the governments of Erhard and Kiesinger, the election of Willy Brandt in September 1969 brought a renewed commitment and a more successful strategy. In reply to the Soviet contention that Western 'bridge building' was merely a strategy by which to divide the Eastern bloc, Brandt began to pursue normalisation directly with the Soviet Union in the hope of establishing a model upon which further agreements could be reached. At the turn of the decade, West Germany and the Soviet Union had initiated talks aimed at producing a bilateral treaty. Less than one year later, a treaty of non-aggression was signed renouncing the use of force and recognising existing borders, most significantly, the Oder-Neisse Boundary between East Germany and Poland. Four months later, a similar agreement was signed with Poland, thereby allowing the establishment of formal diplomatic relations between the two countries.

Brandt's policy of *Ostpolitik* was initially greeted with mixed reactions from the superpowers. While, from the United States, France and Great Britain, German diplomacy was to receive support and encouragement, the fear existed that Bonn's 'all-German, Eastern policy' could take priority over Western European integration and therefore reinforce the traditional German interest in manoeuvring 'freely between East and West'. In response, Pompidou changed course and welcomed Britain's entry into the Common Market.[7] In this way, Brandt's policy ironically had the unintended effect of 'spurring West European integration'.[8]

The United States government feared, however, that Brandt would make concessions to Moscow which could threaten the alliance.[9] Kissinger claimed that 'the deeper motivation of Soviet overtures . . . was to practice selective détente – to ease tension with some allies while maintaining an intransigent position toward us'.[10] For this reason, the United States pressed for a four-power settlement in Berlin as a condition for final Western approval of the Soviet–West German treaty. In September 1971, a preliminary four-power agreement on Berlin was signed between the United States, Britain, France and the Soviet Union. The agreement specified various rights and responsibilities including the Soviet guarantee of the unimpeded flow of traffic between West Germany and West Berlin.

Kissinger claimed in his memoirs that by linking key issues to each other and thereby prohibiting a Soviet policy of selective détente, 'we were in a position to encourage détente and to control its pace . . .'.[11] For the United States, the sole option available regarding *Ostpolitik* 'was to give the inevitable a positive direction'.[12] Brandt recorded somewhat bitterly in his memoirs, Kissinger 'would rather have taken personal charge of the delicate complex of East/West problems in its entirety'.[13]

Concurrently, it is likely that the Soviet government had mixed feelings about *Ostpolitik*. On the one hand, Brandt's policy did offer the opportunity to pursue 'selective détente' and weaken the Western alliance. Furthermore, Bonn's gradual acceptance of the status quo and abandonment of its 'policy of strength' opened up the opportunity to gain Western recognition of East Germany and its borders, regulate crises in Berlin and gain the economic and technical advantages of economic relations with the West. On the other hand, the 'lifting' of the 'Iron Curtain' involved a series of problems in terms of maintaining unity within the socialist camp. While recent events in Czechoslovakia represented the source of Soviet concern, they also demonstrated a need to come to terms with the West. Lawrence Whetten claimed that this factor, in addition to the Chinese threat and the need to reach a *modus vivendi* with the United States, caused the Soviet Union to respond favourably to Bonn's approaches.[14] In fact, Philip Windsor contends that the Soviet Union was really seeking superpower détente and simply had to pay the price of European détente; since the problem of détente rested on the German problem, it was necessary for the Federal Republic of Germany to make a move before superpower détente could proceed.[15]

In assessing the relationship between German diplomacy and superpower détente during this period, it becomes clear that progress on the German question was a prerequisite for any significant progress on the superpower level. In a strange way, both Germanies had held a subtle kind of veto power over the actions of their senior allied partners. While Brandt's *Ostpolitik* complicated the pursuit of superpower détente, its success removed some of the obstacles to it. For instance, the settlement of the Berlin question removed an issue that had been a perennial source of East–West tension. In the Soviet press, the agreement was heralded as an 'important step toward détente'[16] while Nixon identified the agreement as the turning point leading to the Moscow summit in 1972.[17]

A second factor representing this complementary relationship between superpower and European détente came in the form of progress toward a European Security Conference. Since the mid-1960s, Brezhnev had been calling for a European conference of solely European powers. Seen as an obvious attempt to exclude the United States and neutralise Western Europe, Brezhnev's proposal was rejected outright by the West until the Soviet government agreed to American participation. Still, the positions of East and West were far apart. The Soviet leadership wanted a security conference which would provide formal Western recognition of the post-war status quo in Europe. While this recognition was all but formal, the Nixon Administration had little to gain from such a conference and would face domestic opposition from East European ethnic groups within the United States. On the other hand, the West was interested in an agreement guaranteeing a freer exchange of ideas and people between East and West. Furthermore, under domestic pressure to withdraw troops from Europe, Nixon was especially interested in an agreement providing for mutual and balanced force reductions in Europe. Realising this American need, and secure in the knowledge of their superior conventional forces in Europe, the Soviet government was not anxious to alter the status quo.

The deadlock was broken when, in May 1971, Brezhnev accepted the idea of two separate conferences. Once again, the stage was set for establishing a dialogue on issues causing tension. Talks began in 1972.

The next major factor serving to neutralise tension involved the mutual policy decisions to pursue arms control negotiations with renewed vigour. In November 1969, the superpowers met for preliminary SALT discussions in Helsinki. As some observers noted, the success or failure of the SALT negotiations would be a 'make or break factor' for superpower détente in the 1970s.[18]

For the first eighteen months, no progress was made. Problems ranged from varying definitions of parity to methods of verification. The largest obstacle, however, involved whether offensive weapons should be included in the first treaty with defensive weapons. In May 1971, a compromise was reached when it was agreed that the first treaty would focus on defensive weapons while providing some limitation on numbers of offensive missiles (ICBMs) through an interim agreement.[19]

While the SALT negotiations were not completed until the Moscow summit of 1972,[20] two other agreements were reached via the process. The first established further measures designed to limit the danger of accidental nuclear war. The second established improved 'hotline' communication by use of advanced satellites. The progress made in the SALT negotiations coupled with the two agreements produced by those involved served to build faith in superpower negotiations between 1969 and 1971.

The fourth factor contributing to the reduction of tension during this period was the common willingness to liberalise and expand commercial ties between East and West. While the most significant steps in US–Soviet economic relations were not taken until late 1971 and 1972, the general increase in the flow of goods between East and West grew with the success of European détente. Ironically, while the rise in economic intercourse signified an easing of tension between the East and the West, renewed Western competition for Eastern markets caused strains within the Western alliance. Western businessmen and their governments were making increasingly liberal interpretations of the 'COCOM' Export Council List which had been issued to prevent the export of strategically viable goods to Communist countries. Trapped within an economy hardened by a $100 billion war in Indochina, and faced with the rising economic challenge from Western Europe and Japan, American businessmen were anxious to reap their share of the new Eastern markets. With the 1949 Export Control Act due to expire on 30 June the issue of East–West trade received special Congressional hearings. While many restrictions were maintained, the United States moved to cut down its Export Control list by 1800 items over the next three years.

In terms of superpower relations, the renewed interest in trade

| | US–Soviet trade (in millions of US$) | |
	USSR exports to US	US exports to USSR
1967	41	60
1968	58	58
1969	52	106
1970	72	119
1971	57	162
1972	96	542
1973	220	1195

SOURCE   Data from *Yearbook of International Trade Statistics 1970–1 and 1974* (N.Y.: United Nations) pp, 796 and 957.

was exemplified by a massive increase in the volume of trade between the United States and the USSR in 1969. After almost ten years of relatively low levels, the total volume of trade jumped dramatically. Trade continued to rise in 1970 and 1971 until major new steps were taken to expand economic exchange as part of US–Soviet détente.

The final factor contributing to this building period in US–Soviet relations was the series of minor agreements and statements made with the aim of establishing the groundwork for détente. While the agreements were more quantitative than qualitative and the statements calling for détente were laced with various conditions, the collective impact was extremely positive.

Of the minor agreements signed, the most notable were the expanded cultural agreement (February 1970), the Joint Space Mission Agreement (October 1970), and the agreement to prevent incidents at sea (October 1971). Other agreements involved the establishment of new consulates, protection of rights for nationals, banning of nuclear weapons on the ocean floor, and the prevention of accidental nuclear war. Collectively, these agreements demonstrated the primacy of the negotiating process and the possibilities of achieving major agreements through the same means.

The desire of both sides for improved relations was voiced time and time again through various policy messages and statements in both countries. After declaring the era of negotiation, Nixon used his annual 'state of the world' messages to clarify United States policy and establish the coming year's strategy for peace. In his report entitled United States Foreign Policy in the 1970s: 'A New Strategy for Peace', Nixon assured the Soviet Union that the United States would take any opportunity to improve relations between East and West and promised not to exploit nationalism in Eastern Europe. In October 1970, Nixon told the United Nations General Assembly that US–Soviet co-operation was a prerequisite for solving world problems and pledged his energies toward achieving such co-operation.

At Twenty-Fourth Communist Party Congress in March/ April 1971, Brezhnev restated the Soviet intention to 'implement in practice the principles of peaceful coexistence, to develop mutually advantageous ties and . . . to co-operate in the field of strengthening peace, making mutual relations . . . as stable as possible'.[21] He also stated the Soviet willingness to negotiate mutual troop reductions in Europe thereby raising hopes for MBFR talks. Even Brezhnev's declaration of the ninth five year plan had significance for superpower relations. By setting the goal of modernising the Soviet economy through major technological advances, increases in the efficiency of planning and management and improvements in the quality and availability of consumer goods, Brezhnev was revealing the Soviet need for expanded East–West trade. The massive and intensified build-up of Soviet military power throughout the late 1960s had not been achieved without extensive economic consequences. All of these factors served to promote co-operation and provide proof that the desire of the superpowers for accommodation was mutual.

In conclusion, the period from Nixon's inauguration in January 1969 to the latter part of 1971 can be characterised as one in which stability was maintained through a number of factors. The deleterious effects of various crises and other tension-producing factors were mitigated by the progress being achieved in other areas. Ultimately, the positive trends had greater influence.

'HIGH' DÉTENTE: 1972 TO THE MIDDLE OF 1975

The first signs of the emerging period of 'high' détente appeared on 12 October 1971 with the announcement of Nixon's trip to Moscow. Unlike Khrushchev, neither Brezhnev nor Nixon placed much favour or hope in the summit process as a means for settling outstanding issues. After all, the landmark achievements of détente in the 1960s had been achieved through traditional diplomatic channels. Having been Eisenhower's Vice President during the 1950s, Nixon was especially sceptical about the 'summit-trip' approach to superpower relations. Upon coming to power, he spoke often about his intention to seek a substantive détente, without atmospherics dominating the scene. Therefore, when the Moscow summit was announced in October, there was reason to believe major agreements were in the making and that Nixon and Brezhnev would meet to formalise and highlight those agreements. The recent breakthrough in the SALT negotiations, the agreement on convening the European Security Conference, and the substantial progress being made in European détente contributed to the credibility of this view.

Within one month, the first major step characterising the

emerging détente was taken. A substantial grain deal worth $136 million was negotiated. On 20 November, United States Secretary of Commerce Maurice Stans met with Soviet leaders in Moscow for exploratory talks on expanded trade. At the conclusion of his visit, the Soviet press announced that major contracts worth $125 million had been signed with American firms.[22] Both sides expressed their commitment to the expansion and normalisation of trade relations and Western businessmen moved to exploit the new mood. On 16 February 1972, the United States Department of Commerce announced approval of export licences for $397 million worth of truck manufacturing equipment to the Soviet Union. The following day the State Department announced that the Soviet government had agreed to reopen lend-lease settlement talks as part of a larger trade agreement. For its part, the Nixon Administration made clear its intention to seek removal of some of the restrictions on the export of items whose strategic relevance was questionable, as well as Congressional approval for the granting of 'Most Favoured Nation' status to the Soviet Union. The expansion of trade was one way in which the superpowers sought to gain mutual advantage and construct a framework of interdependence thereby increasing their common stake in peace.

Between the positive events of October/November 1971 and the Moscow summit in May 1972, two events occurred which threatened to disrupt the embryonic stages of détente. First, the Soviet hesitancy to co-operate in ending the Indo-Pakistani war (December 1971) was upsetting to the United States and viewed as being inconsistent with détente. As Kissinger recalled, the Soviet government was using the Indo-Pakistani conflict to humiliate China, frustrate Sino-American openings and demonstrate the futility of having China and the United States as allies.[23] Secondly, Nixon's decision to mine and blockade North Vietnamese harbours (8 May 1972) was a highly provocative step, labelled by the Soviet leaders as being contrary to détente and international law. The significance of these two events, however, is that, despite causing a temporary rise in tension, they failed to upset plans for the Moscow summit meeting. Neither side allowed these incidents to interrupt what was considered the main priority – superpower détente.

Perhaps the most significant factor influencing the emergence of détente relates to Nixon's trip to China in February 1972 and the developing triangular relationship. While initial progress in Sino-American relations promoted tension, the addition of China into the superpower equation eventually caused a complete reassessment in Soviet strategic thinking and planning. The thought of 800 million Chinese situated across the border from the vast empty spaces of Siberia had become a nightmare for the Soviet Union.[24] Following the simple maxim that 'in a threesome it is folly to constitute a minority', the Soviet leaders no doubt felt it prudent to upgrade their own advances to Washington. As Coral Bell suggests in *The Diplomacy of Détente*, this motivation was fundamental in the Soviet Union's pursuit of détente. In strategic terms, détente was promoted by Soviet concerns about the dangerous potentialities of a two-front war. In political terms, superpower détente was aided by the Soviet determination not to be the isolated side of the emerging triangular relationship.

In the months leading up to the Moscow summit, détente continued to progress. On 10 April the United States, the Soviet Union and Great Britain signed a treaty banning biological warfare and calling for the destruction of stockpiles of any such weapons. The following day, the superpowers expanded their cultural agreement allowing for a greater amount of cultural, educational and scientific co-operation. Ten days later, a maritime agreement was announced giving the ships of each nation greater access to the ports of the other. As these agreements were being made, the United States was offering additional grain sales to the USSR. From great to small, the agreements came with increasing frequency. This environment provided a fitting prelude for the Moscow summit in May 1972.

When Nixon travelled to Moscow to meet with Brezhnev for eight days in the end of May, the optimistic expectations of various observers throughout the East and West were not disappointed. After months of careful preparation, the leaders put their signatures to numerous agreements marking the significant strides that had been taken. On 23 May, health and environmental research agreements were signed. The following day government officials signed agreements on space exploration and technological co-operation thereby extending the cultural exchange accord (signed in April). On 25 May, government officials signed an agreement designed to avoid possible problems between each other's ships at sea. This accord marked the first military agreement between the United States and the Soviet Union since the Second World War.

The following day, both sides announced the formation of a joint trade commission with the aim of resolving outstanding differences on economic issues and supervising the initiation of large-scale economic interchange between the countries. While this step was a secondary achievement taken in lieu of a full trade pact, such a pact was in the making and would be concluded before the end of the year.

Perhaps the most significant achievement of the Moscow summit was the signing of the SALT treaty and interim agreement on 26 May, limiting the deployment of various defensive and offensive weapons. Each superpower was limited to two ABM systems and existing levels of fixed land-based intercontinental ballistic missile (ICBM) launchers, submarine-launched ballistic missiles (SLBM) and modern ballistic missile submarines. SALT was a landmark achievement because the perennial issue of arms control was a major centrepiece and gauge of détente. While it was limited, the agreement was viewed by the participants as a major first step. Speaking at a state dinner on the day of the signing, Nixon described it as 'an enormously important agreement', one that was 'only an indication of what can happen in the future as we work towards peace in the world'. Soviet Premier Kosygin responded by calling the agreement 'a great victory for the Soviet and American peoples in the matter of easing international tension'. The general feeling about SALT in relation to détente was aptly summed up in *Pravda* two weeks later: 'In the history of international relations it is difficult to find another example of such fruitful results achieved through negotiations.' In short, the SALT agreement represented an important step in arms control and, as a result, a landmark of détente. It provided firsthand evidence that détente could work to the mutual advantage of both supepowers in difficult areas of contention.

The Moscow summit was concluded with the signing of a US–Soviet declaration of principles. The declaration of principles was designed as a loose code of behaviour or set of guidelines in an effort to institutionalise détente. In the agreement, the superpowers promised to pursue coexistence on the basis of respect for 'sovereignty, equality, noninterference in internal affairs and mutual advantage'. Major emphasis was placed on the necessity of preventing 'exacerbation of their relations' and both sides promised to 'do their utmost to avoid military confrontations' and to adhere to the 'renunciation of the use or threat of force'.

The significance of the summit was partly revealed in the amount of 'press' it received throughout the world and, especially, in the Soviet Union. The press campaign appeared to be a sign of unreserved official approval for the 'new relationship' with the United States and the benefits emerging from it.

This 'new relationship' was also the subject of Nixon's report to Congress. Less than an hour following his return to the United States, he urged Congress to inspect and approve the Moscow arrangements, especially the SALT accords.

In short, both the Soviet and American governments appeared committed to backing their newly achieved agreements all the way, thereby increasing confidence in the permanence of détente. In fact, during the next fifteen months, the continuing process of negotiations paid high returns. On 3 June, the final protocol of the Four-Power Berlin agreement was signed, thereby formally settling the Berlin question and clearing the way for the ratification of the Soviet–West German treaty.

During the summer and autumn of 1972, a number of advances took place in US–Soviet economic relations. First, several American businesses signed contracts with the Soviet government. Second, a record-setting grain deal was signed between the two countries to meet Soviet consumer demands after the massive crop failure of the previous winter. On 8 July, United States Secretary of Agriculture Butz and Soviet Deputy Foreign Trade Minister Kusmin signed a three-year agreement in which the Soviet Union would purchase over $750 million worth of grain with an additional $500 million worth of credits available through the Commodity Credit Corporation (CCC). The deal was augmented on 14 October by a US–Soviet maritime agreement establishing premium rates for United States vessels carrying grain to Soviet ports. The maritime agreement also substantially increased the number of ports in each country open to ships of the other nation.

Finally, a comprehensive trade agreement was signed on 18 October, thereby settling outstanding problems and clearing the way for large scale economic intercourse governed by a common set of guidelines. The Soviet government agreed to repay $722 million in World War II lend-lease debts thereby satisfying the American demand that the issue be settled before an expansion of trade relations. In exchange, the Soviet Union was promised most-favoured-nation trading status, a provision which was subject to the approval of the United States Congress. Furthermore, the United States Import–Export Bank would extend credits enabling the Soviet Union to increase its level of trade despite the lack of a market for Soviet goods in the United States. Additionally, a permanent representative trade office was to be established in the capitals of both nations. Finally, a series of other guidelines were established covering commercial payments and safeguards, the settlement of commercial disputes, the expansion of business facilities and the status of Soviet foreign organisations.

While the expansion of commercial relations was a primary area of détente in the second half of 1972, the US–Soviet relationship was moving forward in other areas as well. On 21 September, an agreement on joint environmental projects was announced which included the exchange of seismic detector installations – a move believed to have significance beyond environmental protection (i.e. monitoring the Test-Ban Agreement).

In an effort to maintain the momentum in the field of arms control, SALT II negotiations were opened in Geneva on 21 November. These talks were aimed at broadening the categories of weapons to be restricted and replacing the five year interim agreement on offensive weapons with a permanent one. European détente also moved forward as preparatory talks on the European Security and Co-operation Conference opened in Helsinki on 22 November.

Beyond these progressive steps in negotiations on trade, arms control, European security, scientific and cultural exchange and in many other areas, one final factor was contributing to détente during this period. Since 1969, Nixon had been trying to wind down American involvement in Vietnam through 'Vietnamisation'. American troop strength had been reduced from 337 900 in January 1971 to 139 000 by February 1972. At the same time, United States negotiators had been trying desperately to reach a peace agreement with the North Vietnamese at the Paris peace talks. Domestic pressure to terminate American involvement in the war was reflected in every way from Congressional statements to the burning of draft cards and mass demonstrations. By the second half of 1972, the United States had scaled down its involvement dramatically and progress was being made in Paris. While the wind-down in Vietnam was temporarily interrupted by an intensive American bombing campaign during late December to force a peace agreement, the upsurge in fighting was only temporary. On 23 January, the Vietnamese Peace agreements were signed thereby marking an official end to hostilities in Vietnam. While fighting continued in Cambodia and the machinery established by the Vietnam agreement for peace negotiations and a ceasefire was soon to break down, the issue that had distracted the United States and inhibited progress in superpower relations throughout the 1960s and 1970s had been diminished. On 31 January, mutual force reduction preparatory talks opened in Vienna. Representatives of the NATO and Warsaw Pact countries set about the task of writing an agenda for the forthcoming MBFR talks.

In preparation for Brezhnev's visit to the United States, the Soviet Communist Party's Central Committee gave a unanimous vote of endorsement to their leader's policy of détente on 27 April. Nixon pledged his continuing commitment to détente in his annual 'state of the world' message on 3 May 1973. He also called 1973 the 'year of Europe', stressing the United States commitment to the MBFR talks as well as the need for a strengthened Atlantic Alliance.

Brezhnev's visit to the United States in the latter half of June 1973 was symbolic of the developing relationship between the superpowers. Not unlike the Moscow summit in May 1972, the Washington summit was characterised by a number of signing ceremonies where the Soviet and American leaders formalised the final products of previous negotiations. On 19 June, four executive agreements were signed on oceanography, transportation, agricultural research and cultural exchange. The following day, a tax convention was formalised.

On 21 June, Nixon and Brezhnev signed a declaration of principles aimed at accelerating the SALT II negotiations which had stalled in Geneva. Additionally, the two leaders agreed to increase co-operation on nuclear energy research. On 22 June, Nixon and Brezhnev signed an agreement designed to avert nuclear war between the two superpowers, or between one of them and any other country. The agreement obliged the superpowers to begin 'urgent consultations' whenever relations between them or between either of them and another country appeared to involve the risk of nuclear conflict. Other agreements involved the expansion of airline service and the establishment of a Soviet trade mission in Washington.

In short, a great number of agreements were signed at the Washington summit. The agreements, however, were not as significant as the agreements signed at the Moscow summit. Little progress had been made on the central issue of arms control, and the inclusion of some minor agreements in the signing ceremonies accentuated the absence of some more significant agreements. Nonetheless, these agreements provided evidence of the common desire to maintain the momentum of détente.

The final communiqué issued on 25 June summarised the achievements of the Washington summit and praised the important strides taken in US–Soviet economic relations over the past year. Both sides pledged to 'aim at a total of $2–3 billion of trade over the next three years'.

This final section of the summit communiqué had been designed to encourage Congressional approval of the US–Soviet trade agreement. After the agreement had been signed in October 1972, Senator Henry M. Jackson introduced an amendment prohibiting the extension of credits or most-favoured-nation status to non-market economies which restricted or taxed emigration by their citizens. This amendment was specifically aimed at Moscow whose restrictive policies on Jewish emigration provoked vocal opposition within the United States. The co-sponsorship of the amendment by seventy-two other senators reflected a wide-spread concern about extending Eximbank credits to communist countries denying fundamental human rights to their citizens.[25] Trade, with its benefits more readily obvious for the Soviet Union than the United States, soon became the subject of a domestic political debate that was to rage on for the next two years. On one side, the Administration claimed that trade not only produced mutual economic advantages, but also was both a cause and effect of an easing of tension eventually allowing for the liberalisation of hardline domestic policies such as restrictions on emigration.

On the other side, Congressional opponents claimed that trade, with its many advantages for the Soviet Union, could and should be used as an incentive or negotiating tool in persuading Soviet leaders to liberalise their policies. Good Soviet behaviour would be rewarded with the economic benefits of trade.

Both sides agreed on the desirability of US–Soviet trade as well as its potential in achieving liberalisation within the Soviet Union. The debate centred around whether trade itself would bring liberalisation, or whether the reward and promise of trade would bring liberalisation. This 'chicken or the egg' argument was complicated by conflicting signs from the Soviet Union. The Administration's contention was undermined by the Soviet decision on 3 August 1972 to establish an emigration fee. This decision was taken immediately following the Moscow summit when détente was in full swing. Conversely, the emigration figures of Soviet Jews in the early 1970s suggest that détente, augmented by trade, brought a degree of liberalisation. (1970 – 1000; 1971 – 15 000; 1972 – 30 000; 1973 – 35 000). At the height of the debate over the Jackson Amendment, in 1974, the number fell to around 20 000.[26]

On 18 April 1973, the White House announced it had received assurances from Soviet leaders that they would drop the special emigration fee imposed on Jews wishing to leave for Israel. With this announcement, Nixon called again for the granting of most-favoured-nation status to the Soviet Union. The following week, Brezhnev told a group of United States Senators in Moscow that while the Soviet Union was committed to the development of East–West trade, it would not allow the issue of emigration to be linked with a trade agreement.

Neither Nixon's assurances nor Brezhnev's warnings satisfied or deterred the backers of the Jackson Amendment. The contradictory claims emerging from the White House and the Kremlin created suspicion. Nixon's relative exclusion of Congressional representation in these negotiations did not serve the cause of co-operation between the executive and legislative branches of government.

Just as the debate was reaching a climax, the issue of Soviet dissidents and the violation of human rights within the Soviet Union was highlighted, thereby raising the pitch even higher. On 21 August, dissident Soviet physicist Andrei Sakharov issued a warning to Western newsmen about the dangers of pursuing détente on Soviet terms. Stating his support for the Jackson–Vanik amendment, Sakharov claimed that the Soviet leaders would have to be pressured to grant basic human rights as a price for détente.

One week later, the Soviet government launched a large-scale press campaign against Sakharov. This move and the continual harrassment of Alexander Solzhenitsyn only served to exacerbate Western suspicion and concern over Soviet human rights violations.

In an attempt to demonstrate concern for human rights, the Soviet Union took two highly visible steps in September. First, the Soviet government eased the jamming of Voice of America and other Western broadcasts (with the exception of Radio Liberty) directed toward the Warsaw Pact countries.

Second, the Soviet leadership announced ratification of two 1966 United Nations Covenants setting down principles on freedom of communication between countries. The United States had refused to ratify these Covenants due to an escape clause allowing for the abrogation of these freedoms for reasons of national security, public order, health and morals.

These two moves were accompanied by a strong warning from Soviet Foreign Minister Gromyko during a United Nations disarmament speech on 25 September. He warned that the Soviet Union would not allow Western governments to interfere with Soviet internal affairs. This warning was confirmed in early October when Secretary of the Treasury Schultz returned from trade talks in Moscow empty-handed.

During this period, the trade issue was complicated and clouded by two additional factors. First, while the initial opposition to the advancement of US–Soviet trade had rested on a concern for emigration and other human rights, the question of the benefits of such economic exchange was increasingly being raised. The foundations for such doubts lay in the grain deal of 1972. While United States Administration officials had been claiming one more victory for détente, critics were claiming that the United States had come out on the 'short end' of the deal. As time progressed, the facts increasingly fell on the side of the critics. The United States Department of Agriculture had agreed to sell massive quantities of wheat at subsidised prices ($1.63–$1.65 per bushel) without allowing for the subsequent price rises caused by the sudden increase in demand. Therefore, domestic consumer prices jumped dramatically (to $4.30 per bushel) in 1973, causing skyrocketing food prices and general inflation.[27]

A Government Accounting Office report released in early 1973 criticised the Agriculture Department for subsidising United States grain 'much beyond what appeared necessary or desirable' thereby providing the Soviet Union with 'bargain prices'.[28] In a White House press conference on 7 September 1973, Treasury Secretary Schultz admitted that the United States had been 'burned' in the Soviet grain deal.

The embarrassing deal was suddenly turned into a maddening fiasco when Soviet officials turned around and offered to sell the grain back to the United States at the higher market prices. Much of the grain was still sitting in United States ports giving the Soviet Union a clear profit without transportation costs. Other shipments of grain had been sent to drought-stricken India as 'Soviet aid'.

The embarrassing tragedy of the US–Soviet grain deal was not overlooked by Congressional opponents of the unamended version of the Trade Reform Bill. As Senator Jackson stated:

> Fifty years ago, Lenin promised the Soviet people bread and freedom. If American farmers are to provide the bread, is it too much to ask that the Soviet leaders provide their own people a measure of freedom?[29]

The aftermath of the grain deal only served to give fire to the advocates of the Jackson Amendment.

The second factor complicating the trade issue was the United States perception of Soviet actions during the Middle East Crisis in October 1973. The full impact of this crisis will be discussed at length in the following paragraphs because its implications go far beyond the issue of trade. Nonetheless, the Middle East Crisis contributed to growing Congressional concern and on 11 December 1973, the House of Representatives passed a foreign trade bill containing the Jackson–Vanik amendment. This was a significant defeat for Nixon who had promised the Soviet leaders that MFN treatment would be granted without linkage to emigration.

The Middle East crisis began when, on 6 October, during the Yom Kippur holiday, Israel was attacked on two fronts by Syrian and Egyptian forces. As the Arabs made advances against Israel, other Arab nations contributed forces.

For the superpowers, any war in the Middle East was potentially explosive. However, the crisis held significant political and strategic implications, because it involuntarily put the new détente relationship to the test. Unfortunately, on the first count, the new relationship failed as evidenced by Soviet action or inaction at the onset of the crisis. Months before, at the Washington summit, Nixon and Brezhnev had signed an agreement promising to inform one another of potential conflict situations threatening the general peace. Since the Soviet leaders had withdrawn their military personnel hours before the invasion of Israel's occupied territories, it was suspected that the Soviet government held prior knowledge of the military action but had failed to inform the United States. This inaction was in direct violation of the Washington agreement. It was especially irritating to the United States because of the initial Arab advances. However, within a few days the tide turned. Israel staged an effective counter-offensive and was able to solidify new lines on both fronts. As Arab forces began to lose ground, the Soviet government called for the establishment of a joint superpower peace-keeping force and suggested that it would intervene unilaterally if the United States failed to act. Nixon's reply was immediate and decisive. On 25 October, the United States launched a worldwide military alert – the first since 1962. Brezhnev immediately accused the United States of artificially drumming up the crisis but, at the same time, practised restraint and reaffirmed his support for détente. A United Nations resolution was passed, and the superpowers agreed to try to expedite the talks between the parties involved. On 31 October, the United States cancelled its military alert.

While the new superpower relationship failed on the first count in preventing the crisis, it succeeded on the second count in preventing it from exploding into a superpower confrontation. Coral Bell has observed that US–Soviet management of the crisis demonstrated the success of détente.[30] William Quandt agrees that, despite Soviet posturing, the Soviet leaders seemed primarily concerned with ending the conflict.[31] While Soviet actions can be interpreted as being somewhat devious, the most important feature of the crisis was that the superpowers co-operated effectively in its resolution. The nuclear alert did not represent so much an interruption in the process of détente as a reminder of the cold realities upon which the US–Soviet relationship was based.

The most serious outgrowth of the October crisis was the Arab implementation of an embargo on oil exports to those countries supporting Israel. This move held dramatic implications for superpower détente, the Western economy and the Western alliance.

At a ministerial meeting of the Organisation of Arab Petroleum Exporting Countries on 17 October, the members agreed to cut oil production by 5 per cent each month until Israel withdrew from all Arab lands occupied since the 1967 war. On 20 October, following the Nixon Administration's announcement of a $2.2 billion military aid package to Israel, the OAPEC ministers declared a total embargo on oil to the United States and any other supporters of Israel (e.g. the Netherlands). The move was led by America's traditional friend, Saudi Arabia, which found itself in a particularly difficult position balancing the moral and security considerations of Arab solidarity on the one hand and American friendship and the fear of Arab radicalism on the other.[32] Since most of the supplies were controlled by American companies and allocations were simply shifted from different points of origin, the major impact of the embargo appears to have been psychological.[33] Nonetheless Saudi–American relations were strained.[34] To the detriment of détente, the embargo was actively encouraged and supported by the Soviet Union even though it had been initiated by an anti-Soviet state.[35]

The impact of this first major application of the 'oil weapon' was no less than dramatic for the Western alliance. As the United States attempted a massive resupply effort of military equipment to aid Israel in the heat of the battle, the NATO allies (with the exception of Portugal and Greece) refused to participate or even co-operate. The Arab leaders, with their economic weapons, had done more to divide the Western allies (including Japan) than the Soviet government could ever hope to do.

For the Western allies, the issue was viewed in terms of basic economic well-being. As the Arabs proceeded to levy embargoes, the alliance broke down into 'each nation for itself'. This unfortunate spectacle vividly demonstrated the narrow limits of allied co-operation. The simple fact was that the West had become overly dependent on Middle East oil and was paying the price. The potency of the oil weapon was demonstrated the following year when chronic shortages and skyrocketing prices thrust the Western economies into a severe recession.

In the final analysis, the Arab Embargo strained superpower relations as the Soviet government actively encouraged and rejoiced in the economic blackmail of the West. Secondly, the price rises which accompanied the embargo were a primary factor contributing to the economic difficulties of the Western powers and many other countries in the following period. Finally, the embargo demonstrated and accentuated the lack of unity and cohesion within the Western alliance.

The breakdown in the Western alliance also highlighted one other emerging trend that was to influence détente. This trend was 'polycentrism', and it partly grew out of the success of détente.

By nature of the Western alliance, the tendency toward independent decision-making had always existed. However, the rise of West European and Japanese economic power in the 1970s brought increased competition among the Western powers. Therefore, decisions affecting various aspects of Western policy and relations were increasingly being taken independently of Washington. This was demonstrated vividly during the 1973 Middle East War.

In addition, the trend toward independent action was augmented by European and superpower détente. As the Western powers began to establish independent relationships with their Eastern counterparts and as the United States focused an increasing amount of attention on its new relationship with the Soviet Union, there was a decline in the factors binding the Western powers together. In this way, Nixon's declaration of 1973 as the 'year of Europe' was rendered ineffective.

For the Soviet Union, the problem was not as initially obvious but involved a greater potential for problems. The split with China had demonstrated this. As in the West, détente led to an increasing number of contacts between East European countries and their Western counterparts – including the United States. The year 1973 alone had witnessed the establishment of new relationships involving Britain, France, East Germany, West Germany, Czechoslovakia, Bulgaria, Hungary and the United States. While the Soviet leaders hoped to diminish United States influence and divide the Western allies by promoting European détente, they ran the risk of subverting their own influence over their Eastern European allies. When, in mid-1973, the West made its participation in the European Security Conference contingent upon the inclusion of the question of freer exchanges of people, ideas and information on the agenda, it became clear that the growth of East–West contacts and co-operation would come at a price. It was probably this realisation and concern that prompted the Soviet government to tighten the controls of internal security and intensify the ideological struggle.

In short, détente contributed to divisions within both blocs and threw new complications into the alliance relationships upon which European security and stability were based. As this trend developed, 'polycentrism' was to become an increasingly important factor on the balance sheet of détente.

Despite the events in the Middle East and the controversy over trade, the US–Soviet commitment to détente remained firm. While more problems emerged and others grew more intense during 1974, the superpowers continued to engage in efforts aimed at advancing their relationship.

In January 1974, the Conference on European Security and Co-operation reconvened in Geneva and the MBFR talks resumed in Vienna. Throughout the first half of 1974, Kissinger and Gromyko travelled between capitals and met wherever possible in an effort to speed up completion of the SALT II agreement.

Meanwhile, the superpowers co-operated in promoting peace in the Middle East. With the aid of Kissinger's direct mediation, ceasefire and troop disengagement agreements were signed in May between Egypt, Israel and the superpowers.

The trend toward increased US–Soviet trade also continued. The extent to which commercial relations had grown as a result of détente was revealed in February when United States government trade figures showed that US–Soviet trade had risen from $642 million in 1972 to over $1.4 billion in 1973.

Despite these factors, progress in superpower relations was not as forthcoming as it had been during the previous two years. This 'wind-down' of détente became evident during Nixon's second visit to Moscow in June 1974 when no major agreements were reached. While Nixon and Brezhnev signed three minor nuclear agreements, a SALT II agreement was conspicuously absent.

The progress made in other areas was equally unimpressive. Agreements on housing, energy, medical research, environmental protection, space ventures, cultural exchanges and transportation generally complemented already-existing accords signed in 1972.

In the area of trade, an economic agreement was signed aimed at establishing a broad framework for US–Soviet trade over the next ten years. The future of US–Soviet trade, however, was still being decided in Congress and no optimistic executive agreement could change that reality. Throughout the first half of 1974, the trade question had been complicated by the growing concern over human rights in the Soviet Union. In February, dissident author Alexander Solzhenitsyn was arrested and deported in response to the publication of *Gulag Archipelago* by the Western press. In March, the Arabs agreed to lift the oil embargo which had been choking the United States economy since October 1973. After having encouraged the Arabs in their embargo against the United States, Soviet leaders were highly critical of the Arab decision. This Soviet attitude did little to encourage support for the granting of MFN treatment and credits to the Soviet Union.

In July, a more serious issue emerged to complicate the trade question with the Soviet Union. On 19 July, a declassified CIA report revealed the Soviet Union was increasingly outspending the United States on defence. The report estimated Soviet military spending had been increasing on the average of 3 per cent each year since 1960 while American increases had been offset by inflation. The successful testing of a Soviet MIRV the previous January was one in a series of incidents demonstrating the Soviet ability to match United States strategic power qualitatively as well as quantitatively. A series of other studies published during this period supported this conclusion. The rise in Soviet military spending lent credence to the allegation that Soviet leaders were seeking military superiority. This growing realisation suddenly cast a shadow over the question of détente as a whole and especially US–Soviet trade. The debate revolved around whether by providing the 'butter', the West was supporting and assisting Soviet acquisition of the 'guns'. Suddenly, Lenin's 'rope theory' gained credibility: 'When it becomes time to hang the capitalists they will compete as to who will sell us the rope.' While the West had mutually agreed to prohibit the sale of certain strategic goods to communist countries, the list of strategic items had been increasingly liberalised with the progress of détente and the growth of Western economic competition and economic difficulties. The declared Soviet interest in Western technology, as opposed to Western goods, increased the suspicion that the Soviet government not only wanted to build their own competitive industrial machine but were interested in the military application of those technologies. Suddenly, the definition of 'strategic goods' again fell into question. Indeed, under the guns and butter argument, every item of trade had the potential of contributing to the Soviet military effort.

On the opposite side of the debate were those advocating a type of convergence theory. They claimed that only through increased economic, cultural, educational, scientific and social intercourse would the Soviet Union gain a greater stake in the status quo and hence, promote the cause of peace. As the massive build-up of the Soviet military arsenal became increasingly evident, this type of convergence theory lost credibility.

The entire question of trade and the future of US–Soviet relations were complicated by the resignation of Richard Nixon in August 1974. Under the threat of impeachment for his role in the Watergate scandals, Nixon stepped aside and his appointed Vice President, Gerald Ford, became President. This move held both positive and negative implications for US–Soviet détente. On one hand, the Watergate scandals had been increasingly distracting Americans from the pursuit of détente, as well as undermining Nixon's authority and ability to carry it out. Nixon's resignation settled the major issue of the Watergate question thereby removing this obstacle. On the other hand, there was doubt as to the new President's ability to achieve further progress in a superpower relationship that seemed to be fading. Ford's commitment was made clear upon his taking the oath of office on 9 August as he pledged to continue his predecessor's policies. His decision to keep Henry Kissinger as Secretary of State was viewed partly as a move to assure the Soviet government of the continuing United States commitment to détente.

In late November 1974, Ford and Brezhnev met in Vladivostok. The two leaders reached a tentative agreement to limit the numbers of all strategic offensive nuclear weapons and delivery vehicles (including MIRVs) through 1975. Kissinger hailed the agreement as a 'breakthrough' which would 'mean that a cap has been put on the arms race for a period of ten years'.[36] Based on the principle of absolute equality in the reduction of weaponry, a provision demanded by a Jackson amendment to SALT I, the agreement represented a significant step. However, Jackson's amendment had represented a turning point, in terms of the doubts expressed by some that SALT had been unequal. Therefore, the Vladivostok accords elicited a rising chorus of accusations and complaints in the United States that the Soviet leaders were violating SALT I and that the new accords gave them a strategic advantage. This line of analysis was to figure prominently in the American debate throughout 1975 and 1976.

The last major event of 1974 in US–Soviet relations was a harbinger of the following period in the superpower relationship. On 20 December 1974, the United States Congress passed a final and comprehensive version of the foreign trade bill. A controversial rider granting trade benefits to the Soviet Union was based on the understanding that the Soviet Union had agreed to end restrictions on the emigration of its Jewish citizens. When the Soviet government announced that no such understanding had been reached, congressmen brushed aside the comment as a face-saving gesture by the Soviet leaders.

On 10 January 1975, the Soviet leaders announced their decision to cancel the 1972 trade pact in light of the restrictions placed on US–Soviet trade by the foreign trade bill. The Soviet action was highly significant because it clearly stated Soviet priorities. While the improvement of US–Soviet relations through trade was important, it was secondary to the Soviet Union's right to determine its own internal policies. Not even the promise of credits and MFN treatment would be allowed to challenge that right. While both sides announced that the cancellation of the trade pact would not interfere with the further development of US–Soviet détente, a major element in the foundation of détente had been removed.

The final nail would be driven into 'the coffin of US–Soviet trade' in January 1976 when President Ford withdrew his support for MFN trading status with the Soviet Union. This move was taken in response to Soviet actions in Angola.

A further issue served to complicate détente in the spring of 1975. After the machinery of the Paris agreements had broken down during the previous year, Communist forces made substantial gains and finally, on 30 April, captured Saigon. Given the amount of American blood that had been shed in this seemingly senseless conflict, the fall of Saigon was no less than traumatic and humiliating for the American people. America's 'peace with honour' was shown to be less than honourable. While both sides had violated the peace agreements, the whole event took on the appearance of communist deception. Clearly, the unwillingness of the American people to continue providing sufficient support to the South Vietnamese government played a significant part in the events but this was not a convincing explanation at the time. The Ford Administration immediately froze all South Vietnamese assets and placed an embargo on trade but this was an unsatisfying punishment under the circumstances.

Despite these setbacks in US–Soviet relations, two major events occurred in the summer of 1975 that served to neutralise the impact of this failure of détente temporarily. First, the joint Soviet–American space mission took place bringing almost five years of political, scientific and technological efforts to fruition. The Apollo–Soyuz mission was not only a marvellous achievement but served as an impressive demonstration of superpower co-operation in a fiercely competitive field.

The second and most important event was the signing of the Helsinki accords on 1 August, marking the culmination and conclusion of the Conference on Security and Co-operation in Europe. The meeting in Helsinki of thirty-five national leaders from the Soviet Union, the United States, Canada and thirty-two European states symbolically represented the climax of European détente. The Final Act consisted of four sections (called 'baskets') – the first setting out general declarations on such topics as European security and human rights; the second calling for increased East–West co-operation in economics, science, technology and the environment; the third setting forth principles on the international movement of people and ideas; the fourth making arrangements for a follow-up to the agreements. For the East, the Conference symbolised American and West European acceptance of the division of Germany and the political status of Eastern Europe. For the West, the agreements on the freer movements of people and ideas, East–West economic, scientific and technological exchange, and human rights, seemed to open up new possibilities for European détente. The French government welcomed the agreements as a means to promote the traditional French view of *l'Europe des Etats* and British leaders welcomed them as yet another means by which to transcend the cold war. For the West Germans, the Conference represented a confirmation of the results of Brandt's policy of *Ostpolitik* on a multilateral level.

For the superpowers, the agreements were much less significant in real terms but held the potential for contributing to détente. The Soviet Union 'gained' Western recognition of the political and territorial status quo in Europe – a fact that had been already implicit in the policy considerations of many Western governments. In fact, four months after Helsinki the American State Department advisor on communist affairs, Helmut Sonnenfeldt, officially stated that it was in American long term interests to encourage East European states to develop 'a more natural and organic' relationship with the Soviet Union and to support 'the clearly visible aspirations in Eastern Europe for a more autonomous existence within the context of a strong Soviet geopolitical influence'.[37] The American government not only recognised the status quo in Europe but viewed Western security in terms of its maintenance.

In a different environment, the Helsinki accords might have had a more positive influence on superpower relations. However, while the agreement augmented European détente, it highlighted the failures and drawbacks to the American policy of détente. The Helsinki agreement initially met with a large amount of support in the United States, but its critics were vocal and persistent. Senator Jackson, a presidential challenger and champion of ethnic minority groups, claimed Ford had 'sold out' Eastern Europe while receiving nothing more than dubious promises in return. As the year progressed and the Soviet government proceeded to arrest dissidents in violation of the Helsinki accords, Senator Jackson's accusations gained credibility. The issue was sucked into the realm of presidential politics putting Ford and Kissinger on the defensive. The issue would reach a climax when, during the Carter–Ford debate on international relations, Ford awkwardly denied that Eastern Europe was under the domination of the Soviet Union. This weak rationalisation for Helsinki offended large members of East European immigrant voting groups in the United States and, in the analysis of many political observers, eventually cost Ford the presidential election. The American public reaction to the Helsinki accords, and the failure of the trade agreements several months before, eventually worked to turn the course of superpower détente.

THE AFTERMATH: LATE 1975 UNTIL 1976

Throughout the final months of 1975, the US–Soviet relationship suffered set-backs in other essential areas. In arms control, little progress was made. The MBFR talks were deadlocked. Despite the Vladivostok accords, the SALT II negotiators had made little headway during the two sessions of 1975. In mid-1974, the Soviet government had toughened its stand in an effort to test the authority of the politically weakened Nixon presidency. This tactic was also used to test the credibility and determination of the new Ford Administration which had come to power without a popular mandate. Ironically, just as the Soviet Union became interested in completing the SALT II agreement, the issue became entwined with American presidential politics. In January 1976, Kissinger flew to Moscow for talks with Brezhnev on SALT II. This meeting was successful and both sides announced the likelihood of a SALT II agreement by mid-1976. However, as the presidential primary season progressed and Ford was successfully challenged from the right by Ronald Reagan, the political wisdom of signing a controversial arms agreement with the Soviet Union fell into question. To Kissinger's extreme disappointment, the Ford Administration was forced to engage in delay tactics with the Soviet government until after the November elections. When Jimmy Carter emerged victorious, the Soviet leaders showed no more interest in dealing with the lame-duck Ford Administration, and the opportunity for a SALT II agreement in 1976 was lost.

Ford's political problems were exacerbated by a growing American awareness of the Soviet arms build-up. An increasing number of studies supported the contention that the Soviet Union was engaged in an effort to obtain military superiority under the guise of détente. The attack was not only coming from Reagan and his advocates on the right, but from within the Ford Administration. Secretary of Defense Rumsfeld warned that the United States would have to increase its military budget dramatically in order to keep pace with the Soviet Union. The CIA doubled its estimates of the ratio of GNP the Soviet Union was spending on defence. Throughout the NATO alliance, military specialists were sending out warning signals in response to the growing strength and preparedness of the Warsaw Pact. The sudden withdrawal of Greece from NATO in August 1974, in addition to the rising spectre of 'Eurocommunism' in Italy had already served to augment fears about the vulnerability of Western defences. To the alarm and disillusionment of all Westerners, this massive build-up in Soviet military strength had taken place during the period of 'high détente'.

This image of Soviet deception, as well as the overall significance of the Soviet military build-up, became clearer and more threatening when the Soviet government actively backed and aided rebel forces in the Angolan civil war. When Ford stated in an NBC interview on 3 January 1976 that Soviet involvement in Angola was 'inconsistent with the aims and objectives of détente', the Soviet government reiterated its support for 'wars of national liberation'. At the Twenty-Fifth Party Congress in Moscow in February, Brezhnev pledged 'redoubled energy' to the pursuit of détente while, at the same time, voicing his commitment to an intensification of the ideological struggle and Soviet support of national liberation movements. Suddenly, the disturbing spectre of Soviet adventurism based on the Khrushchev model rose again – but with one difference. This time Soviet adventurism would be backed up by the new realities of Soviet military power. Furthermore, any 'problem areas' too sensitive for superpower involvement could be dealt with by use of Cuban proxy forces. The Soviet Union's new-found military strength and the apparent willingness to use it created fear and provided more ammunition for the critics of détente.

If Soviet actions in Angola served to highlight a duality in the Soviet concept of détente, these actions only served to highlight a trend that had been emerging since the inception of the Moscow summit in 1972. Time and time again, Brezhnev had stated his support for détente and his commitment to an intensification of the ideological struggle in the same breath. Western observers viewed this as a concession to hardliners within the Kremlin in exchange for their support for détente. Nonetheless, as the Soviet leaders upgraded ideological warfare and increased their measure of internal repression, Westerners increasingly viewed these actions as inimical to détente. Angola was seen as a manifestation of such asymmetrical policies. These actions were made all the more apparent and damaging by countertrends occurring in the United States. First, Nixon and Kissinger had purposely subordinated moral and ideological considerations in United States foreign policy. Upon joining the Nixon Administration, Kissinger claimed that his 'overriding problem was to free our foreign policy from its violent fluctuations between euphoria and panic'.[38] For this reason, foreign policy making would be kept from the public so as to allow Kissinger maximum flexibility – a prerequisite for his policy of 'linkage'. This approach found favour with Nixon who held the 'conviction that secrecy was needed for successful negotiations'.[39] The quest for secrecy and a centralisation of power was further augmented by Nixon's distrust of the Eastern liberal-dominated State Department and bureaucracy – a group Kissinger claims 'is attracted to the fashionable' and when thwarted, engages in 'political warfare against the President'.[40] Foreign policy making was centralised in the White House and Nixon and Kissinger 'introduced on a grand scale maneuver, shock tactics and surprise'.[41]

While remarkable diplomatic strides were taken by means of secret diplomacy, progress was achieved at the expense of building a strong foundation upon which these achievements could rest. Nixon and Kissinger had misunderstood the American political system by failing to build a new foreign policy consensus based on American ideological traditions. Not unlike the First World War, Vietnam was widely viewed as being the product of deceptive, secretive and elitist decision making – a direct result of too much Presidential power. The Administration's pleas for 'basic trust' went unheard as Congress denied important sticks and carrots at essential times. As Stanley Hoffman observed, Nixon and Kissinger's style of diplomacy 'sacrificed solidarity to immediate efficiency' and allowed them to get too far ahead of public opinion.[42] Their deliberate subordination of American ideological traditions brought on a public revolt which would be reflected in the Presidential elections of 1976.

A second trend served to complicate the first. As Soviet 'adventurism' was on the rise, the United States was withdrawing from its world commitments, largely in reaction to the American tragedy in Vietnam. When Ford sought military aid for Western-backed forces in Angola, Congress voted to prohibit American participation in the conflict. The combination of these two countertrends was the cause and effect of a failing foreign policy consensus that had served to unite Americans since the end of World War II.

The Soviet victory in Angola had profound effects upon the American perception of détente. It not only reinforced the image of Soviet deception, but contributed to the decline of American confidence. In the guilt-ridden aftermath of Vietnam and Watergate, many Americans tended to view the failures of détente in the light of American naïveté and the declining adherence to moral principles. In reality, Americans were being increasingly exposed to the consequences of the decline of American power. The growing reaction against détente was, in part, an inability or an unwillingness to acknowledge this decline.

Throughout the remainder of 1976, détente increasingly became a liability. From many quarters in American politics came the accusation that détente had been a 'one-way street'. Americans had supposedly given a lot and received little in return. This 'era of goodwill' had been achieved at the expense of American and Western security.

The political pressure grew so intense that Ford decided to drop the word 'détente' from his political nomenclature. The word had taken on a pejorative colouration not unlike the word 'appeasement'. In search of an explanation and scapegoat for the decline of American power and its consequences, the American people turned on the policies of détente. While the majority of Americans appeared to remain in favour of détente on a whole, there was a general consensus that the US–Soviet relationship had to be placed back on an equal footing. Détente could only be made acceptable by making it a two-way street.

FACTORS CONTRIBUTING TO, AND DETRACTING FROM, DÉTENTE

In retrospect, the factors contributing to the Moscow détente appear to be five-fold. First, the strategic and political implications of the emerging Sino-American relationship in 1971 had a profound influence on the development of US–Soviet détente. Since the fall of Khrushchev in October 1964 and the growth of United States involvement in Vietnam, the new Soviet leadership had been reluctant to expand relations with the United States. When, in March 1971, China suddenly began to seek accommodation with the United States, a dramatic reassessment of Soviet foreign policy took place. Strategically, the possibility of Sino-American collusion raised a frightening prospect – Western strategic power on one front and 800 million Chinese on the other. The option of increasing ties with Washington became all the more attractive, if not essential.

Politically, this option was attractive because of the consequences of being left on the short side of the emerging triangular relationship. With increasing pressure for expanded relations with the West coming from within the Eastern Bloc, Soviet leaders were not anxious to have any of their satellites follow the Chinese or Rumanian examples. The upgrading of relations with Washington was partly viewed as a means to enhance stability in Eastern Europe and gain recognition of the status quo. Additionally, the recognition of Soviet influence and 'super' power by the West would serve to put China in its place.

For its part, the United States sought to gain leverage by way of the emerging triangular relationship. United States strategy during this 'era of negotiation' was to increase the adversary's stake in the status quo thereby enhancing stability and peace. After Nixon's announcement regarding the limitations of United States commitments around the world, the opportunities for diplomacy through accommodation became even more attractive.

When the Soviet government expressed an urgent interest in the improvement of US–Soviet relations immediately following the initiation of Sino-American contacts, both sides appeared ready for progress. The negotiating mechanisms, already established during the 1960s, took on new life. Soon, the overall importance of the superpower relationship took priority over relations with China, and superpower détente moved forward.

Second, the steady American withdrawal from Vietnam removed a major barrier which had served to inhibit superpower accommodation and progress throughout the latter half of the 1960s. It enabled Soviet leaders to seek an improvement of superpower relations without facing serious charges of selling out their Vietnamese communist brothers. Furthermore, Chinese overtures to the United States weakened the base from which ideological purists could complain.

For the United States, the steady withdrawal from Vietnam enabled the Nixon Administration to focus on the development of superpower relations, an area at the top of Nixon's list of international priorities. In light of the United States experience in Vietnam and the profound influence it had on Americans, Nixon's commitment to the pursuit of détente gained additional significance. The war had shattered the domestic consensus surrounding America's role in the world. In this uncertainty were the seeds of isolationism or, at least, a trend towards limiting United States involvement in world affairs. Nixon and Kissinger's policy of détente provided another and less costly means by which to contain communism and maintain United States influence in the world. With declining popular support for an activist foreign policy, détente provided the opportunity for managing the Soviet Union and China through negotiation without the cost of confrontation. In this way, détente complemented the needs of American foreign policy.

Third, the relative achievement of strategic parity between the superpowers in the late 1960s and early 1970s helped to set the stage for détente. Acceptance of the principle of parity in the United States was augmented by the declining faith in American wisdom for the world and in the effectiveness of military power. Furthermore, the military costs of fighting a war in Vietnam had been staggering and the popular support for additional investments in military might was low. Arms control negotiations bcame the focal point of hope, and the establishment and maintenance of parity was viewed as the key to stability and peace.

For the Soviet Union, the achievement of parity enabled it to negotiate with the United States on an equal strategic footing. On this basis, détente was viewed as a means to be recognised as a superpower equal to the United States. With their unbending faith in the power and influence of military strength, the Soviet leaders sought to rid themselves of a traditional Russian inferiority complex.

Fourth, economic considerations had a particularly significant influence on the development of détente. Since 1965, the economies of both the Soviet Union and the United States had been overburdened by the demands of the arms race. The Soviet Union faced the awesome challenge of 'catching up' with the United States by way of an economy half the size. The Soviet leaders were under pressure to place more resources into the consumer sector. To complicate things, the Soviet economy had been experiencing a steady decline in its growth rate (from 5.3 per cent in 1958–67 to 3.7 per cent in 1967–73)[43] due to poor management and a lack of technological development.

Part of the solution involved putting a halt to the arms race. The SALT negotiations and a general relaxation of tension provided the means by which the Soviet leaders could cut their heavy investment in arms development and procurement. The rest of the solution involved developing trade relations with the West. Soviet development and prosperity was seen in terms of applying successful Western technological methods to the lethargic and backward Soviet economy. With this aim in mind, the Politburo decided during the Twenty-Fourth Party Congress in March 1971 to improve relations with the United States in the hope of gaining credits and establishing a beneficial economic relationship.

For the United States, economic problems appeared equally as serious. By the end of the 1960s, American economic preeminence was coming to an end. The rise of Japan and Western Europe brought new levels of competition to the international economic system, and the added burden of the war effort led to a serious decline of the American dollar. For the first time, the United States was experiencing successive trade deficits, and hence, a nagging inflation rate. Funds which should have been invested in industrial development were diverted to the war effort and the arms race. Given these factors, the United States was anxious to 'cap' the arms race through the SALT and MBFR negotiations and reap the benefits of growing trade relations with the Eastern Bloc. Détente offered the potential for both achievements.

The fifth and final factor contributing to détente involved the insights, personalities and abilities of the leaders at the time. The remarkable line of successful achievements during this period can be greatly credited to the political abilities and political reputations of Nixon and Brezhnev. Both men were creative and able statesmen in international affairs and were assisted by two exceptionally competent foreign secretaries in the persons of Kissinger and Gromyko. Furthermore, both leaders had the confidence and support of most political elements in their respective countries. Brezhnev apparently had the backing of hardliners in the Kremlin and Nixon had the backing of most liberal and conservative groups in his policies toward the Soviet Union. Both leaders took a creative approach to foreign policy and were fully committed to their policies of détente.

The factors contributing to the decline of détente are four-fold. First, a number of unanticipated obstacles to US–Soviet cooperation in trade and other areas arose, thereby invoking a higher price than the superpowers were willing to pay. When the United States Congress voted in December 1974 to link the issues of human rights and trade, and when the Soviet government decided to reject such a linkage the following month, both sides were, in effect, placing a price on their co-operation. With each side unwilling to meet the terms of the other, the limits of détente through trade became clear.

Trade was not the only area where the limits of superpower co-operation were exposed. In the vital area of arms control, progress had been stalled since the euphoric aftermath of the Moscow summit when the SALT I agreement had been signed. With each additional summit, minor agreements were elevated in an attempt to demonstrate the continuing superpower commitment to détente. This exercise had the dual effect of illuminating the failure of negotiations in the important areas, while promoting atmospherics to fill the gap. While both sides had been careful to make 'real progress', not atmospherics, the prominent feature of the Moscow Summit (1972), the latter characteristic emerged as both leaders struggled under the political pressure of portraying détente as an 'irreversible process'. As various obstacles re-emerged in the US–Soviet relationship, doubts began to mount over the authenticity and viability of détente.

Second, the failure to achieve a mutually acceptable definition of a code of détente, or the rules of international behaviour, contributed to the decline of détente as both sides attacked each other for violating its nebulous code. In reality, the Soviet and the American views of détente were shaped by the trends in their respective foreign policies at the time. The Soviet leaders had achieved full military and strategic superpower status and were anxious to reap the political benefits of that achievement. Conversely, the American people had been shaken by their participation in the Vietnam War and were anxious to place limits on their world commitments. It is within this context that both sides perceived détente. For the Soviet leaders, détente promised a peaceful environment in which to pursue the goals of their foreign policy by means of their growing superpower status. Furthermore, détente promised mutual restraint on attempts to influence the internal policies within nation-states and alliances, a particularly sensitive area among Soviet leaders. Finally, détente promised numerous economic benefits in terms of technology and credits.

For the Americans, détente promised a stable and predictable international environment in which both sides would practise mutual restraint in their political, strategic–military and ideological competition. Such restraint would be encouraged by establishing co-operative ties in many areas thereby giving the Soviet

Union a larger stake in the status quo. By restricting the Soviet tendency to upset the status quo, the United States could withdraw from some of its world commitments. Détente promised a peaceful international atmosphere where the costs of maintaining peace were limited.

Given these diverging views of détente and its guidelines, it is no surprise that superpower détente experienced problems. Nowhere was this divergence more apparent than in the three following areas – superpower involvement in the Third World, the arms race and ideological competition. Soviet support for 'national liberation' groups on the African continent in 1974–75 caused a complete reassessment of the political viability and advantages of détente within the administration and the entire United States. The successful Soviet intervention in Angola was precisely the type of activity Kissinger had hoped détente would prevent. Despite Soviet actions, the United States chose not to respond and this indirectly reinforced Soviet 'adventurism'. When the United States criticised the Soviet Union for pursuing policies contrary to détente, the Soviet leaders replied that they were simply performing their ideological duty of aiding national liberation movements, and dismissed the possibility that Soviet ideology could be contrary to détente. The fall of Saigon in 1975 was a painful reminder of the Soviet Union's commitment to selected 'national liberation movements'. Conversely, the Soviet government was critical of America's 'one man show' in the Middle East peace process. Kissinger's shuttle diplomacy was seen as an attempt unilaterally to extend United States influence in the Middle East by excluding the Soviet Union.

The spectre of Soviet 'adventurism' was made more frightening to American observers by developments occurring in a second area of contention – the arms race. As the extent of the Soviet arms build-up became known, Western political analysts asked why the Soviet Union was attempting to build its arsenal beyond parity in an age of détente.

Once again, the problem was exacerbated because Soviet and American policies were proceeding in opposite directions. While the United States was paring down its military budget in real terms, the Soviet Union was realising the fruits of its military investments throughout the late 1960s and early 1970s. Because détente was based upon the principle of parity, these trends were dangerous.

Finally, the divergence in the superpower views of détente was most apparent in the area of ideological competition. While Nixon and Kissinger had moved to de-idealise and amoralise American foreign policy, Brezhnev had moved to upgrade Soviet ideological competition. The United States administration was supporting the Soviet demand that a trade agreement be unaccompanied by any American ideologically-inspired provisions; Brezhnev was calling for an intensification of the ideological struggle. When President Ford decided against receiving Soviet dissident Alexander Solzenhitsyn for fear of offending the Soviet government, the American people had had enough.

The American interest in détente coupled with the post-Vietnam and Watergate upheaval in the American 'moral consensus' enabled Kissinger temporarily to downgrade considerations of ideology in American foreign policy-making. However, as Soviet intentions became known, Nixon and Kissinger's 'amoral' approach to foreign policy was sharply criticised. Brezhnev's intensification of the ideological struggle and internal police measures was seen in the United States as further evidence of Soviet insincerity. Subsequently, moral considerations were reasserted in American foreign policy, by way of the Jackson amendment, thereby raising the price of détente – a price the Soviet government was not willing to pay.

In retrospect, the reasons behind Brezhnev's intensification of the ideological struggle do not seem devious. His policies were grounded in political realism. As détente progressed, bringing an expansion of East–West contacts on all levels, the threat of 'ideological pollution' grew more intense. Because much of the legitimacy and power of the Soviet and East European communist régimes depended upon a strict adherence to 'state created' ideology, expanded contacts with the West posed a serious threat. In the interests of national security and in exchange for support from conservative elements within the Kremlin, Brezhnev wisely coupled his policy of détente with one of intensifying ideological competition. While this dualism was viewed by Americans as being antithetical to détente, Brezhnev made no secret of his position. The intensification of ideological competition was simply one more price tag placed on détente. Soon, it became too high a price to pay.

The third major factor contributing to the decline of détente involved the joint realisation that in some areas, détente worked against the interests of national security. For instance, détente had tended to promote polycentrism or pluralism within the alliances. As in previous periods, détente served to undermine those mechanisms upon which East–West security was based. The logical result of growing insecurity was an increase of tension – and the decline of détente.

In the West, this problem was most obvious during the 1973 Middle East War and the Arab oil embargo. The primary characteristic of the NATO alliance at that time was complete disunity – a dangerous state of affairs in terms of Western security. This lack of cohesion was also a problem in the area of East–West trade as the Western democracies competed fiercely for the new markets in the East.

As Western alarm spread over the Soviet military build-up, and the NATO governments became increasingly cognisant of the vulnerability of NATO defences, the trend of pluralism was reversed and the allies worked together to upgrade their forces. Unfortunately, this was achieved somewhat at the expense of détente.

As previously mentioned, polycentrism in the Soviet bloc is a far more serious matter. The trend of polycentrism within the socialist bloc, beginning with China in 1960, had already augmented Soviet feelings of vulnerability. The Soviet invasions of Hungary (1956) and Czechoslovakia (1968) served as cold reminders of the Soviet Union's intention to maintain its buffer zone against 'Western aggression'.

As stated earlier, it was upon these philosophical lines that Brezhnev coupled his policy of détente with a call for the intensification of the ideological struggle. It was probably on this premise that the Soviet government decided to reject the terms of the US–Soviet trade agreement. And it was probably on this line of analysis that the Soviet leadership chose to tighten internal security measures within the Soviet Union and the Eastern bloc in flagrant violation of the Helsinki accords. For fear of stirring up East European nationalism and encouraging the so-called 'revisionist' trends of Titoism, the Soviet government chose to maintain absolute control. This control was maintained greatly at the expense of détente. It was apparently decided that the potential problems brought by polycentrism were too high a price for détente.

The fourth and final factor contributing to the decline of

détente was its 'overselling', which was augmented by the fall of President Nixon. Just as the 'leadership factor' contributed to the rise of détente, it played a part in the gradual decline of détente. The issue goes far beyond the question of Ford's political credentials or competency. The fact that Ford was not a hardliner, lacked finesse in foreign policy and took office without a popular mandate did not help the cause of détente. However, the stage had been set for the decline of détente before Ford took office. Among the other factors working against détente, US–Soviet relations indirectly suffered as a result of Nixon's attempts to survive Watergate. In this way, the United States contributed foremost to the collapse of détente during this period.

From the start, Nixon had been careful not to 'over-personalise' détente in the hope of basing it solely on substantive achievements. While he welcomed personal credit for the achievements, he wished to see détente based on a lasting foundation that would enable him to pass on the new relationship to his successor after two terms in office. Unfortunately, when the prospect of finishing a second term became threatened by impeachment, Nixon clung to his former successes in a desperate attempt to retain office. At a time when US–Soviet détente was beginning to face difficulties, Nixon was announcing its continuing success and 'irreversible qualities'. As a result, throughout the latter half of 1973 and into 1974, détente was oversold to the American people.[44] This overselling inflated popular expectations and set the stage for widespread disillusionment.

The responsibility for the 'overselling' of détente does not rest exclusively with Nixon, however, nor does it rest with Kissinger, who has often been criticised for over-personalising and over-politicising détente. The process of 'overselling' détente has its roots in the nature of American foreign policy making. Due to the widespread democratisation of foreign policy making in the United States, new policies have to be 'sold' to the people. Due to the nature of political plurality, whether in Congress or across the country, policies often have to be oversold in order to survive the bartering of political life. When faced with the prospect of 'selling' a complicated policy to millions of people, there is a natural tendency, if not necessity, to oversimplify. Because the American people do not have the time, interest or ability to digest the immense complexities of international problems, but on the other hand share the responsibility for deciding the American response to them, complicated policies are often summed up in oversimplistic rhetorical absurdities. Television journalism, with its allotted one minute time spots for complex issues, can reinforce this problem.

Such was the case with détente. After two decades of pursuing a foreign policy based on the American consensus of anticommunism, Nixon and Kissinger were faced with the challenge of persuading the American people of the benefits of the 'new era of negotiation' with the Soviet Union. Despite Nixon's attempts to transcend atmospherics, the nature and magnitude of the change in directions could not be underplayed. Support for SALT I and the trade bill depended upon American acceptance of the new relationship with the Soviet Union.

The American people were generally forthcoming in their acceptance of the new détente relationship. However, because there are dominant tendencies in most societies to see things in black and white, it was difficult to portray the 'grey areas' of détente. Accordingly, people began to expect too much from détente, and the administration's tendency to present it as the only rational alternative to nuclear war reinforced those expectations. When the expectations for détente failed to materialise, the natural reaction was one of disillusionment and fear.

THE LEGACY OF THE MOSCOW DÉTENTE

Despite the many disappointments of the Moscow détente, it left a legacy that went far beyond the collective achievements of the previous three periods. The Moscow détente not only strengthened and institutionalised the common superpower commitment to avoid nuclear war, but served to establish a precedent for superpower co-operation in the face of common challenges.

The second and equally significant legacy of the Moscow détente involves the establishment of a type of 'adversary partnership' between the superpowers. The changing political, economic and military trends of the 1970s increased the difficulties of superpower leadership and hence the potential for conflict. In an attempt to introduce a significant element of predictability and stability into this changing international environment, the superpowers established a series of political and strategic–military principles aimed at preventing developments which threatened to upset the balance of power. Some of these principles included the following: a joint acknowledgement of parity as the foundation of a stable relationship; a mutual restraint on efforts to achieve unilateral advantages at the expense of the other super-power; the prevention of incidents which might exacerbate superpower relations; the prevention of developments which might lead to superpower military confrontation at any level; and a mutual commitment to prevent the development and applica-tion of nuclear capabilities among smaller powers. Because the nature of superpower competition would not yet allow a common definition of détente and hence, the establishment of a 'code of détente', these principles have not served to eradicate superpower conflict. However, these 'principles' have been generally success-ful in moderating superpower competition in an age of change. This legacy will most certainly face greater tests as the dynamic forces creating uncertainty in the contemporary international environment continue to exert their influence.

7 Conclusion: The Nature of Détente

The preceding discussion of the meaning, setting and historical experience of superpower détente has provided a framework through which to assess the nature of détente. In this concluding chapter, we will summarise the meaning and experience of détente. Second, we will identify those common elements which have worked for and against détente. Finally, we will discuss the logic of détente – whether it is cyclical or progressive in character.

THE MEANING AND EXPERIENCE OF DÉTENTE

First, we have argued that détente should be regarded as a process – not a condition, policy or historical period. Furthermore we have seen that détente involves an easing of tension, but not simply in any relationship; rather, détente has been defined as the *process of easing tension between states whose interests are so radically divergent that reconciliation is inherently limited*. In other words, détente presupposes a relationship governed by basic underlying factors which produce conflicting interests and perceptions. The relationship between the United States and the Soviet Union in the post-1945 era is one such relationship. Détente is the easing of tension within this context.

Throughout the last three decades in US–Soviet relations, such an easing of tension has occurred four times: in 1955, the 'spirit of Geneva'; in 1959, the 'spirit of Camp David'; in 1963–4, the Post-Missile Crisis détente; and in 1972–5, the Moscow détente. During this era, détente has taken on many different forms. In the 1950s, it was based almost entirely upon atmospherics. While the 'spirit of Geneva' and the 'spirit of Camp David' re-established US–Soviet dialogue and clarified the joint desire to avoid nuclear war, nothing substantial was achieved. During the 1960s, by contrast, détente was founded on substantive accomplishments including the Test-Ban Treaty, Hotline Agreement and Non-Proliferation Treaty. Through these agreements, the architects of détente attempted to introduce an element of restraint into superpower relations. In the 1970s, détente was characterised by a comprehensive series of agreements spanning the entire sphere of US–Soviet political, strategic, economic, scientific, cultural and social relations. Not only did the superpowers attempt to define and regulate their relationship; détente was employed as a means by which to settle issues of joint concern. In addition to these varying features, a variety of diverse elements contributed to the rise and fall of détente.

COMMON ELEMENTS CONTRIBUTING TO, AND DETRACTING FROM, DÉTENTE

While the preceding chapters have accentuated factors working for and against détente that were peculiar to each period, a significant number of recurrent factors have also emerged. In fact, four common elements appear to have contributed to the 'spirit of Geneva', the 'spirit of Camp David', the Post-Missile Crisis détente and the Moscow détente.

The first and most fundamental element was the *fear of nuclear war*. It seems likely that, without this fear, détente would not have emerged. Holding in their hands the potential power to destroy each other and perhaps human civilisation, the United States and the Soviet Union were well aware of their mutual responsibility to keep the superpower contest within rational bounds. At times, the fear of failing in this responsibility outweighed their fear of each other. Therefore, détente was founded on the mutual fear of destruction. Out of this fear, and the realisation that there could be no winners in a nuclear war, emerged a consensus that some means had to be found to move towards a safer relationship. As a result, détente was pursued in an attempt to introduce an element of mutual restraint into the superpower relationship.

The second common element contributing to US–Soviet détente was the *self-perceived strength and security of each superpower vis-à-vis the other*. At no point did either side feel capable of pursuing détente from a position of weakness or inferiority. Each superpower was willing only to negotiate from a position in which it felt it was itself strong and secure. This perception of strength did not necessarily rest on the belief that superiority had been achieved, but rather required a minimum degree of confidence in national security. Neither side was prepared to go naked into the conference chamber.

When this perception of relative strength was added to the fear of nuclear war, the motivation for détente was augmented. The combined influence of these two common elements can be identified in each period of superpower détente. For instance, one of the major factors contributing to the 'spirit of Geneva' was the acquisition of the hydrogen bomb by both sides by the latter half of 1953. Despite the limited ability of both sides – especially the Soviet Union – to deliver the weapon effectively, the creation of a weapon many times more powerful than those dropped on Japan had great psychological effects on both countries. Suddenly, the United States, which had held a monopoly on these weapons a few years earlier, became vulnerable. For the first time since the beginning of the cold war, both sides were perceived as being capable of destroying each other. Despite the disparity of strategic power between the United States and the Soviet Union at this time, the acquisition of the hydrogen bomb worked as an equaliser. Furthermore, as Khrushchev and Eisenhower recorded in their respective memoirs, the consolidation of Eastern and Western security pacts in May 1955 (the addition of West Germany to NATO and the creation of the Warsaw Pact) augmented their security, thereby enabling them to negotiate at Geneva from a self-perceived position of strength. This factor was primary in each leader's decision to pursue détente at Geneva.

In a similar sense, the perceived shift and reinstatement of relative power positions in 1959 contributed to the 'spirit of Camp David'. The Soviet Union's technological successes in 1957 were perceived as having thrown the superpower relationship out of balance. Only after the United States had reasserted its power through the Eisenhower Doctrine and the placing of nuclear weapons in Europe did the pursuit of détente become feasible. Khrushchev's inability to exploit the new Soviet 'missile lead' probably contributed to this perceived equalisation process. After Khrushchev's Berlin Ultimatum had only succeeded in pushing the world to the brink of war, both sides sought a safer means by which to settle their differences.

At no time was the threat of war more overwhelming than during the Cuban Missile Crisis. Having gone to the brink, the superpowers were more aware than ever of the need to make their contest safer. As a result, the Post-Missile Crisis détente was marked by progress in methods of crisis control. The one notable exception to the rule of negotiating from strength lies with Khrushchev's willingness to pursue détente in the wake of the Soviet failure in Cuba. On one hand, this can be explained by the fact that the events in Cuba dramatically demonstrated the need for some sort of superpower accommodation. On the other hand, Khrushchev maintained greater control within the centralised Soviet power structure than his Western counterparts and hence had a greater degree of flexibility. Given a similar failure, it seems likely that an American leader would have been forced to call for renewed vigilance. Nonetheless, Khrushchev's flexibility in this area was eventually shown to have its limits. His willingness to pursue détente from a position of weakness was a primary factor in his downfall. With the increasing strategic strength of the United States and the growing schism between the Soviet Union and the Peoples' Republic of China, the new Soviet leadership felt it necessary to diminish the role of détente and call for renewed vigilance.

Finally, the Moscow détente was largely made possible by the achievement of strategic parity in the early 1970s. While the United States had been preoccupied with pouring billions of defence dollars into Vietnam, the Soviet Union had been building its strategic force. By the turn of the decade, the Soviet Union had all but closed the gap.

The third common element contributing to superpower détente was the *influence of the individual leaders involved*. While a variety of factors contributed to periods of relaxed tension, superpower détente only became possible when the present leaders had the qualifications and commitment to pursue it. In Khrushchev and Eisenhower, two leaders emerged who were willing to experiment with alternatives to the cold war. After having achieved their hardline credentials and consolidated their domestic support, both leaders willingly pursued détente. Similarly, the 'spirit of Camp David' was, to a large extent, the product of Eisenhower's and Khrushchev's efforts. They basically 'willed' détente to occur. This contributed both to its success and ultimately to its failure.

The Post-Missile Crisis détente was partly made possible by Kennedy's adept handling of the Cuban Missile Crisis. His success earned him hardline credentials seldom afforded to Democratic Presidents. From this base, he eagerly pursued détente and produced landmark achievements. Concurrently, Khrushchev lost his hardline credentials, partly as a result of the Cuban affair, and was soon removed from office.

Nixon and Brezhnev provide the best examples of two hard-liners whose commitment to détente produced remarkable results. The success of the Moscow détente was greatly credited to the influence of these two leaders, assisted by their skilled foreign secretaries.

The fourth common element contributing to détente was the *convergence of superpower special interests*. This convergence occurred in two ways. First, from mutual respect for spheres of influence in the 1950s, to a mutual fear of the rise of third parties in the 1960s and 1970s, superpower strategic interests had tended to converge. In the 1950s, the outcome of events in Korea, the Middle East, Hungary and Berlin demonstrated that the superpowers had placed limits on their objectives. There was a reluctant but quite evident mutual respect for the spheres of influence and vital interests of the opposing side. The need for crisis control brought the two sides closer together. The control of allies added another factor to the condominium of superpower interests. In fact, throughout the 1960s, the unpredictable 'China factor' led the superpowers to co-operate in maintaining the status quo, at least in some areas of international politics, as evidenced by such agreements as the Test-Ban Treaty and the Non-Proliferation Treaty. As both sides increasingly perceived themselves as guardians of the international order, a community of interests emerged.

In the 1970s, the attraction of détente transcended the hope of making relations safer. The community of superpower interests began to suggest the possibility of settling various outstanding issues. Nonetheless, if dynamic forces augmented this community of interests, they also presented new opportunities for unilateral gains. This gave rise to the apt description of US–Soviet relations as an 'adversary partnership'.

The other way in which converging special interests complemented détente was through the realisation of the mutual advantages to be gained by an easing of tension. In most periods, the possibilities of controlling a costly arms race provided a strong economic incentive for détente. The option of transferring more resources to the consumer sector was politically attractive. Furthermore, the opportunities for expanded trade, cultural, scientific and social relations promised benefits for both sides. Superpower co-operation on these levels was seen also as a way of promoting peaceful relations. For instance, it was on the occasion of an exchange of national exhibitions that Eisenhower extended his invitation to Khrushchev. Through similar contacts, American and Soviet astronauts ventured jointly into space. In short, the convergence of superpower special interests contributed to détente in several ways.

Alongside the common elements that contributed to superpower détente, we may also recognise certain common elements that contributed to its decline in each period. The first of the latter elements was perhaps the *changing perception of the relationship between detente and the national interest*. While the superpowers intially perceived the pursuit of détente as being within the national interest, certain factors arose to alter that perception. These factors represented the influence of what we have called the limits of détente.

In some cases, the binding force that had led the superpowers to seek accommodation began to lose its hold as détente progressed. For instance, during the 1950s and, to some extent, throughout every period of easing tension, the growing ambiguity of the nuclear threat slowly eroded the psychological foundations of détente – especially in the West. As peaceful relations proceeded and détente reduced the expectation of war, the pursuit of détente began to lose urgency. In some cases, as the people became less fearful and more passive, they were less willing to make the necessary sacrifices to maintain an 'adequate' deterrent. This presented a dilemma for Western political leaders.

Furthermore, it seems likely that the longer peace was maintained, the less credible the nuclear threat became, thereby undermining the moratorium on opportunism. There was an increasing temptation to test the boundaries of the nuclear relationship, in order to enhance national security through the pursuit of unilateral advantages. As the basis for mutual restraint declined, opportunism increased and tension began to rise.

In a number of other ways, détente started to militate against various national interests leading the participants to interpret the price of détente as being too high. For instance, the Suez and Hungarian Crises demonstrated the lack of allied unity in both NATO and the Warsaw Pact. This disunity can be partly credited to the influence of the 'spirit of Geneva'. In the West, détente helped to erode the vigilance upon which allied unity and security had been based. As the Soviet threat appeared to decline, so did the psychological underpinnings of the alliance. In the East, détente had eroded Soviet control over the Eastern satellites. Khrushchev's policies of liberalisation and the new cracks in the iron curtain had provided new opportunities for the forces of Eastern European nationalism. When these forces began to threaten the Soviet security system, the price of détente was interpreted as being too high.

On both sides, the subordination of conflicting issues and lessening of ideological warfare were also eventually perceived as militating against the national interest. Even when only one side perceived this, as with the Soviet Union during the Post-Missile Crisis détente or the United States during the Moscow détente, the process of détente suffered. As previously stated, ideological warfare had served to unify both citizens and allies and convince them to make the necessary sacrifices to maintain national security. Furthermore, ideological warfare had provided a peaceful means of superpower competition. As the application of ideological warfare declined, the function that it had served went unfulfilled.

While the subordination of conflicting issues had initially contributed to an easing of tension, those issues often re-emerged with potency as détente began to lose favour. This was especially true in the earlier periods, when 'atmospherics' tended to obscure the lack of progress in superpower relations.

Similarly, in later periods, détente was eventually perceived as being contrary to national interests. During the Post-Missile Crisis détente, Khrushchev was dismissed for pursuing policies seen as working against the best interests of the Soviet state. Likewise, during the Moscow détente, the United States Congress registered its price for détente in such forms as the Jackson Amendment. The Soviet rejection of the amended trade agreement confirmed that the price of détente (at least in the areas of trade, free access and human rights) was too high. A number of other unanticipated obstacles led observers to question the relationship between détente and the national interest.

The second common element contributing to the decline of détente again involved the *influence of individual leaders*. The success or failure of détente was often bound up with the political fortunes of its champions. For instance, internal pressure was influential in Khrushchev's sudden departure from the 'spirit of Camp David'. Less than five years later, his fall facilitated the stagnation of the Post-Missile Crisis détente. A decade earlier, both Khrushchev and Eisenhower had to dissociate themselves from the Geneva détente after the Suez and Hungarian Crises. In the mid-1970s, Nixon's fall from power was closely associated with the decline of the Moscow détente.

Furthermore, for political reasons, détente was sold and oversold on the promise that it was the only rational alternative to nuclear war. Therefore, the pursuit of détente was based on the highest moral claims and was couched in the language of peace. This was not only misleading; it raised unrealistic expectations for peace and led to disillusionment. Because both sides viewed and perceived détente in terms of their own national interest, the motivations for unilateral advantages became increasingly evident. The language of peace gave way to moral indignation. The United States criticised the Soviet Union for using détente as a cover, while pursuing its long range plans for world domination. Likewise, the Soviet Union criticised the United States for using détente as a means to infiltrate, ideologically pollute or otherwise interfere in the internal affairs of socialist states. Because détente was wrapped in the language of peace, the application of détente for reasons of unilateral advantage was viewed as premeditated deception. The constraints of détente contributed to the fear that time was working in favour of the adversary. This suspicion produced more fear and contributed to the rapid decline of détente.

The final element contributing to the decline of détente was the *failure of the superpowers to reach a common code of détente*. Because détente was couched in a moralistic, political language, it did not readily provide a prescription for superpower behaviour. The word 'spirit' was accurately applied to the first two periods of détente because no substantive agreements had been reached to suggest any real change. In the latter periods, substantive achievements did take place. Even the 'Basic Principles' set forth in the Moscow détente, however, allowed for a wide interpretation of the code of détente, as the coming years were to demonstrate. As various events and policies began to militate against the national interest, each side attacked the other for violating its nebulous code. These attacks produced anger, suspicion and fear, thereby causing a reaction against détente.

Ironically, in this failure to reach a common code of détente lay both the strength of détente and its weakness. Given the basic differences on both sides, as well as the power realities dictating their relationship, it may have been impossible for the superpowers to agree on a precise 'common code of détente'. The agreements surrounding détente were generally open to widely different interpretations, because both sides purposely left themselves free to manoeuvre in case détente started to work against the national interest.

THE LOGIC OF DÉTENTE

We finally come to the question of whether détente is cyclical or progressive in nature. Given the experience of détente in US–Soviet relations so far, does the evidence suggest that each détente led to the resumption of the *status quo ante* or can we discern an overall trend toward improved relations?

On the surface, there is much evidence that suggests détente approximates a cyclical process. The preceding review of US–Soviet relations has shown how successive détentes have collapsed and how, at times, what has been done eventually has been undone. Furthermore, despite the US–Soviet experience, there is no compelling logic guaranteeing that any legacy of détente will be permanent or that future periods of détente will prove more enduring than previous ones. These factors are supported by the observation that détente has a unique, circular logic behind it. In other words, the progress and success of détente tends to undermine the premise on which it rests. As the superpower relationship becomes safer, the principal stimulus for détente – the mutual fear of destruction – declines. For instance, the fear of nuclear war set détente in motion and fuelled its progress. By reducing tension, détente was seen as the means of reducing the risk of nuclear war. As tension eased, so did the chances of war – but only up to a point. When the reduction in tension and the expectation of war fell below a certain point, it seems likely that the superpowers became less fearful of war and more willing to take risks in the pursuit and protection of their national interests. In short, the fear that initiated and made possible the progress of détente was eventually negated by the very success of that process.

In a number of similar ways, détente automatically undermines itself when the easing of tension proceeds beyond certain limits. Détente slowly undermines allied cohesiveness by diminishing the sense of a common threat upon which allied unity is based. As discord grows the price of détente becomes too high. Likewise, the subordination of disputes or issues causing conflict, and the decline in application of ideological warfare serve both to encourage détente and eventually to undermine it. It is only a matter of time before important issues re-emerge and the function once played by ideological warfare goes unfulfilled and threatens security. In the mid-1950s, liberalisation in the foreign and domestic policies of the superpowers initially contributed to détente, but eventually detracted from it. The problems of the Soviet Union in Eastern Europe are most instructive on this point. From the Khrushchev policies of 1956 to the Helsinki agreements of 1975, détente has been said to involve the increasing flow of information and people between East and West. However, as cracks in the Iron Curtain began to appear, the forces of dissidence and East European nationalism began to threaten Soviet security. Brezhnev's attempt to escape this dilemma by pursuing détente on one hand and calling for an intensification of the ideological struggle on the other, eventually contributed to the American rejection of détente.

Whatever the legacy left by détente, each period has ended as a result of one or both sides perceiving the price of détente as being too high. Policies of détente, whether they arise from concern about peace, the pursuit of unilateral advantages or other considerations, grow out of the belief that they serve the national interest. The endless debate about whether détente is 'good' or 'bad' is fundamentally about the relationship between détente and the national interest. As a phenomenon of international relations, détente is neither good or bad. As a policy option, it can be either desirable or undesirable, depending upon whether it serves the objectives concerned or not. When factors once seen as working in favour of the national interest eventually are perceived as being contrary to it, suitable action is taken.

This opposite reaction to an identical stimulus is caused by the inherent limitations of détente. Those fundamental realities contributing to tension in the US–Soviet relationship appear to have an effect comparable with that of gravity on a pendulum. The needle swings freely until it passes the centre point. As it swings past the centre point, it is only a matter of time before the needle loses momentum, stalls and reverses its swing.

For this reason, it seems safe to assume that given the underlying conditions affecting the US–Soviet relationship, to which reference was made in Chapter 1, a certain amount of tension is not only inevitable, but fulfils a certain function in this relationship. Because peace and stability are based, at least partly, on deterrence, a certain degree of vigilance must be maintained on both sides. As a psychological phenomenon, the success of deterrence is closely tied to the level of tension maintained. If, at any time, a potential aggressor considers the risk of war to be acceptable, peace and stability become gravely threatened. In short, tension plays a vital role in US–Soviet relations. This role is not unlike the role tension plays in maintaining stability on a tight-rope. If tension is too great, the tight-rope snaps. If there is insufficient tension, the rope becomes unstable and the walker is likely to fall to his doom. In this way, the superpowers have been forced to find the proper balance in a relationship constantly threatened by destabilising factors. As Hedley Bull has written:

> It is doubtful whether the stability of the Soviet-American strategic balance ever has been, or ever could be, absolute: It is maintained only by constant attention to standards of warning, invulnerability, penetration capacity, accuracy, political determination etc. which, if it were not forthcoming, would place the balance in jeopardy.[1]

Given this seemingly essential relationship between tension and stability in the US–Soviet relationship, the logic of détente cannot be viewed as being progressive in a linear sense. The episodic nature of US–Soviet détente suggests that there has not been a steady or absolute decline in tension. In fact, as has been shown, such a decline would violate the very premise upon which détente rests.

The widespread expectation of linear progress seems to have

grown out of the symbols and rhetoric surrounding détente. For example, the symbols of détente – the establishment of greater co-operation, the rise of negotiation in the place of confrontation, the declining expectation of war, among others, contributed to the optimistic view that the superpowers were on the verge of a new relationship in which co-operation would grow and competition decline. Furthermore, the rhetoric surrounding détente often portrayed it as the only rational alternative to nuclear war. Khrushchev claimed, 'There are only two ways: either peaceful coexistence or the most destructive war in history. There is no third way.'[2] Nixon claimed, 'We must either live together, or we will all die together.'[3] Similar appeals were issued by other leaders as well as by apologists for détente. This approach, however, was laced with fallacies. As Theodore Draper observed:

> The promoters of détente sought to save it by reducing it to a hard core avoidance nuclear warfare. They were in fact exposing its essential hollowness. They were giving it the self-same function that the cold war of unblessed memory used to have – as an alternative to hot war. They were giving détente undeserved credit for an impasse that had been brought about by the mutual destructiveness of nuclear warfare. The linkage of détente with nuclear war betrayed a misunderstanding of both.[4]

In short, the view that détente was progressive in a linear sense or that the relationship was in some state of evolution was augmented by its portrayal as the only alternative to nuclear war.

In reality, détente has not served to eradicate those factors causing tension in the superpower relationship. In many ways, only the perceptions have changed. The adversary is perceived as being less threatening and more rational. The language of peace is employed, and hopes for reconciliation are fostered. However, despite the conclusion of 'exchange' agreements, the expansion of economic relations, the commitment to negotiate arms limitation treaties and the promise to practise political restraint, full reconciliation is proved to be impossible because the basic underlying factors causing tension are still limiting the relationship. While significant strides have been taken, superpower competition remains as intense as ever. Over a period of time, vital interests are tested and the adversaries are forced to compete for advantages in a contest where one side's loss is perceived as the other side's gain.

Because détente is tied so closely to changes in perception, 'atmospherics' have played a major role. While the 'spirit of Geneva' and the 'spirit of Camp David' failed to produce any substantive accomplishments, they represented a general feeling or attitude among peoples that, for some reason, tension was easing. The rhetoric and symbolism surrounding these periods augmented this feeling and the mere expectation of détente became a self-fulfilling prophecy. Even during the Moscow détente, the 'atmospherics' produced by the Nixon–Brezhnev summits contributed to the expectations for détente. Both images and substantive accomplishments characterised an easing of tension in superpower relations. In these ways, 'atmospherics' helped to produce and characterise the process of détente.

As previously stated, however, 'atmospherics' have also had a negative impact on détente; they have raised the expectations for détente far beyond its potential. Therefore, détente is often viewed not as a pragmatic arrangement to control tension, but as a prelude to a closer relationship. When this 'closer relationship' fails to materialise, disillusion results.

The unrealistic expectations surrounding détente are perpetuated by the politics of promoting it internally. For instance, in the 1950s, after years of portraying the adversary as a monolith of unredeemed evil, the Soviet and American governments attempted to convince their citizens that a new relationship was possible. While this challenge was much less difficult for the Soviet Union, Khrushchev still found it necessary to wage a 'peace campaign' through the party press in order to gain support. In the United States, where public opinion exercises far greater influence over policy decisions, Eisenhower found it necessary to justify his détente policy on the grounds that the Soviet leaders had changed. Both sides claimed that given the proper honest negotiation and mediation, major problems could be solved. This optimism raised expectations beyond practical limits. When these expectations were disappointed, disillusion was the result. To some extent, this scenario was repeated throughout all four periods of superpower détente.

In short, the overselling of détente has served further to promote a linear view of the process. To the detriment of détente, it has been portrayed and/or viewed as being the fundamental step on the road to the 'millenium' in superpower relations.

Our brief review of the history of US–Soviet détente then clearly suggests that Soviet–American relations have not followed a linear pattern of progress. It is also true, however, that the evidence does not support the idea of a merely cyclical process, in which successive attempts to achieve détente lead inexorably to the *status quo ante*. Each attempt at détente has in fact left a legacy; the collapse of each attempt has led not to the *status quo ante*, but rather to a new situation, on which later attempts to promote détente have sometimes been able to build. For instance, since the inception of the 'spirit of Geneva', the increasingly 'explicit' superpower commitment to avoid nuclear war has reinforced a mutual perception of rational decision making. Furthermore, the development of various forms of crisis management appear to have reduced the danger of miscalculation.

The substantive accomplishments of détente in the 1960s and 1970s have also proved to be enduring. Both powers have continually supported the Test-Ban Treaty and the Non-Proliferation Treaty, thereby placing certain limits on the unpredictable potentialities of nuclear power. Likewise, with all of its shortcomings, SALT I contributed an additional degree of restraint to the arms race as well as a format by which to pursue further negotiations. Finally, while trade relations have been highly susceptible to changes in the political environment, mutually advantageous cultural, social and scientific contacts have increased the channels of communication between the two countries. Since the 1950s, significant agreements have been reached, US–Soviet dialogue has been re-established, and the process of negotiation has been firmly entrenched as the means to deal with conflicting issues.

In short, the legacy of détente has been cumulative in US–Soviet relations. While this legacy could in principle disappear, in whole or in part, such an occurrence seems highly unlikely. The progress achieved in US–Soviet relations invalidates the purely cyclical view of détente. Therefore, while the logic of détente is neither cyclical nor progressive in a linear sense, it appears to be, nonetheless, progressive in the sense of being cumulative. In fact, the process most closely approximates to the course of a curtain being pulled along a curtain rod. At times the curtain runs freely while at other times it gets stuck and must be temporarily withdrawn in order to make further progress. Likewise, its span is limited and can only proceed within the confines of the distance allowed.

In conclusion, détente has contributed to a type of maturation process between the superpowers and holds the same potential in the decades to come. Despite the many dangers inherent in the superpower conflict today, the postwar world has survived almost four decades without a major nuclear or conventional conflict. It has been the legacy of détente to inject an element of sanity and co-operation into a seemingly insane and bitterly competitive environment. It has shown that despite their competition, the superpowers have been able to co-operate to advance common interests in the areas of arms control, crisis management, international peacekeeping and co-operation, and economic, social, cultural, educational and scientific exchange. The evidence in this study, however, suggests that détente, at least in the US–Soviet relationship, has proved to be a limited process with limited potential. Certain basic factors making for conflict between the superpowers have continuously asserted themselves to impose limits on the extent to which any relaxation of tension can change the relationship. A clear recognition of these limits as well as the potentialities of détente can only serve to augment its utility in the practice and advancement of international relations.

Epilogue: Update, 1977–84

Since the decline of the Moscow détente nearly a decade ago, little has occurred which would suggest the coming of a new era of superpower détente. Indeed, of late, the US–Soviet relationship has been characterised by a higher level of tension than at any time since the Cold War. Due to a lack of historical perspective, the history of this stage has yet to be written. Nonetheless, the last eight years provide an interesting period in which to consider the conclusions of this study.

In terms of superpower behaviour, two salient characteristics emerged. First, the United States attempted, with varying degree of success, to reassert itself ideologically, politically, economically and strategically. President Jimmy Carter initiated this trend with the launching of his human rights campaign on Inauguration Day, 20 January 1977. In direct contrast to the previous administration, Carter openly communicated with Soviet dissidents and championed their cause. He criticised the Soviet government for its poor record on human rights and flagrant disregard for the Helsinki Accords. In turn, the Soviet leaders charged Carter with interfering in their internal affairs and responded with such bitterness that both European and American observers questioned whether or not Carter's crusade was proceeding at the expense of détente. His 'Wilsonian rhetoric' led some to fear that, as in the Latin proverb *Fiat justitia pereat mundus*, he was 'doing good but destroying the world in the process'. Others were troubled by his alienation of traditional allies whose human rights records did not measure up to American standards. In response, Carter and Secretary of State Vance made it clear that the American policy was to be pursued based on the demands of national and international security. Soon the campaign gained popularity among Europeans who had long championed human rights and among Americans who, from conservatives (who enjoyed needling the Soviet Union) to liberals alike (who advocated the primacy of moral considerations in American

203

foreign policy making), saw the policy as evidence of America on the move again.

Indeed, in retrospect, Carter's human rights policy seemed to function most effectively as a means to rebuild an American moral consensus on foreign policy and to reassert American ideological leadership around the world. He was simply rebuilding what Watergate, Vietnam and détente, with its eventual failure, had served to destroy. Instead of threatening what was an already ailing relationship, Carter's policy aimed to make détente more acceptable to Americans by making it seem more equitable.

There was little doubt about President Carter's commitment to superpower co-operation. He agreed to respect the SALT I agreement after its expiration and supported the signing of an agreement on the Exploration and Use of Outer Space. He vigorously pursued a SALT II agreement and unilaterally cancelled or deferred the development of the B-1 bomber and the neutron bomb. Upon officially recognising the Peoples Republic of China in January 1979, Carter made a point to assure the Soviet leaders that the move was not directed at them. The Carter–Brezhnev meeting in Vienna in June 1979 culminated in the signing of SALT II and symbolised the continuing commitment on the part of both leaders to arms control negotiations. Despite such achievements as the Camp David agreements, however, Carter's effectiveness was hampered by the fact that his handling of foreign policy often seemed to be inconsistent, indecisive and confused. This may have indirectly encouraged a series of crises in late 1979. The cycle began with the alleged discovery of a Soviet combat brigade in Cuba. Carter protested and increased American military presence in the Caribbean but he was able to do little else. When Iranian 'students' took over the American embassy in Tehran in November and seized American hostages, his options were even more limited. America's international campaign for political and economic sanctions against Iran failed to gain freedom for the hostages as did a tragically bungled rescue attempt several months later. When the Soviet Union invaded Afghanistan in late December, the Administration could only muster support for a grain embargo and a partial boycott of the 1980 Olympics. With each successive event, the image of American impotence grew. Carter's astonishing admission that the Soviet action in Afghanistan had caused 'a dramatic change in my opinion of what the Soviet Union's ultimate goals are . . .' lent credence to the image of his naïveté. Accordingly, he was forced to request deferment of Senate consideration for SALT II in January 1980. The events of 1979 had led to a decline in his credibility and, ultimately, contributed to the election of Ronald Reagan.

Under the Reagan Administration, the United States reasserted itself in other areas, most notably in the military and strategic spheres. Backed by a strong electoral mandate, Reagan sought to 'get tough with the Soviets' by rebuilding the American arsenal. Claiming that the Soviet arms buildup during the 1970s had left the United States behind in both conventional and strategic arms, Reagan sharply increased the defence budget, and pushed for the deployment of the MX missile and a number of other military programmes. He also pushed unfailingly for the first track of the NATO 'two-track' decision, taken in December 1979, to modernise the allied European missile system. The other track, a commitment to negotiate a reduction in intermediate range nuclear forces (INF), received a lower priority as did the new START negotiations.

Second, Reagan was assertive in countering what he perceived to be Soviet-backed terrorism in Central America, the Middle East and elsewhere around the world. In the face of some domestic opposition, he sought to increase American military assistance to the centre-right government of El Salvador and the rebel 'contras' in Nicaragua. Neighbouring countries also were the recipients of American aid, partly in response to the allged threat from Cuban and Soviet arms. The invasion of Grenada in October 1983 represented the most striking example of Reagan's willingness to assert American military force in response to the growth of Soviet influence near American borders.

In the Middle East, Reagan sought to stabilise a pro-Western regime in Lebanon with the aid of, not only international peace-keeping forces but, American Marines. While his policies proved to be shortsighted if not counterproductive (not unlike Eisenhower's military actions in the Middle East in the late 1950s), they signified a belief in the efficacy of American military intervention to advance and protect American interests.

Revelations of a possible Soviet–Bulgarian connection behind the attempted assassination of Pope John Paul II and the Soviet destruction of an unarmed South Korean civilian jet soon after only seemed to confirm Reagan's charges that Soviet-backed terrorism and barbarism represented an evil force in the world.

Third, while Reagan fulfilled a campaign promise by removing Carter's grain embargo against the Soviet Union, he willingly applied American economic power by tightening export controls on high-technology and other items seen as relevant to the maintenance of Western security. The most notable example involved the Reagan Administration's use of economic sanctions to stop construction of the Soviet–West European Natural Gas Pipeline. While this caused tremendous tension within the alliance and was condemned by West European leaders throughout 1982, Reagan stubbornly pushed the issue to the brink. Another example came in response to the imposition of martial law in Poland in December 1981. The Reagan Administration levied a series of economic sanctions against the Polish Communist regime to protest its violation of human rights.

Finally, Reagan stepped up the rhetorical debate. He spoke out on the 'dark purposes' of 'the evil empire' while, at the same time, countering Soviet peace proposals with proposals of his own. Reagan's plans for peace were no doubt partly inspired by the growing concern, domestically and throughout the alliance, that the superpowers were headed on a collision course. Despite this, the anti-nuclear demonstrations throughout the United States and Europe were not influential enough to dissuade Reagan and other key Western leaders from halting the scheduled deployment of American missiles in Europe in December 1983. In protest, the Soviet government walked out of the MBFR talks, the INF talks and the START talks leaving the superpowers, for the first time in fourteen years, without a forum for arms control negotiations.

The second salient characteristic in superpower behaviour during this eight-year period was the attempt by the Soviet Union to maintain the advantages it had achieved and to demand respect for its superpower status from the United States. Nowhere was this more evident than in the strategic–military sphere. After having pursued a massive defence build-up throughout the 1970s, the Soviet Union sought to convince the United States that rough parity had been achieved and needed to be maintained. As justification for the disparity in the numbers of various conventional and strategic weapons, the Soviet government pointed to encirclement of unfriendly powers (from Norway through Central Europe, Greece, Turkey, Iran, Pakistan, China, South Korea and Japan). SALT II was pursued vigorously and a significant breakthrough came in the MBFR talks in June 1978 when the Soviet Union accepted the principle of equal numbers of troops (though complications arose over verification). Brezhnev launched an effective propaganda campaign in Europe against American development of the neutron bomb which proved to be a harbinger of the Soviet response to NATO's plans for modernisation of missiles in Europe. Throughout this period, as Brezhnev attempted to dissuade the West from engaging in a new arms build-up, the force of Soviet arms was being felt indirectly in the Horn of Africa, Yemen, Cambodia, Central America, the Middle East and directly in Afghanistan. Despite various peace proposals which included the non-first-use of nuclear weapons, despite countless propaganda ploys aimed at exploiting the anti-nuclear movement in Europe and the nuclear freeze movement in the United States and, despite a number of threats including a promise to walkout of arms control talks upon the deployment of new missiles, centre-right governments were given strong mandates in the USA, Britain and West Germany. During his brief tenure in office following Brezhnev's death, Andropov was no more successful in containing this Western response.

In December 1979, the Soviet government attempted to maintain another recent gain by replacing and bolstering a pro-Soviet regime in neighbouring Afghanistan. This direct military intervention has continued to take place at great cost, exacerbated by the effective resistance of the Western-backed Afghan rebels. The Soviet leaders also attempted to halt the deteriorisation of their influence in Poland. When the Solidarity movement challenged communist control, the government imposed martial law – certainly with the support and probably on the advice of the Soviet Union. Despite Western outcries and sanctions, the Soviet and Polish governments stood firm in their actions.

The right to act as a superpower commensurate with its actual conventional and strategic power, was a dominant theme underlying Soviet actions and rhetoric. The application of military power in various areas of interest was consistent with this view. Soviet defensiveness about Carter's human rights allegations, the breakdown of the Belgrade talks in October 1977, and the subsequent crackdown on dissidents in the face of Western criticism was, in part, a reaction to this priority. American economic 'discrimination' against the Soviet Union, whether it be by way of grain, strategic goods or parts for the natural gas pipeline, continued to be a significant source of tension.

The preceding overview of superpower behaviour during the previous eight years suggests why a new period of détente has not emerged in the US–Soviet relationship. First, the American perception of its strength and security *vis-à-vis* the Soviet Union has continued to inhibit the achievement of arms control agreements and other forms of accommodation. Beginning in the latter half of Carter's term and continuing throughout Reagan's Presidency, the United States and its allies have sought to redress the perceived imbalance through a series of military programmes. With the Soviet leaders trying various forms of persuasion to prevent such an outcome, many Soviet attempts at East–West accommodation has been viewed as a ploy to weaken Western unity and determination. Unlike the mid-1970s, when American foreign intervention was inhibited by the tragic experience of Vietnam, the American government has become more outwardly assertive in defence of its interests.

In short, American policy has become less accommodating and more confrontational in an effort to regain and reassert its strength *vis-à-vis* the Soviet Union. Whether or not this level of security can be achieved without significantly upsetting the Soviet perception of its strength and security *vis-à-vis* the United States will in part determine future opportunities for détente.

Second, the leadership factor has not been conducive to the re-emergence of détente. While Carter may have had the desire to pursue détente with Brezhnev, it is questionable as to whether or not he had the credentials to do so. Certainly after the crises of 1979 when he was forced to withdraw the SALT II Treaty from Senate consideration, there was no doubt. While Reagan may possess the hardline credential to pursue détente, he has shown neither the desire nor the ability to do so. Reagan does not view détente as being in the American interest. As Secretary of State Shultz told the Senate Foreign Relations Committee on 16 June 1983: 'Our policy, unlike some versions of détente, assumes that the Soviet Union is more likely to be deterred by our actions . . . than by a delicate web of interdependence.' Furthermore, Reagan's miscalculations in the Middle East and elsewhere suggest an inability to handle the complexities involved in the pursuit of détente.

While Brezhnev seemed always prepared to pursue détente, he

was unwilling to acknowledge Western concerns over the Soviet military build-up. Andropov had little time to experiment with new ventures in foreign policy and whether Chernenko and the future generation of Soviet leaders will have anything new to offer depends upon the outcome of the various power struggles within the Kremlin and the Politboro's view of détente as it relates to the Soviet national interest.

Neither side has viewed détente as being necessarily consistent with the national interest. The events of the last eight years have suggested that, in many incidences, the price of détente has been too high or else its pursuit has been viewed as being detrimental to national security. The Allied decision to proceed with the deployment of modernised missiles throughout Europe in the face of the Soviet arms build-up and the Soviet decision to walk out of the arms control negotiations were decisive and symbolic actions.

Beyond the many special interests shared by the superpowers, such as controlling the high costs of a spiralling arms race, one factor working for détente rises above the rest; the fear of nuclear war. Not since the early 1960s has public concern about nuclear conflict or the arms race been greater. The threatening rhetoric surrounding US–Soviet relations has served to increase concern about the nuclear threat and our common destiny. Whether or not this fear will reach the point where it alters the setting for détente depends upon the influence of those factors, at present, militating against it. What is clear is that as we approach the year 2000 the world, and the demands for peace, justice and order within it, will continue to change rapidly and inject a whole range of new, unforeseen factors. Based on our historical experience, it is not unreasonable to assume that détente will be, at a given place and time, an essential element in the chemistry of some future superpower relationship.

Notes

CHAPTER 1 THE MEANING OF DÉTENTE

1. Arthur M. Schlesinger, Jr., 'Détente: an American Perspective', in *Détente in Historical Perspective*, edited by G. Schwab and H. Friedlander (NY: Ciro Press, 1975) p. 125. From Hamlet, Act III, Scene 2.
2. Gustav Pollak Lecture at Harvard, 14 April 1976; reprinted in James Schlesinger, 'The Evolution of American Policy Towards the Soviet Union', *International Security*, Summer 1976, vol. 1, no. 1, pp. 46–7.
3. Theodore Draper, 'Appeasement and Détente', *Commentary*, Feb. 1976, vol. 61, no. 8, p. 32.
4. Coral Bell, in her book, *The Diplomacy of Détente* (London: Martin Robertson, 1977), has written an extensive analysis of the triangular relationship but points out that, as of yet, no third side to the triangle – the détente between China and the USSR – exists, p. 5.
5. Seyom Brown, 'A Cooling-Off Period for U.S.–Soviet Relations', *Foreign Policy*, Fall 1977, no. 28, p. 12. See also I. Aleksandrov, 'Peking: a Course Aimed at Disrupting International Détente Under Cover of Anti-Sovietism', *Pravda*, 14 May 1977 – translated in *Current Digest of Soviet Press*. Hereafter, only the Soviet publication will be named.
6. Vladimir Petrov, *U.S.—Soviet Détente: Past and Future* (Washington D.C.: American Enterprise Institute for Public Policy Research, 1975) p. 2.
7. N. Kapcheko, 'Socialist Foreign Policy and the Reconstruction of International Relations', *International Affairs* (Moscow), no. 4, Apr. 1975, p. 8.
8. L. Brezhnev, *Report of the Twenty-Fifth Congress of the Communist Party of the Soviet Union*, 24 Feb. 1976.
9. Marshall Shulman, 'Toward a Western Philosophy of Coexistence', *Foreign Affairs*, vol. 52, Oct. 1973, p. 36; and Walter Laqueur, 'Détente: Western and Soviet Interpretations', *Survey*, vol. 19, Summer 1973, p. 74.
10. See Marshal Sergei Biryuzov (Soviet Chief of Staff), *Izvestia*, 11 Dec. 1963. Quoted from Raymond Garthoff, 'Mutual Deterrence, Parity and Strategic Arms Limitation in Soviet Policy', in Derek Leebaert, *Soviet Military Thinking* (London: Allen & Unwin, 1981) pp. 92–4.
11. *Pravda*, 16 Oct. 1974.
12. Fritz Emarth, 'Contrasts in American and Soviet Strategic Thought', in Leebaert, *Soviet Military Thinking*, p. 58.
13. This American inclination is described in George Kennan, *American Diplomacy 1900–1950* (London: Secker & Warburg, 1952) pp. 95–6.
14. Daniel Yergin, *Shattered Peace* (London: Andre Deutsch, 1978) p. 9.
15. Henry Kissinger, *White House Years* (Boston: Little, Brown & Co., 1979) p. 915.

16. Yergin, *Shattered Peace*, pp. 10–12.
17. Douglas Scrivner, 'The Conference on Security and Cooperation in Europe: Implications for Soviet-American Détente', *Denver Journal of International Law and Policy*, Spring 1976, vol. 6, no. 1, pp. 140–50.
18. Robert McGeehan, 'American Policies and the U.S.–Soviet Relationship', *World Today*, Sept. 1978, vol. 34, no. 9, p. 349.
19. James Schlesinger in *Defending America* (N.Y.: Basic Books Inc. Publishers, 1977) p. xii.
20. Paul Seabury, 'Beyond Détente', in *Defending America*, p. 233.
21. Draper, 'Appeasement and Détente', *Commentary*, p. 34.
22. John Herz, 'Détente and Appeasement from a Political Scientist's Vantage Point', in *Détente in Historical Perspective*, p. 26.
23. Edward Kennedy, 'Beyond Détente', *Foreign Policy*, Fall 1974, no. 16, p. 3.
24. Schlesinger, 'The Evolution of American Policy Towards the Soviet Union', *International Security*, pp. 46–7.
25. Harold Nicolson, *Diplomacy* (London: Thornton Butterworth, 1939) p. 242.
26. Keith Eubank, 'Détente 1919–1939: a Study in Failure', in *Détente in Historical Perspective*, p. 6.
27. Bell, *The Diplomacy of Détente*, p. 5.
28. Josef Korbel, 'Détente and World Order', *Denver Journal of International Law and Policy*, Spring 1976, vol. 6, no. 1, p. 13.
29. Schlesinger, 'Détente: an American Perspective', *Détente in Historical Perspective*, p. 125.
30. Walter C. Clemens Jr., 'The Impact of Détente on Chinese and Soviet Communism', *Journal of International Affairs*, 1974, vol. 28, no. 2, p. 134.
31. Kennedy, 'Beyond Détente', *Foreign Policy*, p. 6.
32. *Détente Hearings*, pp. 301–2.
33. Hans Morgenthau, 'Détente: Reality and Illusion', *The Wall Street Journal*, 18 July 1974.
34. *Détente Hearings*, p. 239.
35. Ibid., p. 301.
36. *American–Soviet Détente, Peace and National Security*, edited by Fred Warner Neal (Santa Barbara, California: Fund for the Republic, Inc., 1976) p. 26.
37. Anatoly A. Gromyko, 'The Future of Soviet–American Diplomacy', *Annals*, July 1974, vol. 414, pp. 27–40.
38. Hedley Bull, 'The Scope for Super-Power Agreements', *Arms Control and National Security*, vol. 1, 1969, p. 2.

CHAPTER 2   THE SETTING FOR DÉTENTE

1. Alexis de Tocqueville in *Democracy in America*, 1835, tr. Henry Reeve (N.Y.: Colonial Press, 1899) vol. 1, pp. 441–2.
2. E. H. Carr, *The Bolshevik Revolution 1917–1923*, vol. III (London: Macmillan, 1953) pp. 109–13.
3. Max Beloff, *The Foreign Policy of Soviet Russia 1929–1941* vol. I (London: Oxford University Press, 1947) p. 117.
4. Beloff, *The Foreign Policy of Soviet Russia 1929–1941* vol. I, p. 117.

5. S. Brookhart, *New York Times*, 17 Nov. 1933.
6. Joseph Whelan, 'The United States and Diplomatic Recognition: The Contrasting Cases of Russia and Communist China', *The China Quarterly*, Jan.–Mar. 1961, no. 5, pp. 63–4.
7. Diane Shaver Clemens, *Yalta* (London: Oxford University Press, 1970) pp. 262–3.
8. For the Tripartite Agreement see *Foreign Relations of the United States: Diplomatic Papers: the Conferences at Malta and Yalta* (Washington D.C.: US Government Printing Office, 1955) pp. 968–84.
9. A. W. DePorte, *Europe Between the Superpowers* (New Haven: Yale University Press, 1979) p. 92.
10. DePorte, *Europe Between the Superpowers*, pp. 108–12.
11. DePorte, *Europe Between the Superpowers*, p. 123.
12. Sir John Wheeler-Bennett and Anthony Nicholls, *The Semblance of Peace* (N.Y.: St Martin's Press, 1972) p. 556.
13. Cominform statement regarding expulsion of Yugoslavia, 28 June 1948; Stephen Clissold, ed., *Yugoslavia and the Soviet Union* (London: Oxford University Press, 1975) pp. 202–7.
14. DePorte, *Europe Between the Superpowers*, p. 121.
15. Yergin, *Shattered Peace*, p. 400.
16. Herbert Butterfield, *International Conflict in the Twentieth Century* (London: Routledge & Kegan Paul, 1960) p. 77.

CHAPTER 3   THE 'SPIRIT OF GENEVA'

1. J. Robert Oppenheimer, 'Atomic Weapons and American Policy', *Foreign Affairs*, July 1953, vol. 31, no. 4, p. 529.
2. Quoted in Albert Weeks, *The Troubled Détente* (N.Y.: New York University Press, 1976) p. 86.
3. *Pravda*, 25 Apr. 1953.
4. *Pravda*, 10 July 1953.
5. For details see Walter Lafeber, *America, Russia and the Cold War*, 2nd edn (N.Y.: John Wiley, 1972) pp. 174–5.
6. Lafeber, *America, Russia and the Cold War*, p. 5.
7. Norman Graebner, *The New Isolationism* (N.Y.: The Ronald Press Co., 1956) p. 229.
8. *Pravda*, 11 Aug. 1953.
9. *Pravda*, 4 Dec. 1953.
10. Fontaine, *History of the Cold War*, pp. 64–5.
11. Fontaine, *History of the Cold War*, pp. 66–7.
12. Philippe Devillers and Jean Lacouture, *End of a War* (London: Pall Mall Press, 1969) pp. 104–5.
13. Ibid., pp. 104–5.
14. For full details see Bernhard Bechhofer, *Postwar Negotiations for Arms Control* (Washington D.C.: The Brookings Institution, 1961); see also Philip Noel-Baker, *The Arms Race* (London: Atlantic Books, 1958).
15. Anthony Nutting, *Disarmament* (London: Oxford University Press, 1959) p. 10.

16. Eisenhower, *Mandate for Change*, p. 505.
17. Lafeber, *America, Russia and the Cold War*, pp. 149–50.
18. Graebner, *The New Isolationism*, p. 236.
19. Eisenhower, *Mandate for Change*, p. 508.
20. Richard Rovere, *The Eisenhower Years* (N.Y.: Farra, Straus & Cudahy, 1956) p. 27.
21. Rovere, *The Eisenhower Years*, pp. 269–70.
22. Quoted in *Christian Science Monitor*, 16 July 1955.
23. Alastair Buchan, 'The President's Optimism', *Observer*, 17 July 1955.
24. Ellie Abel, 'Eisenhower Credits Soviets with Earnest Peace Aims', *New York Times*, 21 July 1955.
25. Quoted in *Manchester Guardian*, 25 July 1955.
26. Walter Lippmann, 'Today and Tomorrow', *New York Herald Tribune* (Eur. Ed.), 2 Aug. 1955.
27. *Sunday Times*, 24 July 1955.
28. Eisenhower, *Public Papers*, 1955, p. 725.
29. Rovere, *The Eisenhower Years*, Letter from Geneva, 27 July 1955, p. 283.
30. *Pravda*, 20 August 1955.
31. *Pravda*, 5 August 1955.
32. Quoted in *New York Times*, 26 July 1955.
33. Eisenhower, *Public Papers*, 1955, no. 76, pp. 731–2.
34. John C. Campbell, 'Negotiations with the Soviets', *Foreign Affairs*, January 1956, vol. 34, no. 2, p. 305.
35. Roscoe Drummond, 'Behind Soviet Smiles', *New York Herald Tribune* (Eur. Ed.), 3 Aug. 1955.
36. Walter Lippmann, *New York Herald Tribune*, 30 August 1955.
37. Lafeber, *America, Russia and the Cold War*, p. 186.
38. M. Mikhailov, *Izvestia*, 17 Nov. 1955.
39. Quoted in 'What Should U.S. Do About Russia?', *Foreign Policy Bulletin*, 15 July 1956, vol. 35, no. 21, p. 166.
40. Graebner, *The New Isolationism*, pp. 230–1.
41. Quoted in Lafeber, *America, Russia and the Cold War*, p. 186.
42. Graebner, *The New Isolationism*, pp. 230–1.
43. Eisenhower, *Public Papers* (1956), no. 23, p. 211.
44. Lafeber, *America, Russia and the Cold War*, pp. 186–7.
45. Bechhoefer, *Postwar Negotiations for Arms Control*, p. 272.
46. *Pravda*, 15 Feb. 1956.
47. Khrushchev, *On Peaceful Coexistence*, p. 10; from Lenin's *Works*, vol. 23, p. 58.
48. Joseph Korbel, *Détente in Europe* (Princeton, New Jersey: Princeton University Press, 1972) pp. 15–6.
49. Lafeber, *America, Russia and the Cold War*, p. 195; from August Campbell, *The American Voter* (N.Y., 1960) pp. 198–200, 526–8.
50. A full discussion of the growth of superpower competition in the Middle East can be found in Chapter 4.
51. *Pravda*, 6 Nov. 1956.
52. Dwight D. Eisenhower, *Waging Peace*, 1959–1961 (London: Heinemann, 1966) p. 90.
53. *Khrushchev Speaks*, ed. by Thomas Whitney, p. 204.
54. *Pravda*, 31 Oct. 1956.

55. For a more detailed account of events see Frene Vali, *Rift and Revolt in Hungary* (London: Oxford University Press, 1961), pp. 364–9; and Tibor Meray, *Thirteen Days That Shook the Kremlin* (London: Thames & Hudson, 1958) pp. 186–96.
56. Eisenhower, *Waging Peace*, p. 87.
57. Ibid., p. 67.
58. Eisenhower, *Waging Peace*, p. 89.
59. *Pravda*, 14 Dec. 1956.
60. *New York Times*, 4 Nov. 1956.
61. *Pravda*, 15 Dec. 1956.
62. *Détente: Cold War Strategies in Transition*, ed. by Eleanor Lansing Dulles and Robert Crane (N.Y.: Frederick A. Praeger, 1965) p. 105.
63. Butterfield, *International Conflict in the Twentieth Century*, p. 63.
64. Rovere, *The Eisenhower Years*, p. 275.
65. See *Current Digest of Soviet Press*, 1953–56.
66. Rovere, *The Eisenhower Years* (Letter from Washington D.C., 7 July 1955) p. 270.
67. Khrushchev, *On Peaceful Coexistence*, p. 8.
68. Quoted in Graebner, *The New Isolationism*, p. 211.
69. Ibid., p. 238.
70. Ibid., p. 210.
71. Eisenhower, *Public Papers* (1956), no. 210, p. 785.
72. Quoted in James P. Warburg, *Turning Point Towards Peace* (N.Y.: Current Affairs Press, 1955), p. 11.
73. *Détente: Cold War Strategies in Transition*, ed. by Dulles and Crane, p. 103.
74. Eisenhower, *Public Papers* (1955), no. 95, p. 488.
75. Eisenhower, *Mandate for Change*, p. 530.
76. Radio Address, 18 Nov. 1955.

CHAPTER 4   THE 'SPIRIT OF CAMP DAVID'

1. *Izvestia*, 17 Sept. 1959.
2. *Department of State Bulletin*, 11 Feb. 1957, vol. 36, no. 920, p. 211.
3. Yair Evron, *The Middle East* (London: Paul Elek, 1973) pp. 130–9.
4. Section Two of Resolution reprinted in Seyom Brown, *The Faces of Power* (N.Y.: Columbia University Press, 1968) p. 128.
5. Tito's speech to the LCY activists at Pula, 11 Nov. 1956, in Clissold, *Yugoslavia and the Soviet Union*, p. 267.
6. Quoted in Dallin, *Soviet Foreign Policy After Stalin*, p. 451.
7. For an account of the power struggle see Adam Ulam, *Expansion and Coexistence* (London: Secker & Warburg, 1968) pp. 604–5.
8. Reprinted in *Pravda* and *Izvestia*.
9. *Pravda*, 4 Oct. 1957.
10. *Pravda* and *Izvestia*, 19 Nov. 1957.
11. *Pravda* and *Izvestia*, 19 Nov. 1957.
12. *Pravda*, 22 Nov. 1957, quoted in Dallin, *Soviet Foreign Policy After Stalin*, p. 457.
13. Ulam, *Expansion and Coexistence*, p. 599.
14. William Zimmerman, 'Russia and the International Order', *Survey*, no. 58,

January 1966, pp. 209–13, quoted in Lafeber, *America, Russia and the Cold War*, p. 202.

15. Eric Goldman, *The Crucial Decade – and After: America 1945–1960* (N.Y.: Random House – Vintage Edition, 1960) pp. 309–10.
16. Lafeber, *America, Russia and the Cold War*, pp. 201–2.
17. Alastair Cooke, 'Survival? – The Great U.S. Debate', *Manchester Guardian*, 1 Jan. 1958.
18. Lafeber, *America, Russia and the Cold War*, pp. 201–2.
19. *Daily Telegraph*, 3 Jan. 1958.
20. Ibid.
21. *Department of State Bulletin*, 3 Feb. 1958, vol. 38, no. 971, p. 163.
22. Ibid., 3 Feb. 1958, vol. 38, no. 971, p. 162.
23. Ibid., 27 Jan. 1958, vol. 38, no. 970, p. 116.
24. Philip Deane, 'Russia Changing Summit Tactics', *Observer Foreign News Service*, 17 June 1958.
25. Quoted in Seyom Brown, *The Faces of Power* (N.Y.: Columbia University Press, 1968) p. 138.
26. Ibid., p. 128.
27. Message from Khrushchev to Eisenhower, *Pravda/Izvestia*, 20 July 1958.
28. Donald Zagoria, *The Sino-Soviet Conflict 1956–1961* (Princeton, New Jersey: Princeton University Press, 1962) p. 39.
29. Klaus Mehnert, *Peking and Moscow* (N.Y.: Mento Books, 1964) p. 349.
30. Quoted in Brown, *The Faces of Power*, p. 148.
31. Zagoria, *The Sino-Soviet Conflict 1956–1961*, pp. 201, 206.
32. Kalicki, *The Pattern of Sino-American Crises*, p. 183.
33. Ibid., p. 160.
34. *Peking Review*, 6 Sept. 1963, quoted in ibid., p. 185.
35. Quoted in Brown, *The Faces of Power*, p. 148.
36. Ibid., p. 148.
37. Kissinger, *White House Years*, p. 67.
38. Khrushchev, *Khrushchev Remembers*, pp. 453–4.
39. Quoted in Ulam, *Expansion and Coexistence*, p. 620.
40. Philip Windsor, *Germany and the Management of Détente* (London: Chatto & Windus, 1971) p. 12.
41. Ulam, *Expansion and Coexistence*, p. 619.
42. Press release 12 Dec. 1958; *United States Department of State Bulletin*, 29 Dec. 1958, vol. 39, no. 1018, p. 1041.
43. *United States Department of State Bulletin*, 19 Jan. 1959, vol. 40, no. 1021, p. 80.
44. *Department of State Bulletin*, 26 Jan. 1959, vol. 40, no. 1025, p. 11.
45. Harold Macmillan, *Riding the Storm 1956–1959* (London: Macmillan, 1971) p. 610.
46. Ibid., p. 631.
47. Quoted in Ulam, *Expansion and Coexistence*, p. 621.
48. Harrison Salisbury, 'Khrushchev and Summit', *New York Times*, 2 Apr. 1959.
49. *Izvestia*, 11 Apr. 1959.
50. Richard Nixon, *The Memoirs of Richard Nixon* (New York: Grosset & Dunlap, 1978) pp. 208–9.
51. *Pravda*, 10 Apr. 1959.

52. Report to Twenty-First Party Congress, *Pravda*, 22 Jan. 1959.
53. Khrushchev's Foreign Policy Report to the Supreme Soviet, 31 Oct. 1959, *Pravda*, 1 Nov. 1959.
54. *Department of State Bulletin*, 28 Sept. 1959, vol. 41, no. 1057, pp. 436–8.
55. Ibid., pp. 436–8.
56. *Izvestia*, 17 Sept. 1959.
57. *Pravda*, 18 Sept. 1959.
58. *Pravda*, 18 Sept. 1959.
59. A. Adzhubei, *Izvestia*, 22 Sept. 1959.
60. *Pravda*, 30 Sept. 1959.
61. *Khrushchev Speaks*, ed. by Thomas Whitney (Ann Arbor, Michigan: The University of Michigan Press, 1963) p. 372.
62. *New York Times*, 29 Sept. 1959.
63. Press Conference, 28 Sept. 1959, reported in the *New York Herald Tribune*, 29 Sept. 1959.
64. *New York Times*, 17 Nov. 1959.
65. Charles de Gaulle, *Memoirs of Hope* (London: Weidenfeld & Nicolson, 1971) p. 202.
66. David Calleo, *Europe's Future: the Grand Alternatives* (N.Y.: Horizon Press, 1965) p. 120.
67. de Gaulle, *Memoirs of Hope*, p. 229.
68. Brian Crozier, *De Gaulle: the Statesman* (London: Eyre Methuen, 1973) p. 547.
69. DePorte, *Europe Between the Superpowers*, p. 234.
70. Mehnert, *Peking and Moscow*, pp. 422–3.
71. Quoted in Ulam, *Expansion and Coexistence*, pp. 610–1.
72. Alastair Buchan, *The End of the Postwar Era* (London: Weidenfeld & Nicolson, 1974) pp. 22–3.
73. Quoted in *New York Times*, 18 Dec. 1959.
74. *United States Department of State Bulletin*, 1 Feb. 1960, vol. 43, no. 1075, p. 146.
75. *United States Department of State Bulletin*, 29 Feb. 1960, vol. 42, no. 1079, p. 320.
76. *New York Herald Tribune*, 10 Mar. 1960.
77. Quoted in Lafeber, *America, Russia and the Cold War*, pp. 213–4.
78. *Pravda/Izvestia*, 26 Apr. 1960.
79. Lafeber, *America, Russia and the Cold War*, p. 214.
80. *New York Times*, 28 Apr. 1960.
81. *Pravda*, 6 May 1960.
82. *New York Times*, 12 May 1960.
83. Speech to Workers Conference, *Pravda*, 29 May 1960.
84. *Izvestia*, 22 May 1960.
85. See Khrushchev's speech, 20 May 1960 in Berlin. Paul Wohl, 'Coexistence Line Braced by Khrushchev', *Christian Science Monitor*, 23 May 1960.
86. Eisenhower, *Waging Peace*, p. 560.
87. Warren Rogers, 'Age of DO-IT-YOURSELF Diplomacy', *New York Herald Tribune*, 15 Nov. 1959.
88. See Elmer Plischke, 'Eisenhower's Correspondence Diplomacy with the Kremlin – Case Study in Summit Diplomatics', *The Journal of Politics*, Feb. 1968, vol. 30, no. 1, pp. 137–59.

89. Robert Stephens, 'Why Khrushchev Did It', *Observer Foreign News Service*, 29 May 1960.
90. James Reston, 'Conflict at the Summit', *New York Times*, 17 May 1960.
91. Eisenhower, *Waging Peace*, pp. 553–4.
92. David Floyd, 'International Politics Cause Khrushchev Switch', *Daily Telegraph*, 17 May 1960.
93. *Khrushchev Speaks*, ed. by Thomas Whitney, p. 37.

CHAPTER 5   THE POST-MISSILE CRISIS DÉTENTE

1. *New York Times*, 11 Aug. 1963.
2. *Izvestia*, 30 July 1963.
3. *New York Times*, 21 Jan. 1961.
4. William Stringer, 'State of the Nations', *Christian Science Monitor*, 6 Jan. 1961.
5. John Hightower, 'Cold War Tactics High on Kennedy Agenda', *New York Herald Tribune*, 10 Jan. 1961.
6. During the 1960 Presidential elections which were dominated by questions of national security, a significant shift had taken place in the American intellectual climate regarding questions of disarmament and arms control. There was a growing belief that the accelerating procurement of sophisticated weaponry was contributing more to American insecurity than security. In the Fall 1960 special issue of *Daedalus*, several of America's leading strategic thinkers agreed that civilisation was faced with an unprecedented crisis and that serious proposals for arms control with attainable goals – essential unto itself – needed to be pursued. This is significant because such influential thinkers were to play a significant role in the Kennedy Administration and lay the foundation for progress in this area.
7. *America and Russia: From Cold War to Confrontation to Coexistence*, ed. by Gary Hess (N.Y.: Thomas Crowell Co., 1973) p. 103.
8. Quoted in *New York Tribune*, 5 Feb. 1961.
9. Seymour Topping, 'Soviets Wary About Kennedy', *New York Tribune*, 15 Mar. 1961.
10. Harry Schwartz, 'Russia and Summitry', *New York Tribune*, 16 Jan. 1961.
11. *Izvestia*, quoted in James McSherry, *Khrushchev and Kennedy in Retrospect* (Palo Alto, CA: The Open Door Press, 1971) p. 65.
12. *Izvestia*, quoted in ibid., p. 65.
13. *Pravda*, quoted in ibid., p. 66.
14. Theodore Sorensen, *Kennedy* (New York: Harper & Row, 1965) p. 550.
15. Sorensen, *Kennedy*, p. 586.
16. *U.S. News and World Report*, 24 July 1961, pp. 31–5.
17. Anatoly Gromyko, *Through Russian Eyes* (Washington D.C.: International Library Inc., 1973) p. 11.
18. Sorensen, *Kennedy*, p. 619.
19. George Gallup, *The Gallup Polls*, vol. 3 (N.Y.: Random House, 1972) p. 1726.
20. John McCloy, Kennedy's disarmament adviser, quoted in McSherry, *Khrushchev and Kennedy in Retrospect*, p. 74.

21. Sorensen, *Kennedy*, p. 726.
22. Harry Schwartz, *New York Times*, 25 Feb. 1962.
23. Richard Scott, *Guardian*, 21 Feb. 1962.
24. Quoted in McSherry, *Khrushchev and Kennedy in Retrospect*, p. 115.
25. Anatol Rapoport, *The Big Two* (N.Y.: Pegasus, 1971) pp. 182–3.
26. Charles Bohlen, *Witness to History* (N.Y.: W. W. Norton, 1973) p. 495.
27. William Griffith, *Cold War and Coexistence: Russia, China and the United States* (Englewood Cliffs, N.J.: Prentice-Hall, Inc., 1971) p. 78.
28. McSherry, *Khrushchev and Kennedy in Retrospect*, p. 103; *Parliamentary Debates*, Commons, vol. 664, col. 1054.
29. Khrushchev, *Khrushchev Remembers*, p. 494.
30. Roger Hilsman, *To Move a Nation* (Garden City, N.Y.: Doubleday & Co., Inc., 1967) p. 228.
31. Max Frankel, 'Washington Sees Balance Shifting', *New York Tribune*, 1 Nov. 1962.
32. *The Times*, 5 Nov. 1962.
33. Ibid.
34. Gordon Brook-Shepherd, 'Big Drive to Get Russian Accord', *Sunday Telegraph*, 18 Nov. 1962.
35. John Hightower, 'Historic Decisions Believed in Making in World Capitals', *New York Herald Tribune* (Eur. Ed.), 23 Nov. 1962.
36. Joseph Alsop, 'Yoo Hoos from Russia', *New York Herald Tribune*, 28 Nov. 1962.
37. Quoted in *The Sunday Times*, 25 Nov. 1962.
38. Quoted in *New York Times* (Int. Ed.), 11 Dec. 1962.
39. Khrushchev's New Year's Message to Kennedy, reprinted in *The Times*, 1 Jan. 1963.
40. Kennedy's New Year's Message to Khrushchev, 3 Jan. 1963, reprinted in United States Information Service bulletin.
41. *New York Times*, 11 Feb. 1963.
42. *New York Times*, 16 Feb. 1963.
43. *New York Times*, 25 Feb. 1963.
44. Seymour Topping, *New York Times*, 13 Mar. 1963.
45. Reprinted in Peter G. Filene (ed.), *American Views of Soviet Russia 1917–1965* (Homewood, Illinois: Dorsey Press, 1968) pp. 386–7.
46. Ibid.
47. *New York Times*, 11 Aug. 1963.
48. *Daily Telegraph*, 12 Aug. 1963.
49. *Izvestia*, 30 July 1963.
50. George Ball, *Diplomacy for a Crowded World* (London: The Bodley Head, 1976) p. 111.
51. McSherry, *Khrushchev and Kennedy in Retrospect*, p. 182.
52. *JFK: Papers of the Presidents* (Washington D.C.: United States Government Printing Office, 1964) pp. 795–6.
53. *Sunday Times*, 20 Oct. 1963.
54. Max Frankel, 'Problems of the Thaw', *New York Times*, 25 Oct. 1963.
55. Sorensen, *Kennedy*, p. 745.
56. *Cold War Strategies in Transition*, ed. by Eleanor Dulles and Robert Crane (N.Y.: Frederick A. Praeger, 1965) p. 114.

57. *New York Times*, 2 Jan. 1964.
58. Walter Lippman, 'The Thaw', *New York Herald Tribune* (Eur. Ed.), 3 Jan. 1964.
59. James Reston, 'The New Soft Mood Music in the Cold War', *New York Times*, 22 Apr. 1964.
60. Radoslav Selucky, *Cezchoslovakia: the Plan That Failed* (London: Thomas Nelson, 1970) pp. 127–34.
61. Edward Cranshaw, 'East and West Enter a New Phase', *New York Times*, 30 Aug. 1964.
62. Roy Medvedev, *Khrushchev: The Years in Power* (Oxford: Oxford University Press, 1977) pp. 143–75.
63. Archie Brown and Michael Kaser (eds), *The Soviet Union Since the Fall of Khrushchev* (London: Macmillan, 1975) p. 218.
64. Weeks, *The Troubled Détente*, p. 186.
65. See Weeks, *The Other Side of Coexistence*, pp. 184–8, 197–209, 212–21.
66. Victor Zorza, 'LBJ Visit: a Soviet Warning', *Guardian*, 13 Feb. 1965.
67. *New York Herald Tribune* (Eur. Ed.), 18 Feb. 1965.
68. Quoted in Zbigniew Brzezinski, 'How the Cold War Was Played', *Foreign Affairs*, Oct. 1972, vol. 51, no. 1, p. 196.
69. It is interesting to note that throughout 1965 and 1966, this calm occurred against the backdrop of United States military intervention in Dominica, Indo-Pakistan fighting in Kashmir, the French withdrawal from the integrated structure of NATO, and other events that might have caused a great deal of tension.
70. Michael Howard and Robert Hunter, 'Israel and the Arab World: the Crisis of 1967', *Adelphi Papers* no. 41, Oct. 1967, pp. 15–16.
71. Mohammed Heikal, *Nasser* (London: New English Library, 1971) p. 217.
72. Howard and Hunter, *Adelphi Papers*, p. 31.
73. Lyndon Johnson, *The Vantage Point* (N.Y.: Holt, Rinehard and Winston, 1971) p. 481.

CHAPTER 6   THE MOSCOW DÉTENTE

1. President Richard Nixon, 'Inaugural Address', 20 Jan. 1969.
2. Kissinger, *White House Years*, pp. 159–62.
3. Kissinger, *White House Years*, p. 156.
4. Barnet, *The Giants*, p. 37.
5. Quoted in House Hearing, *Détente*, p. 91.
6. Quoted in Ian Clark, 'Sino-Soviet Relations in Soviet Perspective', *Orbis*, Summer 1973, vol. 17, no. 2, p. 480.
7. Kissinger, *White House Years*, p. 389.
8. Ibid., p. 422.
9. Stanley Hoffmann, *Primacy or World Order* (N.Y.: McGraw-Hill Book Company, 1978) p. 48.
10. Kissinger, *White House Years*, p. 410.
11. Kissinger, *White House Years*, p. 416.
12. Ibid., p. 520.
13. Willy Brandt, *People and Politics* (London: Collins, 1978) p. 284.

14. Lawrence Whetten, *Germany's Ostpolitik* (London: Oxford University Press, 1971) p. 176.
15. Windsor, *Germany and the Management of Détente*, p. 202.
16. *Pravda*, 29 Aug. 1971.
17. Theodore Draper, 'Détente', *Commentary*, vol. 57, no. 6, June 1974, p. 37.
18. Gerald Steibel, *Détente: Promises and Pitfalls* (N.Y.: Crane, Russak & Co. Inc., 1975) p. 14.
19. Kissinger, *White House Years*, pp. 819–20.
20. For details, see ibid., pp. 1216–22, 1229–46.
21. *Pravda*, 31 Mar. 1971.
22. *Pravda*, 1 Dec. 1971.
23. Kissinger, *White House Years*, pp. 859–916.
24. American Bar Association, *Détente* (Chicago: ABA Press, 1977) p. 8.
25. Vladimir Petrov, *US–Soviet Détente: Past and Future* (Washington D.C.: American Enterprise Institute for Public Policy Research, 1975) p. 18.
26. Stephen Cohen, 'Soviet Domestic Politics and Foreign Policy', in *Common Sense in US–Soviet Relations* (Washington D.C.: American Committee on East–West Accord, 1978) p. 6.
27. Bruno Pitterman, 'The Moral Factor in the Conduct of Foreign Affairs', in G. R. Urban, *Détente* (London: Temple Smith, 1976) pp. 15–6.
28. Quoted in *Kissinger and Détente*, ed. Sobel, p. 139.
29. Quoted in Pitterman, 'The Moral Factor in the Conduct of Foreign Affairs', in Urban, *Détente*, pp. 15–6.
30. Coral Bell, 'The October Middle East War: a Case Study in Crisis Management during Détente', *International Affairs* (London), Oct. 1974, vol. 50, no. 4, pp. 531–43.
31. William Quandt, 'Soviet Policy in the October Middle East War', *International Affairs*, Oct. 1977, vol. 53, no. 4, pp. 602–3. See also William Quandt, *Decade of Decisions* (Berkeley: University of California Press, 1977) p. 192.
32. Henry Kissinger, *Years of Upheaval* (London: Weidenfeld, Nicolson & Joseph, 1982) p. 878.
33. Mohammed Heikal, *The Road to Ramadan* (London: Collins, 1975) pp. 272–3.
34. For a full account see Kissinger, *Years of Upheaval*, pp. 854–95.
35. Quandt, 'Soviet Policy in the October Middle East War', *International Affairs*, pp. 593–4.
36. Quoted in *Kissinger and Détente*, ed. Sobel, p. 176.
37. *New York Times*, 6 Apr. 1976.
38. Kissinger, *White House Years*, p. 12.
39. Ibid., p. 516.
40. Ibid., p. 840.
41. Hoffman, *Primacy or World Order*, p. 50.
42. Hoffman, *Primacy or World Order*, p. 71.
43. Draper, 'Appeasement and Détente', *Commentary*, p. 28.
44. Seyom Brown, 'A Cooling-off Period for US–Soviet Relations', *Foreign Policy*, Fall 1977, p. 21.

CHAPTER 7   THE NATURE OF DÉTENTE

1. Quoted in John Armstrong, 'The Soviet–American Confrontation: A New Stage?', *The Russian Review*, Apr. 1964, vol. 23, no. 2, p. 9.
2. Weeks, *The Troubled Détente*, p. 103.
3. Press Conference, 25 Feb. 1973, *Congressional Quarterly Weekly Report*, 32, no. 9, p. 556.
4. Draper, 'Appeasement and Détente', *Commentary*, p. 33.

Bibliography

Books

Adams, Sherman, *Firsthand Report: the Story of the Eisenhower Administration* (N.Y.: Harper Brothers, 1961).

Bailey, Thomas, *A Diplomatic History of the American People* 9th edn (Englewood Cliffs, N.J.: Prentice-Hall, Inc., 1974).

Ball, George, *Diplomacy for a Crowded World* (London: The Bodley Head, 1976).

Barghoorn, Frederick, *Détente and the Democratic Movement in the USSR* (N.Y.: The Free Press, 1976).

Barnet, Richard, *The Giants* (N.Y.: Simon & Schuster, 1977).

Barraclough, Geoffrey, *An Introduction to Contemporary History* (Middlesex, England: Penguin Books Ltd., 1977).

Bechhoefer, Bernhard, *Postwar Negotiations for Arms Control* (Washington D.C.: Brookings Institute, 1961).

Bell, Coral, *Diplomacy of Détente* (London: Martin Robertson, 1977).

Beloff, Max, *The Foreign Policy of Soviet Russia 1929–1941*, vol. I (London: Oxford University Press, 1947).

Bohlen, Charles, *Witness to History* (N.Y.: W. W. Norton, 1973).

Brennan, Donald (ed.), *Arms Control and Disarmament* (London: Jonathan Cape, 1961).

Brezhnev, Leonid, *Peace, Détente and Soviet–American Relations* (N.Y.: Harcourt Brace Jovanovich, 1976).

Brandt, Willy, *People and Politics* (London: William Collins Sons, 1978).

Brown, Archie and Kaser, Michael (eds), *The Soviet Union since the Fall of Khrushchev* (London: Macmillan, 1975).

Brown, Colin and Mooney, Peter, *Cold War to Détente* (London: Heinemann Educational Books, 1976).

Brown, Seyom, *The Faces of Power* (N.Y.: Columbia University Press, 1969).

Buchan, Alastair, *The End of the Postwar Era* (London: Weidenfeld & Nicolson, 1974).

Butterfield, Herbert, *International Conflict in the Twentieth Century* (London: Routledge & Kegan Paul, 1960).

Calleo, David, *Europe's Future: the Grand Alternatives* (N.Y.: Horizon Press, 1965).

Calvocoressi, Peter, *World Politics Since 1945*, 3rd edn (London and New York: Longman, 1977).

Carr, E. H., *The Bolshevik Revolution 1917–1973* vol. III (London: Macmillan, 1953).

Clemens, Walter, Jr., *The Superpowers and Arms Control* (Lexington, Mass.: Lexington Books, 1973).

Common Sense in US–Soviet Relations, The American Committee on East–West Accord (Washington, 1978).

Crozier, Brian, *De Gaulle: the Statesman* (London: Eyre Methuen, 1973).

Dallin, David, *Soviet Foreign Policy after Stalin* (London: Methuen, 1972).

DePorte, A. W., *Europe Between the Superpowers* (New Haven Conn.: Yale University Press, 1979).

Détente, American Bar Association (Chicago: ABA Press, 1977).

Devillers, Philippe and Lacouture, Jean, *End of a War* (London: Pall Mall Press, 1969).

Dulles, Eleanor Lansing and Crane, Robert (eds), *Détente: Cold War Strategies in Transition* (N.Y.: Frederick Praeger, 1965).

Eidelberg, Paul, *Beyond Détente* (La Salle, Illinois: Sherwood Sugden Co., 1977).

Eisenhower, Dwight D., *Mandate for Change 1953–1956* (London: Heinemann, 1963).

——, *Public Papers of the Presidents of the United States 1954–1956* (Washington: United States Government Printing Office, 1958–1960).

——, *Waging Peace, 1956–1961* (London: Heinemann, 1966).

Evron, Yair, *The Middle East* (London: Paul Elek, 1973).

Filene, Peter (ed.), *American Views of Soviet Russia 1917–1935* (Homewood, Illinois: The Dorsey Press, 1968).

Fontaine, André, *History of the Cold War* (London: Secker & Warburg, 1970).

Graebner, Norman, *The New Isolationism* (N.Y.: The Ronald Press Co., 1965).

Gallup, George, *The Gallup Poll – Public Opinion 1972–1977* (Wilmington, Delaware: Scholarly Resources Inc., 1978).

Gaulle, Charles de, *Memoirs of Hope* (London: Weidenfeld & Nicolson, 1971).

Goldman, Eric, *The Crucial Decade – and After: America 1945–1960* (N.Y.: Random House Vintage Edition, 1960).

Griffith, William, *Cold War and Coexistence: Russia, China and the United States* (Englewood Cliffs, N.J.: Prentice-Hall Inc., 1971).

Griffith, William, *Peking, Moscow and Beyond: the Sino-Soviet–American Triangle* (Washington D.C.: Georgetown University, 1973).

Gromyko, Anatolii, *Through Russian Eyes: President Kennedy's 1036 Days* (Washington: International Library Inc., 1973).

Heikal, Mohammed, *Nasser* (London: New English Library, 1971).

——, *The Road to Ramadan* (London: Collins, 1975).

——, *Sphinx and Commissar* (London: Collins, 1978).

Hess, Gary (ed.), *America and Russia: from Cold War to Confrontation to Coexistence* (N.Y.: Thomas Cromwell, 1973).

Hilsman, Roger, *To Move a Nation* (N.Y.: Doubleday, 1967).

Hoffman, Stanley, *Primary or World Order* (N.Y.: McGraw-Hill, 1978).

Johnson, A. Ross, *The Transformation of Communist Ideology: the Yugoslav Case* (Cambridge, Mass.: MIT Press, 1972).

Johnson, Lyndon Baines, *Public Papers of the Presidents of the United States 1963–1964* (Washington: United States Government Printing Office, 1965).

——, *The Vantage Point* (N.Y.: Holt, Rinehart & Winston, 1971).

Kalicki, Jan, *The Pattern of Sino-American Crises* (London: Cambridge University Press, 1975).

Kennan, George, *American Diplomacy 1900–1950* (London: Secker & Warburg, 1952).

——, *Memoirs 1950–1963* (London: Hutchinson 1973).

Kennedy, John F., *Public Papers of the Presidents of the United States* (Washington: United States Government Printing Office, 1962).

Khrushchev, Nikita, *Khrushchev Remembers*, trans. and ed. by Strobe Talbott (London: Andre Deutsch, 1974).

Khrushchev, N. S., *On Peaceful Coexistence* (Moscow: Foreign Languages Publishing House, 1961).

Kissinger, Henry, *White House Years* (Boston: Little, Brown & Co., 1979).

——, *Years of Upheaval* (London: Weidenfeld & Nicolson and Michael Joseph, 1982).

Knapp, Wilfrid, *A History of War and Peace* (London: Oxford University Press, 1967).

Korbel, Josef, *Détente in Europe* (Princeton, N.J.: Princeton University Press, 1972).

Lafeber, Walter, *America, Russia and the Cold War*, 2nd edn (N.Y.: John Wiley, 1972).

Larson, Thomas, *Soviet–American Rivalry* (N.Y.: W. W. Norton, 1978).

Leebaert, Derek, *Soviet Military Thinking* (London: Allen & Unwin, 1981).

Lukacs, John, *A History of the Cold War* (N.Y.: Anchor Books, 1962).

Macmillan, Harold, *Riding the Storm* (London: Macmillan, 1971).

McSherry, James, *Khrushchev and Kennedy in Retrospect* (Palo Alto, Calif.: The Open Door Press, 1971).

Medvedev, Roy, *Khrushchev: the Years in Power* (Oxford: Oxford University Press, 1977).

Mehnert, Klaus, *Peking and Moscow* (N.Y.: Mentor Books, 1964).

Meray, Tibor, *Thirteen Days that Shook the Kremlin* (London: Thames & Hudson, 1958).

Morgenthau, Hans, *Politics among Nations*, 5th edn rev. (N.Y.: Alfred Knopf, 1978).

National Security and Détente, United States Army War College (N.Y.: Thomas Cromwell, 1976).

Neal, Frederick Warner, *American–Soviet Détente, Peace and National Security* (Santa Barbara, Calif.: Fund for the Republic Inc., 1976).

Nicolson, Harold, *Diplomacy* (London: Thornton Butterworth, 1939).

Nixon, Richard, *The Memoirs of Richard Nixon* (N.Y.: Grosset & Dunlap, 1978).

Noel-Baker, Philip, *The Arms Race* (London: Atlantic Books, 1958).

Nutting, Anthony, *Disarmament* (London: Oxford University Press, 1959).

Osgood, Robert, Tucker, Robert and Dinerstein, H., *America and the World* (Baltimore and London: The Johns Hopkins Press, 1970).

Petrov, Vladimir, *US–Soviet Détente: Past and Future* (Washington: American Enterprise Institute for Public Policy Research, 1975).

Pipes, Richard, *US–Soviet Relations in the Era of Détente* (Boulder, Colorado: Westview Press, 1981).

Potichny, Peter and Shapiro, Jane (eds), *From the Cold War to Détente* (N.Y.: Praeger Publishers, 1976).

Pranger, Robert (ed.), *Détente and Defense* (Washington: American Enterprise Institute for Public Policy Research, 1976).

Quandt, William, *Decade of Decisions* (Berkeley: University of California Press, 1977).

Rapoport, Anatol, *The Big Two* (N.Y.: Pegasus, 1971).

Riasanovsky, Nicholas, *A History of Russia*, 3rd edn (N.Y.: Oxford University Press, 1977).

Rovere, Richard, *The Eisenhower Years* (N.Y.: Farrar, Straus & Cudohy, 1956).

Schwab, George and Friedlander, Henry (eds), *Détente in Historical Perspective* (N.Y.: Cyrco Press, 1975).

Selucky, Radoslav, *Czechoslovakia: the Plan That Failed* (London: Thomas Nelson, 1970).

Sobel, Lester (ed.), *Kissinger and Détente* (N.Y.: Facts on File Inc., 1975).

Sorensen, Theodore, *Kennedy* (N.Y.: Harper & Row, 1965).

Steibel, Gerald, *Détente: Promises and Pitfalls* (N.Y.: Crane, Russak & Co. Inc., 1975).

Ulam, Adam, *Expansion and Coexistence* (London: Secker & Warburg, 1968).

——, *The Rivals* (London: Allen Lane, 1973).

Urban, G. R. (ed.), *Détente* (London: Temple Smith, 1976).

Váli, Ferene, *Rift and Revolt in Hungary* (London: Oxford University Press, 1961).

van den Heuvel, Cornelius Christian, *Soviet Perceptions of East–West Relationships* (American Bar Association Press, 1977).

Weeks, Albert, *The Other Side of Coexistence* (N.Y.: Pitman Publishing Corp., 1970).

——, *The Troubled Détente* (N.Y.: New York University Press, 1976).

Wheeler-Bennett, Sir John and Nicholls, Anthony, *The Semblance of Peace* (N.Y.: St. Martin's Press, 1972).

Whetten, Lawrence, *Germany's Ostpolitik* (London: Oxford University Press, 1971).

Whitney, Thomas (ed.), *Khrushchev Speaks* (Ann Arbor, Michigan: University of Michigan Press, 1963).

Windsor, Philip, *Germany and the Management of Détente* (London: Chatto & Windus, 1971).

Yergin, Daniel, *Shattered Peace* (London: Andre Deutsch, 1978).

Zagoria, Donald, *The Sino-Soviet Conflict 1956–1961* (Princeton, N.J.: Princeton University Press, 1962).

Periodicals

Arbatov, G., 'A Step Serving the Interests of Peace', *Survival*, vol. 14, no. 1, Jan./Feb. 1972, pp. 16–19.

Armstrong, John, 'The Soviet American Confrontation: a New Stage?' *Survey*, vol. 21, no. 4, Autumn 1975, pp. 40–51.

Barghoorn, Frederick, 'America in 1959 – as Seen from Moscow', *Review of Politics*, vol. 22, no. 2, Apr. 1960, pp. 245–54.

Bell, Coral, 'The October Middle East War: a Case Study in Crisis Management during Détente', *International Affairs* (London), vol. 50, no. 4, Oct. 1974, pp. 531–43.

Bloomsfield, Lincoln, 'The United States, the Soviet Union and the Prospects for Peacekeeping', *International Organization*, vol. 24, Summer 1970, pp. 548–65.

Brezaric, J., 'The So-Called Sonnenfeldt Doctrine', *Review of International Affairs*, vol. 27, no. 627, 20 May 1976, p. 941.

Brennan, D. G., 'Soviet–American Communication in Crises', *Arms Control and National Security*, vol. 1, 1969, pp. 18–9.

Brown, Seyom, 'A Cooling-off Period for US–Soviet Relations', *Foreign Policy*, no. 28, Fall 1977, pp. 3–21.

Brzezinski, Zbigniew, 'How the Cold War Played', *Foreign Affairs*, vol. 51, no. 1, Oct. 1972, pp. 181–209.

Buchan, Alastair, 'Strategic Factors and the Summit', *The World Today*, vol. 16, no. 4, Apr. 1960, pp. 141–9.

Bull, Hedley, 'The Scope for Super-Power Agreements', *Arms Control and National Security*, vol. 1, 1969, pp. 1–23.

Callen, Earl, 'US–Soviet Scientific Exchanges in the Age of Détente', *Survey*, vol. 21, no. 4, Autumn 1975.

Campbell, John, 'Negotiation with the Soviets', *Foreign Affairs*, vol. 34, no. 2, Jan. 1956, pp. 305–19.

Clark, Ian, 'Sino-American Relations in Soviet Perspective', *Orbis*, vol. 17, no. 2, Summer 1973, pp. 480–92.

Coffey, J. I., 'Strategic Superiority, Deterrence and Arms Control', *Orbis*, vol. 13, no. 4, Winter 1970, pp. 991–1007.

Djilas, Milovan, 'The Limits of Détente', *The Political Quarterly*, vol. 47, no. 4, Oct./Dec. 1976, pp. 438–47.

Dodd, Thomas, 'If Coexistence Fails: the Khrushchev Visit Evaluated', *Orbis*, vol. 3, no. 4, Winter 1960, pp. 393–423.

Draper, Theodore, 'Appeasement and Détente', *Commentary*, vol. 61, no. 3, Feb. 1976, pp. 27–31.

——, 'Détente', *Commentary*, vol. 57, no. 6, June 1974, pp. 25–47.

Fielder, P. C., 'The Pattern of Super-Power Crises', *International Relations*, vol. 3, no. 7, Apr. 1969, pp. 498–510.

Finley, David, 'Détente and Soviet–American Trade: an Approach to a Political Balance Sheet', *Studies in Comparative Communism*, vol. 8, nos 1 & 2, Spring/Summer 1975, pp. 66–97.

Fleming, D. F., 'Beyond the Cold War', *Annals*, vol. 324, July 1959, pp. 111–26.

Graebner, N., 'World Politics in the New Age', *World Review*, vol. 12, no. 2, July 1973.

Gromyko, Anatoly, 'The Future of Soviet–American Diplomacy', *Annals*, vol. 414, July 1974, pp. 27–40.

Hammond, Thomas, ' "Atomic Diplomacy" Revisited', *Orbis*, vol. 19, no. 4, Winter 1976, pp. 1403–28.

Hill-Norton, Sir Peter, 'Crisis Management', *NATO Review*, vol. 24, no. 5, Oct. 1976, pp. 6–9.

Hoffman, Stanley, 'The Uses of American Power', *Foreign Affairs*, vol. 56, no. 1, Oct. 1977, pp. 27–48.

Holzman, Franklyn and Portes, Richard, 'The Limits of Pressure', *Foreign Policy*, no. 32, Fall 1978, pp. 80–90.

Howard, Michael and Hunter, Robert, 'Israel and the Arab World: the Crisis of 1967', *Adelphi Paper*, no. 41, Oct. 1967.

Hunter, Robert, 'The Future of Soviet–American Détente', *The World Today*, vol. 24, no. 7, July 1968, pp. 281–90.

Huntington, Samuel, 'Trade, Technology and Leverage: Economic Diplomacy', *Foreign Policy*, no. 32, Fall 1978, pp. 63–80.

Ivanov, Ivan, 'Soviet–American Economic Cooperation: Recent Developments, Prospects and Problems' *Annals*, vol. 414, July 1974, pp. 18–26.

Kennan, George, 'America and the Russian Future', *Foreign Affairs*, vol. 29, no. 3, Apr. 1951, pp. 351–70.

——, 'Peaceful Coexistence: a Western View', *Foreign Affairs*, vol. 38, no. 2, Jan. 1960.

——, 'The United States and the Soviet Union, 1917–1976', *Foreign Affairs*, vol. 54, nos 3–4, July 1976, pp. 670–90.

Kennedy, E., 'Beyond Détente', *Foreign Policy*, no. 16, Fall 1974, pp. 3–29.

Korbel, Josef, 'Détente and World Order', *Denver Journal of International Law and Policy*, vol. 6, no. 1, Spring 1976, pp. 9–18.

Laqueur, Walter, 'Détente: Western and Soviet Interpretations', *Survey*, vol. 19, Summer 1973, pp. 74–88.

Lay, S. Houston, 'The US–Soviet Consular Convention', *American Journal of International Law*, vol. 59, Oct. 1965, pp. 876–91.

Levine, Herbert, 'An American View of Economic Relations with the USSR', *Annals*, vol. 414, July 1974, pp. 1–17.

Luns, Joseph, 'The Present State of East–West Relations', *NATO Review*, vol. 24, no. 2, Apr. 1976, pp. 3–7.

Manning, Bayless, 'Goals, Ideology and Foreign Policy', *Foreign Affairs*, vol. 54, no. 2, Jan. 1976, pp. 271–84.

McGeehan, Robert, 'A New American Foreign Policy', *The World Today*, vol. 33, July 1977, pp. 241–3.

Metzl, Lothar, 'The Ideological Struggle: a Case of Soviet Linkage', *Orbis*, vol. 17, no. 2, Summer 1973, pp. 364–84.

Morgenthau, Hans, 'Changes and Chances in American–Soviet Relations', *Foreign Affairs*, vol. 49, no. 3, Apr. 1971, pp. 429–41.

Mosely, Philip, 'The United States and East–West Détente: the Range of Choice', *Journal of International Affairs*, vol. 22, no. 1, 1968, pp. 5–15.

Osgood, Robert, 'The Consequences of Détente', *School of Advanced International Studies Review*, vol. 17, no. 2, Winter 1973.

Plischke, Elmer, 'Eisenhower's "Correspondence Diplomacy" with the Kremlin – Case Study on Summit Diplomatics', *The Journal of Politics*, vol. 30, no. 1, Feb. 1968, pp. 137–59.

Quandt, William, 'Soviet Policy in the October Middle East War', *International Affairs*, vol. 53, nos 3 & 4, pp. 377–89, 587–603.

Rubinstein, Alvin, 'The Elusive Parameters of Détente, *Orbis*, vol. 19, no. 4, Winter 1976, pp. 1344–58.

Schlesinger, Arthur, Jr., 'The Origins of the Cold War', *Foreign Affairs*, vol. 46, no. 1, Oct. 1967, pp. 22–52.

Schlesinger, James, 'The Evolution of American Policy towards the Soviet Union', *International Security*, vol. 1, no. 1, Summer 1976, pp. 37–48.

Schwartz, Harry, 'The Moscow–Peking–Washington Triangle', *Annals*, vol. 414, July 1974, pp. 41–50.

Scrivner, Douglas, 'The Conference on Security and Cooperation in Europe: Implications for Soviet–American Détente', *Denver Journal of International Law and Policy*, vol. 6, no. 1, Spring 1976, pp. 122–58.

Shulman, Marshall, 'Arms Control and Disarmament: a View from the USA', *Annals*, vol. 313, July 1974, pp. 64–72.

——, 'Europe versus Détente', *Foreign Affairs*, vol. 45, no. 3, Apr. 1967, pp. 389–402.

——, 'Toward a Western Philosophy of Coexistence', *Foreign Affairs*, vol. 52, no. 1, Oct. 1973, pp. 35–58.

Simes, Dimitri, 'Détente Russian-Style', *Foreign Policy*, no. 32, Fall 1978, pp. 47–62.

Toynbee, Arnold, 'Russian–American Relations: the Case for Second Thoughts', *Journal of International Affairs*, vol. 22, no. 1, 1968, pp. 1–4.

Trout, Thomas, 'Rhetoric Revisited: Political Legitimization and the Cold War', *International Studies Quarterly*, vol. 19, no. 3, Sept. 1975, pp. 251–84.

Tucker, Robert, 'Beyond Détente', *Commentary*, vol. 63, no. 3, Mar. 1977, pp. 42–50.

Ulam, Adam, 'Détente under Soviet Eyes', *Foreign Policy*, no. 24, Fall 1976, pp. 145–59.

W, J. F. A., 'Ten Years of East–West Relations in Europe', *The World Today*, vol. 11, no. 6, June 1955, pp. 246–54.

Watt, D. C., 'Henry Kissinger: an Interim Judgement', *The Political Quarterly*, vol. 48, no. 1, Jan./Mar. 1977, pp. 3–13.

Wesson, Robert, 'The Soviet–American Arms Limitation Agreement', *The Russian Review*, vol. 31, no. 4, Oct. 1972.

Whelan, Joseph G., 'The United States and Diplomatic Recognition: the Contrasting Cases of Russia and Communist China', *The China Quarterly*, no. 5, Jan.–Mar. 1961.

Windsor, Philip, 'The Boundaries of Détente', *The World Today*, vol. 25, no. 6, June 1969.

Wolfe, Thomas, 'Soviet Approaches to SALT', *Problems of Communism*, Sept.–Oct. 1970, pp. 1–10.

Wright, Quincy, 'American Policy toward Russia', *World Politics*, vol. 2, no. 4, July 1950, pp. 463–81.

Zakhmatov, M., 'USSR–USA: Prospects for Economic Cooperation', *International Affairs* (Moscow), Nov. 1973, pp. 41–6.

Government Publications

Bell, Robert, 'Implications of Extending the SALT I Interim Agreement', United States Congressional Research Service, 16 May 1977.

United States Department of State Bulletin (consulted regularly).

Détente: Hearings before the Committee on Foreign Relations, United States Senate, Washington D.C.: United States Government Printing Office, Aug.–Sept. 1974.

Détente Hearings before the Subcommittee on Europe of the Committee on Foreign Affairs, United States House of Representatives, 93rd Congress, 2nd Session (Washington D.C.: United States Government Printing Office, 1974).

Foreign Relations of the United States (Washington D.C.: United States Government Printing Office).

Fraser, Donald, *Tension and Détente: Congressional Perspectives on Soviet–American Relations*, Subcommittee on International Organization and Movements and Subcommittee on Europe of the Committee on Foreign Affairs, United States

House of Representatives, April 1973 (Washington D.C.: United States Government Printing Office).

Miko, Francis, 'Soviet Strategic Objectives and SALT: American Perceptions', Congressional Research Service, 25 May 1978.

Military Implications of the Treaty on the Limitations of Anti-Ballistic Missile Systems and the Interim Agreement on Limitation of Strategic Offensive Arms, Hearings before the Committee on Armed Services, United States Senate, 92nd Congress, 2nd Session (Washington D.C.: United States Government Printing Office, 1972).

Public Papers of the Presidents of the United States (consulted regularly).

Sloan, Stanley, 'SALT II: Some Foreign Policy Considerations', Congressional Research Service, 25 April 1979.

Texts of Final Communiqués 1949–1974 (Brussels: NATO Information Service).

'The Changing American–Soviet Strategic Balance: Some Political Implications', Memorandum prepared by the Subcommittee on National Security and International Operations of the Committee on Government Operations, United States Senate (Washington D.C.: United States Government Printing Office, 1972).

Newspapers (consulted regularly)

Christian Science Monitor
Financial Times
Guardian
International Herald Tribune
Izvestia (Current Digest of Soviet Press)
New York Times
Observer
Pravda (Current Digest of Soviet Press)
The Times

References

Keesing's Contemporary Archives.

Index